MARINE AIR

Also by the Author

CHOPPER

AIR COMBAT

The History of the Flying Leathernecks
in Words and Photos

Marine Air

ROBERT F. DORR

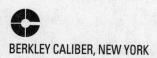
BERKLEY CALIBER, NEW YORK

THE BERKLEY PUBLISHING GROUP
Published by the Penguin Group
Penguin Group (USA) Inc.
375 Hudson Street, New York, New York 10014, USA
Penguin Group (Canada), 90 Eglinton Avenue East, Suite 700, Toronto, Ontario M4P 2Y3, Canada
(a division of Pearson Penguin Canada Inc.)
Penguin Books Ltd., 80 Strand, London WC2R 0RL, England
Penguin Group Ireland, 25 St. Stephen's Green, Dublin 2, Ireland (a division of Penguin Books Ltd.)
Penguin Group (Australia), 250 Camberwell Road, Camberwell, Victoria 3124, Australia
(a division of Pearson Australia Group Pty. Ltd.)
Penguin Books India Pvt. Ltd., 11 Community Centre, Panchsheel Park, New Delhi—110 017, India
Penguin Group (NZ), Cnr. Airborne and Rosedale Roads, Albany, Auckland 1310, New Zealand
(a division of Pearson New Zealand Ltd.)
Penguin Books (South Africa) (Pty.) Ltd., 24 Sturdee Avenue, Rosebank, Johannesburg 2196,
South Africa

Penguin Books Ltd., Registered Offices: 80 Strand, London WC2R 0RL, England

The publisher does not have any control over and does not assume any responsibility for author or third-party websites or their content.

PRINTING HISTORY
Berkley Caliber hardcover edition / December 2005
Berkley Caliber trade paperback edition / January 2007

Berkley Caliber trade ISBN: 978-0-425-21364-3

The Library of Congress has catalogued the Berkley Caliber hardcover edition as follows:

Dorr, Robert F.
        Marine Air / Robert F. Dorr.—1st ed.
            p.   cm.
        ISBN: 0-425-20725-0
            1. Air pilots, Military—United States—Biography. 2. United States. Marine Corps—Aviation—History—Sources. I. Title.

    VE24.D6 2005
    359.9'6—dc22
                                                                                    2005048292

PRINTED IN THE UNITED STATES OF AMERICA

10   9   8   7   6   5   4   3   2   1

Author's Note

These first-person accounts of U.S. Marine Corps pilots and crews in combat are the result of seventy-three interviews and several flights aboard aircraft, completed in 2004 and 2005. Any errors are the fault of the author. However, this book would have been impossible without the help of many.

The following Marine Air combat veterans were interviewed for this book: Walter Attebery, Jim Bailey, Mark Austin Byrd, Howard J. Christenson, John Paul Cress, John D. Cummings, Sarah Deal, Willis "Bud" Dworzak, J. J. Geuss, Jim Henshaw, Eugene S. "Mule" Holmberg, D. N. "Red" James, Cliff J. Judkins, Frank Lang, Bill Luplow, Ernie Lutz, Jim Martin, Paul Moore, James T. O'Kelley, Bud Page, Bill Parks, John "Gordo" Phelps, John Scanlan, John Roxbury, Warren R. Smith, Jay A. Stout, Frank Sturgeon, Thomas M. Tomlinson, David Van Esselstyn, Bill Woolman, and John Zuppan.

The following people also provided interviews and assistance for this book: Dean Abbott, Hal Andrews, William Bartsch, Nancy Bolt, Robert Bolt, Thomas N. Bland, Jr., Alan C. Carey, John Gourley, Frank Haas, Jim Hawkins, Thomas Hudner, James L. "Mac" McWhorter, David W. Menard, Al Noll, Dale Norris, Norman Polmar, Scott Stebbins, Norman Taylor, Barrett Tillman, Nicholas A. Veronico, H. E. "Bucky" Walters, and Mark Wery.

There are some who warrant a special nod for extraordinary assistance. Douglas E. Slowiak of Vortex Photo Graphics has a unique artistry as a portraitist of aircraft. James T. D'Angina, Michael E. Starn, and Ken Smith-Christmas of the National Museum of the Marine Corps provided invaluable assistance. I also want to thank Bill Fawcett and Tom Colgan.

The contribution by John Bolt is drawn from an interview in May 1994. The contribution by Kent Smith is drawn from an interview in August 1964.

Some veterans interviewed for this volume have written their own books. F4F Wildcat and F4U Corsair pilot Thomas M. Tomlinson is author of *The Threadbare Buzzard* (Osceola, Wisconsin: Zenith Press, 2004), an account of World War II fighter flying. An excellent source for PBJ Mitchell operations in the Pacific is *Leatherneck Bombers*, by Alan C. Carey (Altglen, Pennsylvania: Schiffer Press, 2002). An excellent source for further reading on the HO3S-1 and HO5S-1 helicopter is the Marine Corps's official history, *Whirlybirds: U.S. Marine Helicopters in Korea*, by Lt. Col. Ronald J. Brown (Quantico, Virginia: Marine Corps History Center, 2003). F/A-18A Hornet pilot Capt. Jay A. Stout is the author of *Hornets over Kuwait* (Annapolis, Maryland: Naval Institute Press, 1997), a personal account of combat action in Operation Desert Storm.

Robert F. Dorr
Oakton, Virginia

Contents

Chapter One

Battling the Zero in the South Pacific

What Happened

The first hint of morning light seeped over the horizon at 5:45 a.m. on Sunday, December 7, 1941. The warships of Japan's First Air Fleet turned into the wind to launch their first Mitsubishi A6M2 Zero fighters. Fifteen minutes later at 6:00 a.m., Comdr. Mitsuo Fuchida took off from the wind-lashed wooden deck of the aircraft carrier and flagship, *Akagi,* to lead 189 Zeros, dive-bombers, and torpedo bombers from six carriers that would attack the Hawaiian Islands.

At 6:43 a.m., the sun came up. It silhouetted Fuchida's warplanes high over the ocean en route to the principal Hawaiian island of Oahu. At 7:15 a.m., Lt. Comdr. Shigekazu Shimazaki led a second wave of 170 aircraft launching from carrier decks.

When he'd originated the plan 11 months earlier, Adm. Isoroku Yamamoto, commander of Japan's Combined Fleet, used brush, ink, rice paper, and the rich flourish of calligraphy to write down his preliminary idea in a letter to Navy Minister Koshiro Oikawa.

Yamamoto's letter was hand delivered. It was marked "to be burned without showing anyone else." Japan had more aircraft carriers and bet-

Capt. William P. Boland, Jr.
August 8, 1943
Grumman F4F-4 Wildcat
Marine Fighter Squadron
**   VMF-441, "Black Jacks"**
Funafuti, Ellice Islands

Capt. William P. Boland wasn't at Pearl Harbor, but some of his buddies thought he was looking for revenge when he mounted a weeks-long, one-man campaign against a Japanese "Nell" bomber in the South Pacific. Boland was in one of the last squadrons to operate the Grumman F4F-4 Wildcat, the corpulent combat plane that was the standard Marine Corps fighter on December 7, 1941.

[U.S. Marine Corps]

ter carrier-based warplanes than any other nation. Japan also had the formidable Zero fighter, regarded as markedly superior to the F4F Wildcat operated by the U.S. Navy and Marine Corps. But despite advantages, secrecy was vital. The planned attack had to be a surprise. Although the Americans were reading Japan's diplomatic codes, they did not detect the Japanese carrier task force when it set forth from the Kurile Islands and crossed the North Pacific in secret. The Americans did not know about the carriers until 7:53 a.m. at Pearl Harbor.

Pearl was a Navy outpost, home of the U.S. fleet. It had a significant Army presence. Adm. Husband E. Kimmel and Lt. Gen. Walter C. Short later sustained career-ending criticism because the Navy and Army were unprepared for a Sunday-morning assault that sank or crippled 21 vessels and killed 2,388 Americans.

Marine Corps aviation came under attack at Pearl Harbor, too. In fact, Fuchida's airmen found their first target in the Marine Corps air station at Ewa Plantation on Oahu. Some Zeros strafed Ewa while the bulk of the strike force continued across the island. Marines were thus among the first to come under fire.

The Japanese attack force at Pearl Harbor was spearheaded by the famous Zero fighter, otherwise known as the Mitsubishi A6M, which became the nemesis of Marine fighter pilots in the Pacific. This is a late-model A6M5 Zero of the kind introduced in 1941 and used until the end of the war. It was not a Zero but a "Nell" bomber that captured the ire of Marines in the Ellice Islands in 1943.

[U.S. Navy]

Marines had been flying in support of their own troops since long before this war. Marine aviation was a maturing military arm. About a hundred Marine aviators were stationed on Oahu, most at Ewa, where the SBD Dauntless dive-bombers of squadron VMSB-232 were parked in the open. Other Marine aviators, on the morning of the Pearl Harbor attack, belonged to squadron VMF-211 with F4F-3 Wildcat fighters and were hundreds of miles away aboard the carrier USS *Enterprise* (CV 6). Still other Marine aviators were out in the Pacific with SB2U Vindicator scout bombers aboard the USS *Lexington* (CV 2).

As the scream of aircraft engines and the boom of guns resounded over Oahu, Marine Capt. Richard C. Mangrum was reading the Sunday comics in his bungalow at Ewa beach, near the air station. The sounds were not unusual in a location where men practiced at war frequently. Still, Mangrum told himself, it seemed to be a lot of gunfire. Mangrum dropped the newspaper, walked to a window, and saw a Japanese aircraft passing by at low level en route to Battleship Row at Pearl Harbor. In the weeks to come, Mangrum pinned on major's leaves and commanded a Marine air group in the South Pacific. He was a Dauntless pilot, but other Marines were flying the F4F-4 Wildcat, the principal Marine fighter of the era. One of them was Capt. Robert E. Galer. Also at Ewa that morning, Galer looked up and shook his head vigorously at the sight of the red "meatball" painted on the wings of the Japanese planes. Galer had no idea that his own experiences would symbolize Marine aviation over the next 20 years.

At Ewa Field, four Marines were killed and 33 aircraft were torched. The contingent of squadron VMF-211 that hadn't gone to sea on the *Lexington* lost nine Wildcats on the ground. Although a handful of Army P-36 and P-40 fighters got into the air to challenge the attackers, not a single Marine fighter engaged the foe as the Pearl Harbor attack unfolded.

Wake Island

The Japanese also launched immediate attacks on the American outpost at Wake Island. VMF-211 followed up its Pearl Harbor losses by losing seven more Wildcats on the ground at Wake on December 8, 1941. But Wildcats also scored victories: a pair of twin-engine Mitsubishi G3M2 Type 96 "Nell" bombers were shot down by 1st Lt. David S. Kliever and Tech. Sgt. William Hamilton of VMF-211, flying from Wake on December 9. Capt. Henry T. "Hammerin' Hank" Elrod, also of VMF-211 and soon to be briefly the most famous Marine pilot in the world, also shot down a Japanese aircraft that day.

During the heated defense of Wake Island, Marines kept their Wildcats flying by cannibalizing wrecked aircraft, improvising tools, and handmaking some parts. When the Japanese attempted their first landings on Wake early on the morning of December 11, 1941, four Wildcats attacked the invasion force with 100-pound (45-kilogram) bombs and .50-caliber (12.7-millimeter) machine gun fire. That's when Elrod achieved a direct hit on the Japanese destroyer *Kisaragi* with a bomb dropped from his Wildcat, apparently sinking the ship and forcing the Japanese invasion fleet to retire.

In the months after Pearl Harbor, the F4F-4 Wildcat was the best fighter Marine aviators could lay their hands on, although it was usually not a match for the Japanese A6M Zero. Seen taxiing at Henderson Field on Guadalcanal, this Wildcat displays the "raffish" and "disreputable" look attributed to it by pilot Capt. Thomas M. Tomlinson, as well as the narrow track of its landing gear and a 58 US-gallon extra fuel tank carried under the right wing only.

[U.S. Marine Corps]

It was a temporary stay. On December 21, 1941, the Japanese returned, reinforced by carrier aircraft. Just two Wildcats survived to attack a 39-aircraft raid from the Japanese carriers *Soryu* and *Hiryu*. Zeros quickly shot down one Wildcat, but the second ship shot down two of the raiders before the pilot, Capt. Herb Frueler, was wounded. Frueler struggled back to the island where he crash-landed, wrecking Wake's last Wildcat.

When Hammerin' Hank Elrod no longer had a Wildcat to fly, the 36-year-old captain demonstrated that Marines are, first and foremost, riflemen: Elrod assumed command of a flank of the line set up to make a last stand against the Japanese landing. He conducted a spirited defense, enabling his fellow Marines to hold their positions and repulse waves of attacking Japanese and to provide covering fire for unarmed ammunition carriers. Elrod seized a discarded automatic weapon, gave his own firearm to one of his men, and fought on, losing his life but earning the Medal of Honor plus a posthumous promotion to major.

Aerial duels with the vaunted Japanese Zero fighter at Wake, Coral Sea, and Midway became the stuff of legend. The Wildcat became the standard fighter amid the heat, stench, and muck at Henderson Field on Guadalcanal.

The First Marine Division captured the nearly completed airfield on August 7, 1942. Marines named the field for Maj. Lofton Henderson, the first Marine pilot killed in action in World War II when his squadron engaged the Japanese fleet that was attacking Midway. Henderson was commander of Marine Scout Bomber Squadron VMSB-241.

At Guadalcanal, Marine aviators did some of the toughest flying of the war. To stand against the Japanese, they had to struggle not with one enemy but with many. To the pilot of an F4F Wildcat taxiing at Guadalcanal's Henderson Field in a torrential downpour, struggling through geysers of water and mud, the list of enemies included bad weather, corrosion, primitive conditions, and even tropical disease. Marine fliers sometimes needed a roll of toilet paper or a protective bunker—or a hot meal—as much as anything else. It was hard to stay ready to repel the next wave of Japanese bombers when you had to spend time plucking leeches from your skin with a bayonet or running to the latrine to disgorge the foul water and poor food.

Maj. John L. Smith's VMF-223, "Rainbow" squadron, was launched from the escort carrier USS *Long Island* (CVE 1) on August 20, 1942, and landed at Henderson. The next day, Smith's squadron was strafing Japanese troops along the Tenaru River. On August 24, accompanied by five Army Bell P-400 Airacobras, Smith intercepted a Japanese flight of 15 bombers and 12 fighters. VMF-223 pilots shot down ten bombers and six fighters, with Capt. Marion Carl scoring three of the kills. Soon Carl became the first Marine air ace of the war while Smith became the second Marine Wildcat pilot to rate the Medal of Honor. Another Marine, Capt. Joe Foss, racked up 26 aerial victories and received the nation's highest award, too. So did Maj. (later Brig. Gen.) Robert E. Galer, the Pearl Harbor survivor and veteran of VMF-211 who now commanded squadron VMF-224 and who scored 13 aerial victories and waged a point-blank campaign against the Japanese for 29 days. Smith, Carl, Foss, and Galer operated from an airfield that an official history called a "bowl of blast dust or a quagmire of mud" while piloting the stubby, square-wing Grumman fighter that Marines loved and hated. Galer will reappear in this narrative in a subsequent war.

Guadalcanal

At Guadalcanal, Japanese bombers typically approached 26 at a time in V formation, and Wildcat pilots refined their technique of trying to avoid Zeros and get at the bombers. Wildcats dived on the bombers, seeking to destroy some before the Zeros pounced them. These hit-and-run tactics forced the Zero pilots to overuse precious fuel. Once dogfighting began, the Americans learned the importance of teamwork, finding that reliance on one's wingman was crucial and that no "lone wolf" survived for very long.

The Wildcat was no Zero. The Japanese fighter was light and fast and had cannons instead of machine guns. The American fighter was sturdier and gave the pilot a much better chance of surviving if he were hit. As they gained experience, Marines (and the Navy fliers who fought in the Wildcat) learned how to coax greater maneuverability from their ships. They learned how to make better gunnery compensate for the lesser killing power of their guns. And because their aircraft was tough, they stayed in the fight, day after day. The Hellcat and Corsair came along in time to give hard-pressed pilots a better craft in their hands, but before that, the Wildcat became one of the near-great fighters of the war.

In the same class as Carl, Smith, Foss, and Galer, one of the great Wildcat pilots at Guadalcanal was Lt. Col. Harold W. "Indian Joe" Bauer.

Bauer was a Naval Academy graduate and athlete who commanded Marine Fighter Squadron VMF-212, "Devil Cats," shot down eleven Japanese aircraft, and paid the highest price to win the nation's highest award.

When Marines landed on Guadalcanal and seized Henderson Field in the first U.S. offensive action of the war, Bauer's squadron was at Efate, New Hebrides, preparing to enter the fray. Bauer left them there and flew down to Guadalcanal to inspect the airfield, which was under constant Japanese air attack. On September 27, 1942, he borrowed a Wildcat from friend and rival Carl, took off to intercept approaching Japanese bombers, and shot one of them down.

Also during his inspection visit, Bauer shot down four Japanese Zero fighters on October 3, 1942. His squadron hadn't reached the combat zone yet and he was already an ace.

The Japanese mounted a major effort to dislodge the Marines in a furious counterattack. It happened just when Bauer was bringing in the Wildcats of his Devil Cats on October 8, 1942.

He arrived to find a Japanese air raid under way. In the waters off the great island, Japanese Aichi D3A "Val" dive-bombers were swarming down on the USS *McFarland* (AVD 14), a destroyer transformed into a freighter and carrying aviation fuel and ammunition that was desperately needed on Guadalcanal.

Bauer spotted the dive-bombers withdrawing. He was low on fuel. Nevertheless, he gave chase. There was a 55-gallon external fuel tank stuck beneath the right wing of his Wildcat, reducing his airspeed and maneuverability. Still, Bauer dived from 3,000 to 200 feet and closed on the Japanese warplanes. He had superb targets and a full load of ammunition. Bauer shoved throttle, mixture, and prop controls to the fire wall, overtook the dive-bombers from behind, and began squeezing off bursts. In a matter of minutes, he sent three Vals falling in flames into the sea near Savo Island.

On the day of that fight, Bauer was placed in charge of all fighter operations on Guadalcanal. On November 14, 1942, he took off to investigate a Japanese convoy of 11 troop transports escorted by 11 destroyers bearing down on Guadalcanal—the big heft behind the enemy's planned counteroffensive.

Bauer attacked the ships and was met by Japanese fighters. He battled Zeros and shot two down. But bullets ripped into his Wildcat. Unable to maintain control of the F4F-4, he parachuted into the sea.

Also in the air with him during that slugfest were Foss and Maj. Joe Renner. Foss and Renner raced back to Guadalcanal, traded their Wildcats for a J2F Duck amphibian able to land on water, and set forth to attempt to locate Bauer at sea. They were defeated by the arrival of darkness.

Bauer was never seen again. A recommendation for a Medal of Honor for him was approved in May 1943.

THOMAS M. TOMLINSON A fire hydrant with wings, somebody said. The barrel-like, mid-wing configuration of the F4F-3 Wildcat gave it a certain raffish appearance. It was anything but a beauty, and it didn't handle well in the wrong hands. For takeoff, the Wildcat required especially careful handling because the fuselage blanked the rudder, and it had a nasty tendency to veer to port. The tail wheel had to be locked and checked, and the plane didn't perform well in a crosswind. Until you got the tail off the ground, you had to concentrate on stick and throttle every second.

In a dogfight with a Zero, the Wildcat could not maneuver the way the Zero could. It wasn't fast enough or heavily armed enough. It did have some advantages over the Zero, including armor for the pilot and self-sealing fuel tanks which—unlike the Zero—prevented it from being transformed into a burning torch when it sustained hits. The F4F-3 also was a solid, stable gun platform. Once you got past the awkward arrangement of some of the instruments and controls, the F4F-3 was probably about as good an airplane as you were going to get in the early days of the war. It was sturdy and the cockpit had plenty of room. It was responsive. If you mastered it, you could probably stand a chance of beating that Zero, but the real answer was a newer and better fighting machine.

FRANK C. LANG This was very elementary flying. Grumman made the F4F-3 and it was simple and tough, but out of date. I think I logged all of five or ten hours in it.

Sitting in the cockpit, you had to roll the landing gear down and roll the landing gear up, manually. When it was on the way up, you got your hand out of the way real fast because the handle really twisted around while it was coming up.

The Marines also had a few F2A Buffalo fighters at the start of the war. The Buffalo was very similar and it wasn't very effective in combat, but at least you could raise and lower its landing gear hydraulically. The F2A had a very small tail section and you could actually fly that airplane in a spin. It had an electric prop, as did the Wildcat. Previously, a manifold controlled our props. On the F2A and F4F-3, you had an electric prop, but the difficulty with that was it could get away from you.

The F4F-3 flew wonderfully for an airplane of its day, but it couldn't fly effectively against the Japanese Zero. That's why we developed newer fighters like the F6F Hellcat and the F4U Corsair, which the Japanese called the "Whispering Death."

THOMAS M. TOMLINSON I was one of the Americans who volunteered to fly with the Royal Canadian Air Force before the United States entered World War II, so I didn't undergo the flight training at Pensacola, Florida, that most Marines experienced. I went directly into the Marine Corps when the opportunity arose and took a circuitous route into fighters, but I found myself at Ewa and then at Guadalcanal as a member of fighter squadron VMF-214, "Swashbucklers," flying the F4F-4 Wildcat.

No, I don't mean the squadron you've heard about that had another name, the Black Sheep, and had its identity heisted by the ambitious Gregory "Pappy" Boyington. That came later. Those of us who were in the squadron at the beginning saw more fighting and shot down more Japanese airplanes than the squadron did later when its identity was swapped and it became Boyington's outfit. I was in VMF-214 when it began, at Henderson Field on Guadalcanal, living in a coconut grove with an outdoor head and not much in the way of amenities. The commander of VMF-214 "Swashbucklers" was Maj. George Britt.

On April 7, 1943, after the Japanese no longer had any hope of taking back Guadalcanal, they launched the biggest raid they ever sent against the island—67 Aichi D3A Type 99 Val dive-bombers escorted by 110 Zeros. We intercepted them with portions of three Army and four Marine squadrons flying Wildcats, F4U Corsairs, P-38 Lightnings,

A mechanic works on an F4F-4 Wildcat in the southwest Pacific. When Capt. William P. Boland, Jr., took a half-dozen Wildcats to Funafuti in the Ellice Islands, he was able to use the Wildcat to ambush a Japanese bomber.

[U.S. Marine Corps]

P-39 Airacobras, and P-40 Warhawks. Our Swashbucklers squadron was credited with shooting down four Vals and six Zeros over Cape Esperance.

I found myself going after one of those Val dive-bombers. The six .50-caliber guns in the F4F-4 Wildcat were lubricated with Cosmoline, which thickened in the extreme cold at high altitude and could prevent the guns from working. When I locked onto the last Val in the Japanese formation, five of my six guns froze and refused to fire. I gave it some throttle and got up right behind him, which gave me a close-up look at the two men in the Val. I could see the disturbed reaction of the gunner in the rear cockpit of the Val. He was shooting at me when my bullets hit him and chewed him up. This was not pretty at all. I knocked off pieces of the Val and got it smoking, then banked near Lunga Point just in time to get away from a brace of Zeros.

That battle over Guadalcanal was one of the last major actions in the Pacific for the Wildcat. Thereafter, only two squadrons in the Ellice Islands continued to fly the F4F. In June 1943, my squadron converted to the F4U Corsair.

WILLIAM P. BOLAND Ours was the last squadron to fly the Wildcat fighter in combat. We were still flying Wildcats when other Marines were defeating the Japanese in air battles while flying Corsairs and Hellcats.

My squadron was VMF-441. It was one of the very few Marine squadrons to actually be commissioned in the combat zone, organized on October 1, 1942, at Tafuna airdrome, Tutuila Island, American Samoa, with Maj. Daniel W. Torrey as our first commander. Torrey was due for assignment elsewhere, so on December 4, Capt. Walter J. Meyer became our commander. Torrey, Meyer, and most of the Marines in Samoa had been fighting on Guadalcanal, and to them, Samoa was a pleasant backwater after months of harsh fighting—a place of respite and refuge. The war was a lot less active there.

I think most of us liked the Wildcat. By this time in the war, we knew a lot about how to use it effectively against the Zero. The cockpit was spacious and comfortable. The plane had a few annoying features, like the hand crank to put down the landing gear, but every airplane had its idiosyncrasies.

From Samoa, we flew missions against bypassed Japanese outposts like Wotje and Maloelap. Later in the war, of course, VMF-441 flew a lot of combat in Corsairs—the squadron produced seven aces—but the Wildcat period was mostly unremarkable. At least, it was unremarkable until they decided to send a bunch of us to Funafuti. That island was only beginning to have an American presence, but it would eventually become a staging base for the invasion of Tarawa.

SMOKE SPANJER We were flying the older F4F Wildcats while the remainder of the fighter squadrons in the Pacific were transitioning to the F4U Corsair. We had a couple of older F4F-3 models, which had only four guns but carried more ammunition—a feature we liked—but we flew combat in the F4F-4 model. Early in March 1943, we were sent to provide air cover, at the urgent request of the Seabees on the island of Funafuti, in the British-owned Ellice Islands in the Southwest Pacific.

I was part of a four-plane advanced echelon flying north from Samoa to the Ellice Islands. With external tanks we flew 700 miles with only one stop at the French island of Wallis and arrived over Funafuti. A PBY Catalina escorted us during the flight.

To our dismay, the Navy Seabees' desire for our protection exceeded their constructive efforts, and we were forced to land on barely 1,500 feet of unprepared coral surface.

The next day we were alerted for our first business and did, in fact, chase a Japanese "Emily" flying boat but lost it in some rather severe weather.

On March 27, 1943, the SCR 270 ground radar operated on Funafuti by the Army's Fifth Defense Battalion detected the approach of unknown aircraft. Captain Boland and I were launched against a possible radar target and ended up in hot pursuit of four twin-engine Mitsubishi G4M Type 1 "Betty" bombers.

This was the latest in high-speed Japanese bombers, and our tired F4F-4s were straining to get in position for an attack. On the first pass, Captain Boland shot down the lead bomber, which exploded under fire from his six .50-calibers. Contrary to the official squadron history, my guns did not jam immediately. I maneuvered behind the number four Betty, got off several bursts, and was able to inflict some damage before my guns froze. Captain Boland and I made one additional flat pass but the bombers outdistanced us.

For the next four months, we hunted in vain during daylight hours. During the dark, we caught accurate strings of Japanese bombs on the installations on Funafuti. The night bombing raids were heaviest with Army Air Corps B-24 Liberators operating from the island. Even after regular bombing attacks by the Japanese became few and far between, a lone "Nell" kept flying reconnaissance missions high over our heads. No one wanted to get that Nell more than Boland. He began what some later interpreted as a one-man campaign to defeat that solitary Japanese bomber.

NORMAN MITCHELL The Japanese were scouting down through Nanumea and sometimes as far as Nukufetau almost daily in a Nell. That's a twin-engine Mitsubishi G3M2 Type 96 attack bomber, dubbed a Nell by the Allies. William P. Boland got aboard a PT boat and had it drop him off with a New Zealand coast watcher on the island of Nanumea, where he observed the Nell's operation for about a week. During that time, we sent up a section of two F4F-4 Wildcats from Funafuti every day to attempt an intercept over Nanumea. Boland tried from his position on the ground to vector the Wildcats up to attack the Nell. The Wildcats carried extra fuel tanks under the wings to give them loiter time and "reach" to catch the bomber.

Our communication seemed to be working. Our radar seemed to be working. We seemed to know where the Nell was, and Boland was giving us excellent guidance over the radio. But somehow that Japanese heckler managed to escape from us every time. Everybody wanted to get the Nell and we began to think it was not going to happen.

We learned a long time after the war that the Nell was from a Japanese unit called the 755 Kokutai and was operating out of Tarawa. While the war was going on, we didn't know the Japanese names of their units or airplanes.

SMOKE SPANJER For weeks, our Wildcats had been trying to catch up with that Nell. Some of the missions were flown from Funafuti to Nui, where the Nell spent a lot of time. That was a round-trip of 280 miles, which meant that, even with wing tanks, the Wildcats wouldn't have time to spend more than a few minutes attempting the kill. We tried for weeks to meet the enemy plane, sometimes missing only by minutes. On July 17, 1943, we believed we came within a minute or two of nailing the Nell.

On August 8, 1944, Boland took off in a two-plane section with 1st Lt. Samuel G. Middleman on his wing. Soon afterward, the Army radar people told us there was an apparent Japanese aircraft over Nui.

WILLIAM P. BOLAND We had to travel about 140 miles each way, from Funafuti to Nui. It was a good thing the F4F-4 Wildcat was so comfortable. On that August 8 mission, everything broke right. Our communications worked. Our ground radar worked. This time, we really knew where the Nell was. We had wanted to get that Nell for a long time.

We managed to come up behind the Japanese bomber. I made a fir-

Who's Who

Capt. Thomas M. Tomlinson, F4F-4 Wildcat pilot, squadron VMF-214, "Swashbucklers," Guadalcanal, Solomon Islands

Maj. (later Brig. Gen.) Robert E. Galer, F4F-4 Wildcat pilot and commander of squadron VMF-224, Guadalcanal, Solomon Islands

Capt. (later Maj.) William P. Boland, Jr., F4F-4 Wildcat pilot, squadron VMF-441, Funafuti, Ellice Islands

1st Lt. (later Maj. Gen.) Ralph H. "Smoke" Spanjer, F4F-4 Wildcat pilot, squadron VMF-441, Funafuti, Ellice Islands

1st Lt. Norman L. Mitchell, F4F-4 Wildcat pilot, squadron VMF-441, Funafuti, Ellice Islands

2nd Lt. (later Maj. Gen.) Frank C. Lang, a night fighter pilot who flew the F4F Wildcat in training and the F4U-2 Corsair (see chapter 2) in combat

ing pass from the left rear quadrant and sent some .50-caliber into him. The Nell started to disintegrate and sent back pieces of debris that narrowly missed me. The pilot somehow had enough control to get the bomber down to very low altitude before he lost it. The Nell went down in the Nui Atoll, in water so shallow it didn't sink. People told me the wreckage of that Nell was still readily visible in the Nui lagoon 30 years later in 1974.

I later commanded fighter squadrons VMF-215 from November 1944 to February 1945 and VMF-321 from March to August 1945. I flew other fighters, but the Wildcat enabled me to bag that bomber after weeks of trying.

Grumman F4F-4 Wildcat

To satisfy a 1936 requirement for a carrier-based fighter, Leroy Grumman's company offered the Navy and Marine Corps a biplane fighter called the F4F-1. But even before Grumman grew into its famous Bethpage, Long Island, facility in April 1937, the Navy said it wanted the

This is an F4F-3 in flight over the South Pacific. Marines extracted every last ounce of performance and maneuverability out of the Wildcat but were often outgunned by their Japanese adversaries. "We didn't fly with the canopy open at Guadalcanal," said pilot Tomlinson. "A pilot only did that if he wanted to have his picture taken."

[U.S. Marine Corps]

Brewster F2A-1 Buffalo instead. The Buffalo was a monoplane. With war clouds still gathering, the Navy had decided that the single-wing design was the wave of the future.

Grumman designed its own monoplane. Engineer and pilot Robert L. Hall took it aloft for the first time on September 2, 1937. The F4F-2 wasn't really the second version of Grumman's fourth fighter, as its designation suggested. It was a new aircraft. A 1,050-horsepower Pratt & Whitney R-1830-66 Twin Wasp engine powered the F4F-2, which acquired the name Wildcat in 1940.

In October 1938, the Navy ordered the bigger F4F-3, with an improved Twin Wasp and a wing having an area of 260 square feet (24.15 square meters). In August 1939, the Navy ordered a batch of F4F-3s and lower-powered F4F-3As (originally designated F4F-6). The first F4F-3 Wildcat took to the air on August 20, 1940. Soon Wildcats with names like Wasp and Ranger were aboard carriers. The Wildcat was the fighter piloted by Lt. Edward "Butch" O'Hare of Navy squadron VF-42 from the USS *Lexington* (CV 2), who shot down five Mitsubishi G4M Betty bombers in five minutes near Rabaul on February 20, 1942.

Wildcats achieved conspicuous success in the battles of Wake Island and Midway and in operations at Guadalcanal. The Wildcat really earned its spurs not on pitching, heaving carrier decks but in the heat, stench, and muck at Henderson Field on Guadalcanal where, slowly, the tide began to turn and Americans mounted the first offensive action of the Pacific conflict.

The designation F4F-4 went to 1,168 production Wildcats, whose wings folded manually, powered by the Wright R-1830-86 Cyclone radial. Delivery of F4F-4 fighters began in November 1941. Navy and Marine squadrons were flying the planes by the time of the Pearl Harbor attack.

At the outset of 1942, the Navy saw that Grumman was going to be

---

Grumman F4F-4 Wildcat

Type: single-seat carrier-based fighter

Power plant: one 1,200-hp (895-kW) Pratt & Whitney R-1830-86 Twin Wasp 14-cylinder radial piston engine with a 2-speed, 2-stage mechanical supercharger or R-1830-90 with a 2-speed, single-stage supercharger, driving a 3-blade, 9-ft 9-in (3.01-m) Curtiss Electric C5315(S) propeller

Performance: maximum speed, 278 mph (447 km/h) at sea level; 318 mph (512 km/h) at 19,400 ft (5915 m); cruising speed, 155 mph (249 km/h); initial climb rate, 1,950 ft (594 m) per minute; service ceiling, 31,000 ft (9448 m); absolute ceiling, 34,400 ft (10485 m); range, 770 mi (1239 km)

Weights: empty, 5,758 lb (2612 kg); maximum takeoff weight, 7,952 lb (3607 kg)

Dimensions: span, 38 ft (11.58 m); span, wings folded, 14 ft 4 in (4.37 m); length, 28 ft 9 in (8.76 m); height, 9 ft 2¼ in (2.81 m); wing area, 260 sq ft (24.15 sq m)

Armament: 6 fixed .50-cal (12.7-mm) Browning M2 machine guns with 450 rounds per gun, plus two 100-lb (45-kg) bombs or two 250-lb (96-kg) bombs or two 58 US-gal. auxiliary fuel tanks, although only one was typically carried under the right wing only

Crew: 1 (pilot)

First flight: September 2, 1937 (XF4F-2); August 20, 1940 (F4F-3); November 7, 1941 (F4F-4)

---

exceedingly busy with the number and variety of warplanes it was producing. Not only was the firm building the F4F-4 Wildcat, TBF Avenger, J2F Duck, and J4F Widgeon, but plans were well advanced toward the F6F Hellcat fighter. General Motors took over Wildcat production. Under wartime pressures, all five GM plants were reorganized and the automaker's Eastern Aircraft Division was created.

The American industrial heartland turned out 7,825 Wildcats, including 1,988 built by Grumman and 5,837 from General Motors. Foster Hailey, correspondent for the *New York Times,* summed up the Wildcat's impact on history in 1943. Hailey wrote, "The Grumman Wildcat, it is no exaggeration to say, did more than any single instrument of war to save the day for the United States in the Pacific."

Chapter Two

Corsair in the Night Sky

FRANK C. LANG Our F4U-2 Corsair had the familiar lines of one of the most respected and beloved fighters of World War II, but it was a unique version. It was the first U.S. single-engine fighter to be equipped specifically for night fighter duties. Our outfit, squadron VMF (N)-532, became the first to shoot down an enemy aircraft at night using night fighting equipment. Our commander, Maj. Everette H. Vaughan, was a guiding force in developing tactics and methods for taking advantage of the superb performance of the radar-equipped Corsair.

Vaughan became commander of the newly formed VMF (N)-532 at Cherry Point, North Carolina, in the spring of 1943. He was an experienced pilot who had flown in the Reserves before the war. He had been an airline pilot at the time of Pearl Harbor. He had thousands of hours in his logbook.

Vaughan really whipped our squadron into shape. He was a real leader who rarely needed to use his powerful personality. He supervised every aspect of our preparations to go to the Pacific with our early F4U-2 night fighters, which had the metal-brace "birdcage" canopy unique to early Corsairs and, of course, the distinctive APS-4 radar housed inside a dome on the right wing.

**1st Lt. Frank C. Lang
April 14, 1944
Vought F4U-2 Corsair
Marine Night Fighter Squadron
    VMF (N)-532
Engebi, Eniwetok Atoll**

Frank C. Lang was a first lieutenant flying the F4U-2 Corsair in the South Pacific when this portrait was taken. He was one of the Marines' first night-fighter pilots. Lang went on to pursue a lengthy career that encompassed three wars and ended in 1978 when he retired as a major general.

[U.S. Marine Corps]

TOMMY TOMLINSON The first Corsairs really were not safe airplanes. The wing would stall near the tip. The mechanics kept taping a carved block of wood out there to make that thing stall evenly. That airplane absolutely would not recover from an inverted spin. One of the astounding things that happened during the war was how rapidly they improved the Corsair, how the engineers kept modifying the bird with incremental changes that improved the plane at every stage.

Nobody ever said the Corsair was uncomfortable. You could get very comfortable in there. The cockpit was roomy. But it was hard to reach the rudder pedals if you were only five foot six.

I wasn't in the night fighter outfit: I flew the F4U-1 with the third squadron to get the Corsair. VMF-124 was the first to operate the plane, followed by VMF-213 and finally our outfit, VMF-214, which was known in the early days on Guadalcanal as the Swashbucklers long before people started calling it the Black Sheep Squadron.

We were flying the F4F-4 Wildcat in combat. They pulled us back to Turtle Bay, New Hebrides, a staging base for fighting in the Solomons, to check out the new fighter, but they initially could give us only two

Corsairs to check out. Maj. Gregory J. Weissenberger, the skipper of VMF-213, came down to Turtle Bay from Guadalcanal. He was one of the greatest Marine fighter pilots that ever lived and was an ace with five aerial victories. They had just started using the bird up there, and he came down to give us a little scholarly advice on how to fly it. Weissenberger knew the Corsair from A to Z. He was a tremendous tutor.

The advice he gave us was, "This airplane has some undesirable characteristics: One is, you can hardly see out of it." The canopy, which had so many crisscrossing bars we called it the birdcage, was too low, and to further obstruct the pilot's forward visibility, the tail wheel oleo strut was too short.

Weissenberger continued: "The best thing to do is land it on its wheels. The only way you can really see out the front is to have the plane level, which means the main landing gear will touch ground first. That means you'll be coming in faster than is really safe, and this strip is pretty short. You might lose control of it when you're landing. If you do get in real trouble, I would aim the damn thing between some of those neat, orderly rows of coconut trees, to shear off the wings and slow you up. Then you'll survive." And then he said, "You'll be okay except for the coconuts that will fall on your head."

Compared to the Wildcat, the Corsair climbed very fast. It ran very fast: It was a different world entirely.

It became one of the great fighters of the war, but the early models frustrated me. Have you noticed that early Marine Corsairs had tape around the cowling? There was a huge, self-sealing gas tank in exactly the wrong place, smack-dab in front of the pilot. It was made of reclaimed rubber and could catch fire if hit by a spark or an enemy round. Fuel leaked out through the seams on the cowling and could come flying back to block your windshield. We put tape around the seams to prevent being blinded by leaks or having escaping vapors ignite and blow the plane to pieces.

FRANK C. LANG Believe it or not, having that fat radar installation out on the right wing actually improved the performance of the Corsair so

These are Marine F4U-1 Corsairs operating from a Pacific island base.

[U.S. Navy]

that the F4U-2 was in some ways easier to fly than the early F4U-1. The radome improved the stall characteristics considerably. There was a noteworthy improvement in left roll performance over the standard F4U-1.

Prior to World War II, when it got dark, aircraft went into the hangar. Fighting at night was a new idea. Marine night fighters got started at the beginning of 1943. I came out of flight school and went directly into night fighters at Cherry Point. Our first commander at VMF (N)-532 was Maj. Ross Mickey. When we first came together, we hadn't received our first aircraft yet.

There were only 36 F4U-2 Corsairs made. Of the 36, we got 18 and the Navy got the rest. The Navy used them to equip its night fighter squadrons, VF (N)-75 and VF (N)-76. They were modified at the Naval Aircraft Factory in Philadelphia, Pennsylvania. They put the radome on there in Philadelphia.

I was born in 1918 in New Rochelle, New York. I worked for

United Aircraft before I came into the service. I had my private pilot's license while I was working for Chance Vought, a division of United and the maker of the Corsair. Getting into the Corsair as a Marine pilot was the fulfillment of a dream. It was really a great airplane.

Like nearly all Marines who became pilots early in the war, I started out by enlisting in the Navy, up in Boston. I went to Pensacola, Florida, for flight training. That was a piece of cake for me because I was already working on a commercial pilot's rating by then.

In training on the East Coast, we wore Navy flight suits. We wore a winter jacket and coveralls that we got from the Army Air Corps because the Navy didn't have any heavy, winter-type gear. After I got overseas, we wore just a flight suit with a pair of shorts underneath. It was pretty warm in the Pacific.

We had our flying helmet with oxygen mask. We always put our oxygen mask on immediately on taking off.

The cockpit of the F4U-2 Corsair was very roomy. I'm a big guy and I had lots of room in the cockpit. I had no difficulty whatever reaching the levers and buttons. The legroom was just fantastic in the Corsair. They had a hole in the bottom of the fuselage with a piece of plexiglass there that you could look through. We had one gent in our squadron, 1st Lt. Don Fenton, who just made it into the service because he was five foot four and a half, something like that, and he had to use a pillow in order to fly the Corsair. Of course, the Corsair had that long nose and the birdcage canopy, so visibility could have been better, especially when taxiing on the ground. They improved visibility later with a different canopy shape, but we only got one of the bubble canopies in my squadron.

It was a difficult aircraft to taxi. Overseas we had a crew chief lie on the wing beside us and communicate with hand signals to help us taxi. Otherwise we had to turn left, right, left, right constantly to make sure there was nothing in front of us.

While we were training in the F4U-2 at Cherry Point on October 19, 1943, I was making an overhead run on a flight of SBD Dauntlesses when one of the SBDs hit my airplane. It was quite an impact. There was

1st Lt. Thomas M. Tomlinson began the war in the cockpit of the F4F-4 Wildcat but graduated quickly to the F4U-1 Corsair. His squadron, VMF-214, became famous as the "Swashbucklers" before Lt. Col. Gregory "Pappy" Boyington came along to reconstitute the outfit as the "Black Sheep" squadron. Here, Tomlinson sits in an F4U-1 cockpit on Guadalcanal.

[U.S. Marine Corps/E. Hart]

a heavy, clunking sound when we collided. I suffered pretty severe damage to my right wing and lost my radome. Fortunately, both the SBD and I managed to land safely.

We started out at Tarawa. January 13, 1944, was the date of our first flying there. On February 15, 1944, we went up Roi-Namur in Kwajalein Atoll, the Marshall Islands, where night intruder flights by Japanese bombers were a pesky and persistent problem. They were flying over Eniwetok Atoll, and that's where we got our first kill. We knocked him down on April 14, 1944. That's when 1st Lt. Edward A. Sovik and Capt. Howard W. Bollman each shot down a Japanese Mitsubishi G4M Betty bomber off Engebi Island, Eniwetok Atoll. They were important victories, but the cost was high. First Lieutenant Joel E. "Pete" Bonner scored hits on another Betty but sustained damage and had to bail out. First Lieutenant Donald A. Spatz was given an incorrect vector by ground controllers and went down in the ocean. A Navy destroyer eventually rescued Bonner, but Spatz was never seen again.

HOWARD W. BOLLMAN I had just returned to my tent after flying combat air patrol from 2100–2400 and was getting ready to hit the sack when the command driver came to pick up 1st Lt. Frank C. Lang. He told me that there was to be an alert, so I rode to the line with Lieutenant Lang, not intending to fly but to help out on the ground. As we arrived at the flight line, Lieutenant Spatz took off (at 0025) and Lang took off shortly afterward.

I stood by the phone as 1st Lt. Edward A. Sovik, the duty officer, was busy elsewhere. About this time the sirens sounded and at 0038 the phone rang requesting another fighter. I ran out and scrambled in F4U-2 number 212 at about 0045, just in time to hear Lieutenant Bonner announce that he was ready to jump. I tested my guns immediately after takeoff. All were okay. So I kept on all switches but the master gun.

I was vectored 270 degrees to Angels 20. When I had reached 20 miles from base, I orbited once in my climb and reached Angels 20 immediately. As soon as I reported "level," I was given a customer, "Vector 260." Approximately a minute later, I picked up a contact at three and one-half miles ahead. It soon became obvious that we were on opposite courses, and at about two miles I commenced a hard starboard, 180-degree turn, informing controllers of my action. I turned a bit past 180 degrees to 100 degrees to get back on my original track and immediately picked up the bogey at two and a half miles, azimuth 30 left above. I turned astern of the target on course 080 degrees.

I informed controllers I still had contact, and they left me as they had two more fighters to watch. I closed rapidly to half a mile while climbing to the target's Angels 22. At a half mile I slowed to the speed of the target to plan my attack. There was a white cloud base below and I had no desire to be seen against it. The moon was between two o'clock and 15 to 20 degrees elevation and me. I played with the idea of getting above the target so as to see him against the clouds, but was afraid he might be lost under a wing or nose of my plane, so I decided to come in at his altitude and 5 or 10 degrees on the down-moon side of the target.

After checking my gun switches, I added speed and crept up on the target. As I was about 10 degrees off, the sight position was inoperative, and I used search all the way. At 300 yards, I looked up and saw the target exactly where he should have been—a twin-engine Betty bomber.

I immediately sped up and closed very rapidly. I opened fire at 150 feet dead astern and 15 feet below, aiming at his right wing root.

I was startled by the lack of tracers. I had the feeling that my bullets were going astray. I fired for less than two seconds, but his starboard engine began smoking. I then transferred my aim to the port side, and after another two-second burst, I observed flame and smoke on his port engine.

At first I mistook white flashes from my incendiaries to be return fire. I instinctively ducked behind my engine. However, at no time did I receive return fire.

By this time the target was in a 15-degree nose-down attitude and I nearly rammed him. Employing what might be termed an outside snap roll to avoid him, I pulled around to one side and above to observe the plane. From this position, it appeared the flame had blown out, so I gave him another short burst from 20 degrees above and astern at 100 yards. Fifteen seconds later, he broke into two pieces and dropped to earth in flames. At the time of the explosion, there were lights, which might have been flares or gizmos (chaff) dropped from the plane. I looked at my watch. It was about 0110, or 20 minutes after takeoff.

FRANK C. LANG The night of that battle with the Betty bombers, radar was the key. We were controlled by a ground radar that had about a 250-mile range and could pick up these bombers coming from Truck, which was south and west of us. On the F4U-2 itself, we had that APS-4 radome hanging in front of the right wing. In the cockpit, we had a radar scope about six and a half inches round that had three settings on it. One was 5 miles, one was 25 miles, and one was 75 miles. So we would pick up our target and as we got closer, we would bring him closer on the scope. Later on, we had a tech rep, Hershel Hammond, from the company that made the radar. He modified the scope so we could see the target at one mile. That made it real easy to see the target and bring him in.

That night, old Howie Bollman and Ed Sovik both shot down Japanese bombers. I was flying around and my radar was picking up fake returns, which we called gizmos, caused by pieces of aluminum, or chaff, that the Japanese released from their airplanes as a decoy to confuse us.

There was one other chap named Bonner, Pete Bonner, who later became an assistant secretary of the Army. He thought he was too close to his Betty bomber when he opened fire. We had tracers in our machine guns. When Bonner fired tracers, the tail gunner in the Betty bomber saw him and shot out Bonner's engine. So he had to bail out.

We spent a day looking for him. But it wasn't until a day and a half later that a B-25 Mitchell bomber, flying from Engebi down to Truk to do some bombing, spotted Pete in the water.

A destroyer later rescued him. He was a man of very light complexion. He had no cover to protect him from the sun. After two days in that raft, he had blisters all over his body. We thought we were going to lose him for a while. Our doc did some miraculous things to treat him. We later made some modifications to the life raft based on his experience.

That same night, we lost a gent by the name of Don Spatz. The radar operator who was controlling us lost Don. It seems the controller gave Don two vector and then forgot what vector he'd given him. I was the last contact with Don. I was up at about 25,000 or 30,000 feet. His engine gave out. He needed to bail out, but he didn't. I tried to tell Don to bail out, but he wouldn't. So he went in with his airplane. He never left the aircraft.

As the war progressed, we moved on up to Saipan in the Mariana Islands. We flew out of two fields in Saipan. The original field was the short field that they later modified for the B-29s. Then we went to another airfield on the island and flew from there. At this point in the war, we saw less night activity. The Japanese knew we were there. The presence of our night fighters was absolutely a deterrent to them. I know we deterred them from operating effectively at night because as soon as we left, they came out in swarms. And then they had to put the Army Air Corps P-61 Black Widows in there to fight them at night. The P-61 wasn't available when we were doing our night work.

In July 1944, we flew from Saipan down to Guam to cover the invasion there so the fleet could have night fighter coverage. The carriers in the fleet didn't want to work their crews both day and night. So for the night missions, we took off from Saipan, flew down to Guam, spent about an hour and a half providing coverage over the fleet, and then flew back to Saipan. This was one time when we really got a sense for the sheer magnitude of a Pacific island invasion. On a moonlit night, we could see vast numbers of our warships and troop ships at sea. On rare occasions, we could glimpse flashes from shooting. There was no doubt that our side was advancing across the Pacific and moving closer to Japan.

JOHN BOLT I guess the F4U Corsair was the plane that every young man wanted to fly. There was just a special feel to the airplane. It looked right. It felt right. In reality, it could be a challenge, especially on the approach to landing with that big nose hanging out in front of you. But when you were first starting and becoming at Marine aviator, the Corsair was the plane that grabbed you.

I was born in Laurens, South Carolina, in 1921. I studied at the University of Florida for two years. In summer 1941, I joined the Marine Corps Reserve to train as a pilot and earn money for college. By then, as my high school friend, retired Air Force Col. James L. "Mac" McWhorter, 83, later reminded me, I had been "powerfully motivated" by an English teacher at Seminole High School, Margaret Lawson. In later years when I was an attorney in New Smyrna, Florida, I created a fund for the school's teacher of the year award in her honor.

I flew the Corsair [as a day fighter]. It took me some time to get into action. After receiving my wings and commission, I was assigned as a flight instructor. I'm sure they had problems filling flight-instructor positions because everybody had an idea of how best to make a contribution and it didn't include instructing. The truth is, they needed instructors and it was an important job.

I eventually drew an assignment to the Pacific, went to Espiritu Santo, moved onward to Munda, and joined squadron VMF-214, the "Black Sheep," commanded by Maj. Greg "Pappy" Boyington, who

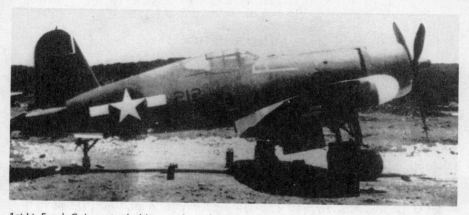

1st Lt. Frank C. Lang took this snapshot of the rare F4U-2 Corsair night fighter with a radome protruding from the leading edge of the right wing. This is airplane no. 212, which was flown by several pilots in Lang's squadron, VMF (N)-532, at Kagman Field, Saipan, in the summer of 1944.

[Frank C. Lang]

had been in the Flying Tigers. In a complex, and common, wartime shuffling of nomenclature, Boyington's fresh outfit was given the name VMF-214, while the exhausted pilots of the original VMF-214, the "Swashbucklers," [Chapter One] were sent home. On September 16, 1943, I was in a division of Corsairs that were drawn into a big fight over Kahili. The first sight of those red "meatball" insignia on the Japanese planes was disturbing, and I can't claim to have accomplished a lot in that initial battle.

A week later, in a fight with a swarm of Zeros, I was able to shoot down two and was closing in on a third when my guns jammed.

On October 16, 1943, I was already approaching the end of my tour when five Black Sheep divisions (20 Corsairs) took off. Three divisions were escorting SBD Dauntless dive-bombers in an attack on Kara Airfield. The other two were making a fighter sweep. As we flew over Kahili's Tonolei Harbor, we saw a huge convoy of Japanese barges. Boyington—usually not one to hesitate—got on the radio and said, "Nobody shoot."

While Boyington proceeded back to Munda, the other seven of us in

Who's Who

1st Lt. (later Maj. Gen.) Frank C. Lang, F4U-2 Corsair night fighter pilot, VMF (N)-532

Maj. (later Col.) Everette H. Vaughan, F4U-2 Corsair pilot and commander of VMF (N)-532

Capt. Howard W. Bollman, F4U-2 Corsair night fighter pilot, VMF (N)-532

1st Lt. Joel E. "Pete" Bonner, Jr., F4U-2 Corsair night fighter pilot, VMF (N)-532

1st Lt. Donald A. Spatz, F4U-2 Corsair night fighter pilot, VMF (N)-532

1st Lt. (later Capt.) Thomas M. Tomlinson, F4U-1 Corsair pilot with squadron VMF-214, "Swashbucklers," on Guadalcanal

1st Lt. (later Lt. Col.) John "Jack" Bolt, F4U-1 Corsair pilot with squadron VMF-214, "Black Sheep," on Munda

that division were able only to make Vella Lavella. There we refueled and I made the decision to swing back to Tonolei Harbor and attack those barges. "The skipper will be pissed," one of the other pilots told me. I went anyway, and at Tonolei we strafed a barge full of troops, an empty barge, a tug, and another small cargo vessel. We left most of the vessels burning and sinking. When we got back to Munda, Boyington expressed his displeasure with me about taking the initiative.

I shot down a couple of more Zeros on the December 23, 1943, raid against Rabaul. I opened my part of the battle with a diving pass at a formation of eight Zeros. I damaged one on the wing, but couldn't confirm anything more. He blew right through our level. Coming back up, I gave chase to another Zero, when a phosphorus bomb blew up near me. Despite the explosion, I caught the Zero in a right turn, scoring hits on its engine cowl. From 8,000 feet up, I watched the plane settle into a long shallow dive. It crashed into New Ireland below.

I flew 94 missions in two tours in the Corsair during the Solomon Islands campaign and was credited with six kills, all Japanese fighters.

That made me an ace. As for defying orders and attacking those Japanese barges, Boyington never forgave me, but Adm. William F. Halsey, Jr., praised me as a "one-man war on Japanese shipping."

The Black Sheep's five-month tour of combat produced eight aces, including Boyington. The Black Sheep were credited with 97 Japanese aircraft downed.

One war later, I flew the F-86 Sabre in Korea on an exchange tour with the Air Force (see chapter 10) and shot down six MiGs. That made me the only Marine to become an ace in two wars.

Vought F4U-2 Corsair

On the eve of World War II, the United States was developing a night fighter version of one of its most famous warplanes.

"Before the war, when night arrived, you put your planes in the hangar," said retired Maj. Gen. Frank C. Lang, 85, of San Diego, California, who was a first lieutenant when he flew the F4U-2 Corsair. "The invention of radar changed all that."

The term *radar* was initially an abbreviation (what would be called an acronym today) for "radio detection and ranging." In 1922, A. Hoyt Taylor and Leo C. Young at the Navy's Aircraft Radio Laboratory in Washington, D.C., were experimenting with radio transmissions between their station and a receiver located across the Anacostia River. During the test, a passing river steamer interrupted their signal. This suggested that radio waves might be used to detect the passage of a ship at night or in fog.

In 1936, R. C. Guthrie and R. M. Page of the Naval Research Laboratory in Washington tested a radar unit that could detect an aircraft 25 miles away. In 1940, the Navy and the Sperry Company developed an air-to-air radar unit that could be carried by a fighter.

Just after Pearl Harbor, the Naval Aircraft Factory at Philadelphia, Pennsylvania, began fitting 34 F4U-1 Corsair fighters with an APS-4 radar using an 18-inch parabolic antenna inside a housing on the leading edge of the right wing of each aircraft. Because of the radar pod, the planes' armament was reduced from six wing .50-caliber machine guns to five.

With these changes, plus a small radarscope on the pilot's instrument panel and flame dampeners to conceal exhaust emissions at night, the planes became F4U-2 models. Later, two more were modified, raising the total to 36, enough for three squadrons.

There were two Navy squadrons, plus Marine Night Fighter Squadron VMF (N)-532, which flew from Tarawa, Roi-Namur on Kwajalein Atoll, and Saipan in the Mariana Islands. Maj. Everette H. Vaughan, who commanded the squadron during much of the war, was a guiding force in developing tactics and methods for taking advantage of the superb performance of the radar-equipped F4U-2.

Apart from its radar, the F4U-2 was indistinguishable from other early F4U-1 Corsair fighters that featured a birdcage canopy with metal braces. Two of the 36 F4U-2 models had the bubble canopy that appeared on every Corsair model except the F4U-1 and F4U-2. The Marines initially received their Corsairs because the Navy was slow to adapt them to use from aircraft carrier decks, but having land-based Corsairs quickly proved to be a blessing for the leathernecks.

The larger story of the Corsair, with its inverted gull wing and powerful radial engine, began in 1938 when the U.S. Navy requested proposals for a single-seat, carrier-based fighter. The Corsair is perceived by some as a backup to the superb Grumman F6F Hellcat fighter. In fact, design work on the Corsair began before the Hellcat came along. In many ways, the Corsair was technically ahead of the Hellcat as well as the famous Japanese Zero.

The Vought Company (named for Chance Milton Vought, who died in 1930) designed the smallest possible airframe that could be tailored to fit the most powerful engine then available, the Pratt & Whitney XR-2800 Double Wasp. Engineer Rex Beisel headed the design team. They came up with the heaviest carrier-based aircraft ever built up to that time. The Corsair was so big its propeller was one-third again the diameter of the German Messerschmitt Bf 109 fighter.

These are Marine F4U-1 Corsairs in flight over the Pacific.

[U.S. Marine Corps]

The Corsair's unusual wing shape resulted from the choice of engine. The large diameter of the propeller (13 feet, 4 inches or 4.06 meters on the F4U-2 model) meant the plane would have a stalky landing gear unsuitable for carrier operations. The highly cranked, inverted gull wing that was adopted allowed the retractable main landing gear units to be located at the pinion joint of the wing, keeping them as short as possible. Apart from its unique wing shape, the Corsair was quite conventional and very much like other fighters of the war.

In June 1938, the Navy ordered an XF4U-1 prototype. The plane first flew on May 29, 1940, piloted by Lyman Bullard. Another Vought test pilot, Boone Guyton, did much of the early flying.

On its fifth flight, the prototype was caught with almost empty fuel tanks amid gathering rainsqualls. Guyton made a courageous effort to save the XF4U-1 on the posh Norwich golf course, but wet grass caused the Corsair to slide and slam into trees, halting with just enough space under the inverted fuselage for Guyton to get out. The prototype flew again and on one test flight reached 422 miles per hour (652 kilometer/hour)—faster than any fighter in the world.

In June 1941, the Navy ordered 585 F4U-1 production airplanes, the first of which flew on June 25, 1942. It was the beginning of one of the longest production runs of any aircraft. Corsairs poured off production lines belonging to Vought (F4U), Goodyear (FG), and Brewster (F3A). The Akron-based Goodyear company also built an advanced version called the F2G-1 with a more powerful engine. In a remarkable show of longevity, production of the Corsair continued for almost 15 years, with the final Corsair rolling off the Vought line in Dallas, Texas, in 1953. There were 12,571 Corsairs in all.

In the Pacific, the Corsair was credited with 2,140 aerial victories

---

Vought F4U-2 Corsair

Type: single-seat fighter, modified for night fighter duty

Power plant: one 2,000-hp (1492-kW) Pratt & Whitney R-2800-8 Double Wasp 18-cylinder radial engine driving a 13 ft 4 in (4.06 m) 3-blade Hamilton Standard propeller

Performance: maximum speed, 417 mph (671 km/h) at 19,900 ft (6065 m); 316 mph (509 km/h) at sea level; initial climb rate, 2,890 ft (881 m) per minute; service ceiling, 36,900 ft (11247 m); range, 1,015 mi (1633 km)

Weights: empty, 8,982 lb (4074 kg); loaded weight, 14,000 lb (6350 kg)

Dimensions: span, 41 ft (12.49 m); length, 33 ft 4 in (10.16 m); height, 16 ft 1 in (4.9 m); wing area, 314 sq ft (29.17 sq m)

Armament: five .50-cal (12.7-mm) Browning M2 machine guns in wing; the usual armament of 6 guns was reduced to accommodate APS-4 radar with an 18-in parabolic antenna on the right wing; other models of the Corsair had 6 machine guns or four 20-mm cannons

Crew: 1 (pilot)

First flight: May 29, 1940 (XF4U-1); June 25, 1942 (F4U-1); ca. January 1, 1943 (F4U-2)

---

against the Japanese, with only 189 air-to-air losses. Corsairs flew 64,051 combat sorties.

Most Corsairs were day fighters, among them the F4U-4 series, including the cannon-armed F4U-4B (see chapter 8). But the scientific advance made by the F4U-2 with its radar and night fighting capability led eventually to the F4U-5N night fighter which, along with the F4U-4 series, added to the Corsair legend in the Korean War.

Chapter Three

Bombing Mission to Fortress Rabaul

DON JEROME The sorriest son of a bitch in the whole Japanese army must have been the guy in charge of their base at Rabaul, and the most miserable moment in his life must have been when he looked up to see our B-25 medium bombers whipping past overhead.

In the early days, fighting in the region, including nearby Guadalcanal, was fierce and casualties were high. When we began bombing Rabaul in our B-25s, which were known in Marine parlance as PBJs, their defenses were formidable. We could expect Zero fighters to rise to meet us. We knew we would face heavy antiaircraft fire no matter what altitude we went in at.

As the Pacific war moved north and west, and the island-hopping campaign went closer to Japan, Rabaul was essentially bypassed and became difficult to supply. The Japanese must have had morale problems after that. But make no mistake: they continued to be serious adversaries. You did not want to be part of a bomber crew going over Rabaul at any time, even in the final months of the war.

A lot of people thought it was funny that Marines were flying medium bombers on a mission that didn't include supporting our own leathernecks on the ground. Our tradition has always been that every

Marine is a rifleman first, and our pilots and aircrews exist for the primary purpose of supporting our guys on the ground. But during the siege of Rabaul, we were flying a mission that was indistinguishable from what the Army Air Corps was doing. We loaded up with bombs, ammo, and gas. We took off. We flew through Zeros and flak and dropped the bombs. No one has ever really explained why this mission wasn't given to the Army.

I guess it was a little funny, too, that I found myself a gunner in a B-25, poking my .50-caliber "Ma Deuce" machine gun out into the slipstream and blasting away at the Japanese. Hell, I'm afraid of heights, and you certainly sense the height when you're shooting at people on the ground. Hell, I wanted to be in the Navy. I'm afraid of heights. I was thinking about being in the Navy where you get good food and live in clean conditions. At least that's what I thought the Navy was like.

I was born in 1922 in Maryland. I was shopping in a store with my dad when they said on the radio that Pearl Harbor had been bombed. I said, "What's a Pearl Harbor?" Within weeks, I was talking to the Navy recruiter. But my buddy was bound and determined to be a Marine, so we talked to the Marine recruiter and signed up so we could be together in the service. We never saw each other again after we got off the railroad car that took us to North Carolina for training.

I was still in North Carolina at Edenton when I went into the B-25 and joined squadron VMB-423, nicknamed the Seahorse Marines. We became one of several Marine B-25 squadrons operating from Emirau Island in the Southwest Pacific and bombing Rabaul on a regular basis. I guess I should add that I was not a member of VMB-433, the "Fork-Tailed Devils," although their planes were parked close to ours.

What Happened

Some outfits have it tough. A Marine squadron called the Fork-Tailed Devils went through a hard-luck phase during the final, hard-fought months of World War II in the South Pacific.

1st Lt. Bill Parks
July 23, 1944
North American PBJ-1 Mitchell
   (B-25)
Marine Bombing Squadron
   VMB-433, "Fork-Tailed
   Devils"
Emirau Island

1st Lt. Bill Parks in a PBJ Mitchell, 1943. Since Parks began as pilot-in-command in the left seat of the PBJ's cockpit, the only time he ever sat in the right seat was to pose for this portrait.

[courtesy Bill Parks]

Marines insist that throughout most of its combat service the squadron was a tip-top outfit with superb leadership and numerous accomplishments. But for a time it wasn't.

The outfit was Marine Bombing Squadron VMB-433, nicknamed the Fork-Tailed Devils. The squadron flew the B-25 Mitchell twin-engine medium bomber, known in Marine Corps lingo as a PBJ [see sidebar].

The squadron stood up at Cherry Point, North Carolina, on September 15, 1943. Commanded by Lt. Col. Gordon "Art" Adams, VMB-433 began its war flying from the Green Islands in the Solomons chain of the Southwest Pacific, not far from Guadalcanal. After a brief period there, VMB-433's Marines moved to Emirau Island. The squadron's job was to bomb Japanese bases in New Britain and New Ireland that were being bypassed by the Allies' island-hopping campaign, especially the famous Japanese base at Rabaul on New Britain.

Today, survivors of the bombing squadron don't like to be told that theirs was a hard-luck outfit, but during the final weeks of the war, it

A PBJ Mitchell medium bomber of squadron VMB-433 drops its bombs on the Japanese base at Rabaul, New Britain, in the South Pacific in late 1944.

[U.S. Marine Corps]

was. "We had high morale most of the time," said retired Lt. Col. Gerard "Jerry" Dethier. "But there were tough days."

VMB-433 suffered both of its combat losses in September 1944. On September 2, a PBJ piloted by 1st Lt. Charles Ingals took off on a night mission and vanished. All six aboard died, but were accounted for only after the war. On September 11, 1st Lt. Eric E. Terry, Jr., and another Marine among his six-man crew were lost after being hit by Japanese gunfire while flying in formation.

According to *Leatherneck Bombers,* by Alan C. Carey, a gunner on another plane had "nightmares for years" over the loss of Terry. "They were 50 yards away when they got hit," the gunner told Carey. "I was looking at Terry's face . . . I saw the dashboard blow up. I saw blood all over him, and the plane go down.'" A Navy seaplane rescued four survivors, but the men's inability to extricate Terry's body from the sinking PBJ hurt morale and bothered one Marine "so much that he was never the same again," Carey wrote. Another member of the squadron claims that Carey exaggerated the psychological impact of seeing a Mitchell crew member killed in action.

The Japanese had no hand in further losses that struck the squadron. On December 4, 1944, VMB-433 lost 1st Lt. Glen H. Ulrich in a swimming mishap at Emirau. On February 27, 1945, the six-man crew led by 1st Lt. Donald R. Hartley was killed in a midair collision with a PBJ from another squadron. The cause of that collision has been debated ever since. Some veterans blame a man who later became a squadron commander.

Altogether, VMB-433 lost 15 Marines in the war zone. The squadron's morale dipped abruptly, veterans say, when Adams left in April 1945. Between April 22 and July 17, the squadron had four commanders. Two who succeeded Adams—each for a few weeks only—were reviled as poor pilots and leaders. VMB-433's fourth and final commander, Maj. Andy "Guy" Smith, was respected.

The squadron transferred to the Philippines after the fighting ended and was disbanded in 1946. It had dealt out severe punishment to Japanese bases in the Pacific and had taken its own blows in the process.

BILL WOOLMAN We never would have dropped a single bomb on Rabaul if it hadn't been for the enlisted Marines who kept the planes flying and kept everything running. As for living quarters, the enlisted flight crews and pilots were in one area and the ground crews were in another, usually closer to the flight line. The metalsmiths took care of mending holes shot through the planes by enemy fire. Some of our planes looked like patchwork quilts with aluminum patches covering shell holes.

The mechanics were responsible to the line chief, who was the senior man in charge of all maintenance of the planes. Ours did a tremendous job by keeping us in the air when we needed to be.

The guys in the radio shack did a fine job keeping all radios and radar units operational. There was a civilian technician assigned to us doing testing on communication gear in the Pacific under those weather conditions. There was also a civilian tech doing research on guns and ammo under tropic conditions. Both these men had made several combat missions.

The armorers and ordnancemen were in charge of taking care of the guns on the planes and loading the bombs before each mission. Some missions were single-plane hecklers, which didn't take long to load up. If there were to be several planes used in an area bombing mission, they had to start sooner and make sure everything was in readiness for the mission. We had a warrant officer in charge of that section. Since we had seven .50-caliber machine guns firing forward, two in the turret, and one in the tail, and maybe six to nine planes in a raid, it required considerable time to keep the guns clean and to have them ready with ammo. There were three guns in the nose and one of them could be turned off from the pilot's gun switch and the bombardier could use it as a free gun. This seemed more effective on low-level strafing missions just above the trees.

While on the Green Islands, we adapted the planes by adding two .30-caliber machine guns to the side windows, which were fired by the radio/radar gunners. They were .50-calibers on some planes. The radio gunner could sit on the chemical toilet and fire from either side or both at once on a strafing run.

Before each mission, we had a briefing for the crew or crews about the purpose of the mission and maybe what we could expect from the Japs. That was usually antiaircraft gunfire. The squadron intelligence officer usually handled briefings. Sometimes an officer from another unit might give us info on the target. We worked with New Zealanders and sometimes a naval officer as we had a PT boat unit there also.

Since we were almost right on the equator, we wore as little as possible because of the heat and humidity. Usually the uniform in the daytime was cutoff pants and shoes and maybe a cap. It did rain quite often. We tried to make good use of the rains for showers as that was all the fresh water we had. We sometimes got all soaped up and just as suddenly the rain quit. That meant we either had to go wash off in the ocean or use the rainwater we caught in a 55-gallon barrel we had erected on a stand for showering. We lived in squad tents and had made a gutter from some boards to catch rainwater that ran down to another barrel. We used this for washing and brushing teeth. The Navy sent a couple of guys by all our tents almost daily to spray an oil scum on the water in the barrels to keep down mosquitoes. If you put your steel helmet in the water and brought it up fast, the oil usually stayed in the barrel.

They had a distillery unit set up to distill seawater, but it didn't taste good. There were only four faucets on it, and when you filled your canteen, you had to let it sit for a while as there was rust in the pipes and it was almost rust-colored water until it settled.

Our chow was at a common mess where all enlisted ate. The pilots and ground officers had another mess tent nearby. We all had to take an Atabrine pill each day to prevent malaria.

Once in a while we got in a load of beer and Cokes and had to put armed guards on it to protect it from our unit and others until it was rationed out.

We got cigarettes free for quite a while. I had never heard of Chelsea brand, but evidently they and Planters had a deal because the cigs came packed 50 in a Planters peanut can. Looked funny with a bunch of guys walking around with a Planters can in their hand. I was lucky in that I had gotten a celluloid cigarette package holder and just filled it as needed.

Later we could buy various brands of cigs at 50 cents per carton of ten packs. These made good trade material in Sydney, Australia, if you could get them down there.

When we went on a mission, we wore either a summer flight suit or dungarees and always wore a Mae West inflatable vest. We usually carried our 38-caliber revolver and survival knife. We didn't have any ID on our person besides our dog tags. We might have a small map just for reference. Wearing your parachute harness was required. Your chute was held on the bulkhead with a bungee cord, always ready to grab.

BILL PARKS Our last stop in the continental United States was El Centro, California, way out in the desert far from Los Angeles. From there we were going to be flying over water, a very long way, to get to the South Pacific.

Prior to leaving El Centro, we removed the secret Norden bombsights from their wooden cases and placed them in the aircraft for the movement overseas. The empty crates did not go to waste. First Sergeant Eaton Golthwaite, using his vast store of ingenuity, utilized the boxes to transport the NCO club's supply of booze and beer along with two questionably acquired slot machines. Things went well until Seabees unloaded these crates marked SECRET from the ship that carried our ground echelon onto a barge in the Espiritu Santo harbor. A loading net broke open and among the crates that came apart on the barge were those containing the two slot machines. The Seabees, being equally as adept at "requisitioning" as the Marines, absconded with the slots before the Marines could climb down the net to save the precious articles. The first sergeant refused to be outdone and negotiated a deal where, for his silence, he got the NCO club's money back plus profit and the club's use of the Seabees' facility.

When our first group of nine aircraft arrived on Espiritu Santo, they were refitted for combat and flown northwest across the Coral Sea, along the west side of Guadalcanal, and up the Solomons' "slot" to Munda on New Georgia island, where the flight echelon spent the night. The following day, we continued northwest along Vella Lavella, the Treasury Islands, Bougainville, and Buka before arriving on the Green Islands, the squadron's first combat station, on July 16, 1944. In August, the second group of aircraft, led by Maj. Art Adams, arrived on Green and joined the first group's combat operations already under way. Ground personnel did not reach us immediately, so we received maintenance help from another squadron.

By August of 1944, the war in the Pacific was moving toward the northwest, and the bloody battles for the Solomons island chain were over. A few Japanese troops remained on those previously unknown but now famous islands where thousands from both sides lost their lives. Guadalcanal, Munda, Bougainville, and Buka were quiet while the few remaining enemy troops hiding in the bush were neutralized by a handful of Allied troops.

The Japanese naval base at Rabaul, New Britain, enemy headquarters in the South Pacific, and its five supporting airfields were mostly abandoned and their ships and planes had moved north to Truk or to some island closer to their homeland. Also partly abandoned were New Ireland and its excellent airfield at Kavieng. Yet some 200,000 Japanese troops remained on New Britain and New Ireland. From time to time, enemy planes would fly in provisions or personnel, mostly at night. Some provisions were brought to the bypassed islands by submarines, and on occasion Japanese troops would be moved between islands at night on motorized barges.

Our Marine Corps squadron equipped with the PBJ Mitchell medium bomber (the naval version of the B-25) operated first from the Green Islands but moved soon afterward to Emirau Island in the Saint Matthias Group, keeping a 24-hour surveillance over these areas, especially Rabaul and Kavieng. Almost every day, Marines carried out bombing and strafing in the PBJ, SBD Dauntless, TBF Avenger, and F4U Corsair. In addition, two to four single-engine planes crisscrossed the enemy-held islands throughout the day. The twin-engine PBJ, well suited for all-weather flying, took the evening watch. We could not have had a better aircraft for this mission.

The PBJ or, if you prefer, the B-25, had tricycle landing gear, high wings, two engines, and a lot of power for a plane that weighed more than 15 tons.

Climbing aboard a PBJ for a mission was a pretty straightforward process. The PBJ had two hatches with built-in steps under the body. One was aft of the waist gunner's windows and the other one was just behind the cockpit. Those of us in the front of the aircraft could climb straight up, slide into our seats, and start the engines. Sixty years after World War II, scratching our collective heads at a reunion of squadron veterans, none of us could remember for certain whether we had seat belts in those days.

These are PBJ Mitchell medium bombers on a bombing mission in the South Pacific.

[U.S. Marine Corps]

Mitchell Medium Bomber

The thing I remember most vividly about the B-25 is the painfully intense, high-pitched scream in the cockpit as the pilot changed the props' pitch during run-up with the windows open. Perhaps the wail of a banshee close by would be a good comparison. However, the noise was not limited to run-up and testing. It was very noisy when flying. Of all the aircraft I have flown, and that is many, the B-25/PBJ is by far the noisiest. In order to get more power from the engines, there was no muffler, and each cylinder had a very short exhaust stack, only long enough to get the exhaust out past the engine nacelle and into the ears of the crew. The noise level was incredible. None of us had earplugs. Most people who flew the B-25/PBJ have a hearing problem. I do! Some of the

R-2600 engines had collector ring exhausts and were less noisy than the ones with individual exhaust stacks. A modern-day analogy would be the Metallica concert my teenaged grandson conned me into taking him to not long ago.

The engine-starting procedure and general checklists were more complicated than any other plane I've been around, although the procedure wasn't any different from most aircraft with radial engines.

I also found the smell of the plane to be very exotic. Scents included hydraulic fluid, insulation, lubricants, and others that I could not identify. There also was a generalized "hot" smell. I would say that the hot smell is about the same on all radial-engine aircraft. A large part of it is lack of good maintenance and leaking gaskets. On the PBJ/B-25, the zinc chromate paint had a distinctive smell, and in hot weather the insulation smelled sort of dry and musty. As I recall, it was quilted nylon filled with asbestos. I can't say it helped much.

Starting procedures were not overly complicated other than the requirement to prime the engines during the starting sequence, with the mixture controls in idle-cutoff. As I recall, we had to energize the starter, engage it, prime the engine, and advance the throttle, all in the same sequence, which made it a three-handed game. It likely looked complicated, but was easy enough once you got the hang of it.

One pilot claimed recently that the B-25/PBJ had a long takeoff roll and needed almost 4,700 feet of runway to get into the air. That caused him to wonder how a B-25 could take off from a World War II aircraft carrier, even with 30-plus knots over the bow.

In fact, we didn't need that much space, even when taking off loaded with our typical load of fourteen 100-pound bombs. Our runway at Emirau was 5,000 feet long and we always got off about halfway down. Maybe the pilot who needed more space didn't know that the manufacturer, North American Aviation, recommended 15 degrees of flap on takeoff to provide more lift. Without 15 degrees, the PBJ/B-25 ate up a lot of runway. As with any aircraft, the takeoff roll varied with ambient temperature, fuel load, weapons, size of the crew, and flap settings, but even in hot weather we could sometimes get off in 2,500 feet.

PBJ Mitchell crew consisting of (back row, left to right) 1st Lt. Bill Parks, pilot; 1st Lt. Chuck Higbie, copilot; Tech. Sgt. Weyman Carter, navigator; (front row, left to right) Corporal Percy Deputy, tail gunner; Staff Sgt. Don Synold, top gunner; and Corporal Henry Leonard, radio gunner.

[Bill Parks]

Once you got that twin-engine bomber off the runway and felt lift building as you climbed out, you had an aircraft that was incredibly responsive to the pilot's hands on the controls. Overall, I felt that it was an easy aircraft to fly. It had a reasonable rate of roll for a bomber, and the controls were positive and responsive in pitch, roll, and yaw. At low airspeeds the nose tended to fall in turns with more than about 25–30 degrees of bank. If you tried to correct this with the top rudder, the plane would snap roll. You didn't want this to happen when you were at traffic-pattern altitude right over the airfield because you wouldn't have enough height to recover. Pilots became accustomed to the aircraft and rarely had any serious problems handling it. When our squadron lost an aircraft in a midair collision during combat operations, there was nothing about the loss that could be attributed to the design of the airplane.

From Emirau down to Rabaul was a couple of hundred miles, so a

Who's Who

1st Lt. Bill Parks, pilot

1st Lt. Chuck Higbie, copilot

Tech Sgt. Weyman Carter, bombardier-navigator

Cpl. Percy Deputy, tail gunner

Sgt. Don Synold, top gunner

Cpl. Henry Leonard, radio gunner

SSgt. Bill Woolman, gunner on scroll mission, VMB-423

SSgt. Don Jerome, gunner, VMB-423

typical mission was two and a half to three hours, during which time you would be exposed to Japanese fighters for perhaps 10 to 15 minutes and to gunfire from the ground for maybe five. I never did see a Japanese fighter myself. We kept the five airstrips at Rabaul so bombed out that the war could move to the north and west without the Japanese at Rabaul being a factor.

A Scroll for the Japanese

On May 27, 1944, a dark blue Marine Corps bomber swooped over the Japanese airfield at Rabaul, New Britain, in the South Pacific. For weeks, PBJ-1 Mitchells had been bombing the Japanese. This plane was carrying bombs, too, but it was also carrying . . . a scroll.

Retired Army Capt. Bill Woolman, 81, of Shell Knob, Missouri, was a Marine staff sergeant and radio/radar operator and gunner aboard the PBJ-1.

Although he was born in Dallas, Texas, Woolman was chosen for the mission because he grew up in Watonga, Oklahoma. "They went through the squadron looking for men from Oklahoma," said Woolman. "There were just two of us."

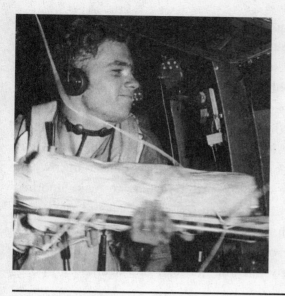

Staff Sgt. Bill Woolman prepares to drop the scroll on the Japanese at the left window of his PBJ Mitchell bomber.

[Bill Woolman]

Thirty-five thousand Oklahoma City schoolchildren had each donated a dime toward the cost of a Marine Corps transport plane. Each child also signed a 65-foot scroll conveying a warning to the Japanese that even the schoolchildren would fight, if necessary, to win the war.

"They felt an Oklahoma boy like me should go on this raid to drop the scroll on the Japanese," Woolman said.

The PBJ-1 was the Marines' version of the B-25 Mitchell medium bomber, best known for its role in the April 1942 attack on the Japanese home islands led by the Army Air Forces' Lt. Col. James Doolittle. The squadron was Marine Bombing Squadron VMB-423, nicknamed the Seahorse Marines, one of seven PBJ-1 outfits that saw combat in the Pacific war, commanded by Lt. Col. John L. Winston. The squadron lost ten aircraft and 37 men during the war. "We had other guys from Oklahoma but by then they were dead," Woolman said.

Although the squadron was operating from the Green Islands in the Solomons, Woolman's PBJ-1 crew was ordered to proceed to Bougainville to pick up the scroll. In mounting the mission against Rabaul, Woolman's crew was asked to go in at low level so the event could be photographed from an accompanying torpedo bomber. "We said we couldn't do that," said Woolman. The PBJ-1 attacked at 7,000 feet with a combat photographer on board to record the event.

Woolman remembers the scroll well. It was written in English and had photos of Germany's Adolf Hitler, Japan's Hideki Tôjô, and Italy's Benito Mussolini. By the time of the mission, Italy had been defeated, "so Mussolini's face was X-ed out."

The scroll-dropping mission enjoyed the support of Maj. Gen. Ralph J. Mitchell, commander of the First Marine Aircraft Wing. When Woolman's crew dropped the scroll (before returning to make another run with six 100-pound bombs), the signatures of Mitchell and two Army generals had been added to those of the Oklahoma schoolchildren.

The crew weighed the scroll down with a burned-out machine gun barrel and dropped it squarely into the midst of the Japanese. In post-

---

North American PBJ-1D Mitchell

Type: 6-place, twin-engine medium bomber

Power plant: two 1,700-hp (1268-kW) Wright R-2600-13 air-cooled, 14-cylinder radial engines

Performance: maximum speed, 275 mph (443 km/h) at 13,000 ft (3960 m); climb to 15,000 ft (4570 m) in 19 minutes; service ceiling, 23,800 ft (7255 m); normal range, 1,350 mi (2173 km)

Weights: empty, 19,975 lb (9061 kg); maximum takeoff, 36,047 lb (16351 kg)

Dimensions: span, 67 ft 7 in (20.60 m); length, 51 ft (15.54 m); height, 15 ft 9 in (4.80 m); wing area, 610 sq ft (56.67 sq m)

Armament: 7 forward-firing .50-cal (12.7-mm) machine guns operated by pilot and top gunner; one .50-cal (12.7-mm) machine gun in the tail position; one or two .30-cal (7.62-mm) machine guns in waist position; bombload of (typically) fourteen 100-lb (45-kg) general-purpose bombs or four 500-lb (227-kg) general-purpose bombs; on some versions: one M4 75-mm cannon weighing 760 lb (348 kg) with 21 rounds

Crew: 6 (pilot, copilot, bombardier-navigator, top gunner, radio gunner, tail gunner)

First flight: August 19, 1940

---

war years, efforts to find a record that the Japanese received and understood the scroll have proven unsuccessful.

Woolman flew a total of 57 missions. In postwar years, Woolman became an Army infantry officer. He served with the 45th Infantry Division, an Oklahoma Guard unit, during the Korean War.

North American PBJ-1D Mitchell (B-25)

The loud, muscular, medium bomber that attacked Tokyo in April 1942 at the hands of Lt. Col. Jimmy Doolittle of the Army Air Corps also became the bulwark of seven Marine Corps squadrons in the Pacific war. It was called the B-25 in Army parlance, but it became the PBJ under the naming system used by the Navy. The letters referred to a patrol bomber (PB) built by North American Aviation, Inc. (J), although the plane wasn't really used on patrols so much as on conventional bombing missions. The Marines retained the popular name Mitchell for the plane, honoring an Army general who had believed in airpower when others didn't. The Navy purchased a total of 706 B-25s to be used by the Marine Corps as PBJ models. During Pacific fighting, the Marines lost 26 of these in combat and 18 more in noncombat mishaps, with a loss of 195 crew members.

When the first squadron came together to fly the twin-engine Mitchell, the Marine Corps did not have a single pilot who had ever before flown an aircraft with more than one engine. So after VMB-413 was formed at Cherry Point, North Carolina, in March 1943, it became not merely a means of introducing men to a new plane but also a training squadron for copilots, radio operators, navigators, and gunners. This first squadron then became the nucleus of the subsequent Marine outfits that took the Corps' largest aircraft to war. When VMB-423, -433, and -443 were formed on September 15, 1943, many of the plank owners came from the initial outfit. Similarly, the initial squadron provided many of the first members of VMB-611, -612, and -613 formed on October 1, 1943. Collectively, these seven squadrons were known as the

Marine Medium Bomber Group, the only such organization in the history of the Corps.

The Marines were fielding a plane built by a company that had never manufactured a bomber before. North American's brilliant chief, James H. "Dutch" Kindleberger, was the moving force behind his company's first bomber, the NA-40 of 1939. The "one of a kind" NA-40 was a shoulder-wing aircraft with tricycle landing gear. In natural metal, it was a shining, silvery machine. It became the NA-40B after an engine change that gave it a pair of 82-kW Wright R-2600 Cyclone radial piston engines. The Cyclone was reliable and was later to win praise from mechanics that worked on it in every climate, often under primitive conditions with inadequate supplies and support. The final design of the B-25 bomber was not yet solidified, but the choice of power plant never changed.

Based on this experience, North American introduced its NA-62 design. The Army air forces quickly gave it the B-25 designation and the name Mitchell followed. It was a nod to Army Brig. Gen. William S. "Billy" Mitchell, who had shown in the 1920s that a bomber could destroy a battleship.

Shining like a newly minted silver dollar, the first B-25 with its unpainted aluminum exterior took off from Los Angeles's Mines Field (the location of today's international airport) for its first flight on August 19, 1940.

Compared to the NA-40, the B-25 Mitchell (the Marine PBJ) had its fuselage widened to provide side-by-side seating for pilot and copilot/navigator. As test-flying progressed, a further change in the B-25 design led to a "bent" or broken-dihedral wing that angled upward from the side of the fuselage but was level outboard of the Cyclone engines. Once the wing was changed, few other modifications were needed to make the B-25 Mitchell a fully operational warplane. As the war progressed, most changes to the B-25 involved its armament. Mitchell carried just about every combination of guns and bombs. A few Army B-25s and Marine PBJs even packed a 75-millimeter cannon—potent during low-level raids on Japanese shipping.

Chapter Four

The Secret Mission No One Told You About

J.J. GEUSS We were scheduled to go to England to attack V-1 buzz bomb launch sites in occupied France and Belgium. We would have been the only Marines in England.

I learned later what Army chief of staff Gen. George C. Marshall said when they briefed him on Project Danny. "Marines in Europe?" were the first words out of Marshall's mouth.

I didn't know any of this at the time. I achieved my boyhood goal of becoming a Marine and a pilot, but nobody was consulting me on secret plans for Europe.

I was born in 1924 in Chicago. My uncle was a retired Marine sergeant who influenced me to join the Marine Corps. At age nine, I could field strip a Springfield .03 rifle and recite every word of the Manual of Arms.

My dream was to fly. Curiously enough, I don't have a memory of where I was when we learned the Japanese had attacked Pearl Harbor on December 7, 1941. Still, I was more interested in military things and in aviation than most kids.

I was 18 when I went in as an aviation cadet on July 24, 1942. Under the arrangement for flight training at that time, we began as seamen

**1st Lt. John "J.J." Geuss
1944–1945
Vought F4U-1C Corsair
Marine Fighter Squadron
   VMF-311 "Hell's Belles"
Yontan Field, Okinawa**

Newly commissioned Corsair pilot
2nd Lt. John J. Geuss with
squadron VMF-511 at Marine
Corps Air Station in 1943. Geuss's
squadron was being readied for a
secret mission, details of which he
did not learn until after the war.

[J.J. Geuss]

second class. We were three or four months into the program when they changed the arrangement and we became aviation cadets.

No other airplane ever entered my mind. I was going to fly the F4U Corsair. It was the plane that inspired every young man—the neatest, sleekest, fastest thing in the sky.

In our final training squadron we requested to be either a multi-engine or single-engine fighter pilot. I wanted to be a fighter pilot. I was able to stay on the single-engine track, graduate from flight school, and receive my wings and second lieutenant's commission on August 28, 1943. My wings were pinned on my uniform by Lt. Col. Richard C. Mangrum, who had been at Pearl Harbor. He had a brushed mustache and a very distinguished look.

The Corsair was under development even before we got into the war. But production was slow and the Marine Corps temporarily had a lot of pilots, so they sent my group of newly minted aviators to Miami, Florida, for "preflying." At Miami, while waiting for the Marines to receive the Corsairs, we flew the SNJ trainer. Miami even had a few of the old SBC-3 Helldiver biplanes, being used to guide other aircraft in over-water navigation. We also flew the F2A Buffalo, which was a real dog and was used by the Marines in combat only at Midway. I flew the F2A four times in training. I figure we flew the last Brewster Buffalos in the service. There were no spare parts for them. Ours were retired soon after that.

I think the Buffalo reflects the contempt that some in the Navy held toward Marine aviation. We were supposed to get secondhand equipment. That was how they saw it. The only reason we got the Corsair—the newest, most advanced thing in the air—was that the Corsair hadn't been cleared for carrier operations yet.

Danny Preparation

After Miami, I went to Cherry Point, North Carolina, to join fighter squadron VMF-511 and fly the F4U-1 Corsair, the airplane of my dreams. The squadron was part of Marine Air Group 51, or MAG-51.

The Corsair was just coming out when I was in flight school. The Corsair was like anything we achieve in life, whether it's becoming an Eagle Scout or whatever. It was the ultimate. I wanted to get over there and do some good with the airplane.

I felt a lot of trepidation when I climbed in. That thing was so huge. And the torque was so powerful. I had to apply power very gradually or the thing would pull me off to the left of the runway. Landing was very tricky in the old F4U-1 with the "birdcage" cockpit. Visibility wasn't good at all. They ended up putting a higher tail wheel in it so the pilot could see better. But the Navy found it bounced on the deck and didn't want it on carriers.

VMF-511 moved to Simmons Knott Auxiliary Airfield, New Bern, North Carolina. It had a 3,200-foot runway and that was sufficient, but we had to be exact every time. We couldn't land "long." We had to set it down on the numbers.

Ours was the only Marine squadron ever to fly from Simmons Knott. We were all thinking about dogfighting Japanese Zeros. Air-to-ground combat was the last thing on our minds. Yet when we arrived at Simmons, they started talking to us about a new air-to-ground weapon.

For Project Danny, the secret program they were setting up for us, the Corsair was to carry the 11.75-inch Tiny Tim rocket projectile.

The Tiny Tim looked like a naval torpedo. It was powered by a 3,000-pound thrust solid-fuel rocket motor and had a 150-pound explosive warhead.

Tiny Tim was 10 feet, 3 inches long and weighed a whopping 1,285 pounds. This was obviously not what I had in mind when I became a fighter pilot. It was something for which Marines had no precedent.

A rocket this size couldn't be launched from directly beneath our Corsairs because the blast would damage the aircraft. Navy weapons experts tested two unorthodox launching methods. The first was a displacement launcher, which moved the rocket some feet below the aircraft's fuselage prior to ignition. This didn't work. Using the second method, we dropped the rocket, and a lanyard extended between plane and weapon. When the lanyard connection broke, the rocket ignited. The solid-propellant rocket accelerated the fin-stabilized Tiny Tim to about 550 miles per hour. Range during a low-altitude launch was about 1500 meters.

When we first heard about the Tiny Tim, we thought, "Are you kidding?" Then we began to wonder, "What kind of target are they planning to use this on?"

RED JAMES We didn't learn the reason for the Tiny Tim until after the war.

Many years after J.J. Geuss and I trained as Corsair pilots in VMF-511, we learned that the Corsair–Tiny Tim combination was intended for use against German submarine pens at Brest, France.

I was imagining shooting down Zeros and becoming an ace like my friend J.J., so it was a shock to be told we'd be using an unproven air-to-ground weapon against a target that wasn't revealed to us at the time.

I was born in 1922 in Bruton, Alabama, but grew up in West Virginia. I eventually logged more hours in the Corsair than almost any other Marine, namely 1,270 hours.

On December 7, 1941, I was a student at West Virginia Wesleyan

2nd Lt. Eugene N. "Red" James stands on his Corsair as a member of squadron VMF-511 in July 1944. Secret plans were being made to send Corsair pilots to England to battle German V-1 buzz bombs, but as it turned out James went to the Pacific instead.

[Red James]

College, and my father was a Presbyterian minister. I had two years of college, which was more than the Corsair guys.

I came from a really straitlaced family. You can't imagine. I wasn't allowed to have a deck of cards or to dance. My dad gave me a hard time for practicing a dance step when I heard about it on the radio.

When I heard about the Japanese attack, I didn't know where Pearl Harbor was. When the Marines decided to send me to Cherry Point, North Carolina, I didn't know where that was, either.

When the war began, because the courthouse burned down in Bruton in 1926, I had to get a replacement birth certificate. After the delay, I entered the V-5 flight training program in July 1942. I went through pilot training and received my naval aviator wings and second lieutenant's commission on October 5, 1943. For reasons having to do with the climate at my training field, flight training took me a couple of months longer than it did many Marines.

Getting into the F4U Corsair at Lee Field in Jacksonville, Florida, was the biggest thrill of my life. That was where we went to make the transition from trainers to real combat planes, and it was a real awakening. I threw that throttle home and those 2,000 horses got ahold of me and I was going down the runway and it was excitement, I'll tell you. In fact, I was so excited I didn't raise the landing gear when I was supposed to on my first takeoff. I got some ribbing for that, but they did an excellent job of teaching us how to fly a heavily armed, single-seat fighter.

I went to Cherry Point in January 1944 to join VMF-511. We initially had the early F4U-1 version of the Corsair, and it had flaws. The F4U-1 had shock absorbers that were too sensitive. The seats were too low. The tail wheel was too low for carrier operations, which is why they gave the Corsair in hand-me-down fashion to the British and the Marines, in that order.

On the right wing of the Corsair, right above the right wheel, there's a spoiler, about four inches long, so that both wings can stall at the same time. That gadget turned the Corsair into a gorgeous airplane. It was a "fix" they needed to make. Everybody wanted to fly the Corsair, but we had problems teaching people to fly it without killing themselves. It would cartwheel. But when it did have an accident, the wing would come off, the nose would come off, and the pilot would still be sitting there.

I don't think any of our Corsair experiences were as difficult as J.J. Geuss's brief exposure to the Brewster Buffalo. I'm glad I never flew the Buffalo. And I'm glad we weren't placed under too much pressure in the Corsair. At Cherry Point one day, our commanding officer took off, stalled, lost control, cartwheeled, and tore the thing up, so after that he was very understanding of our predicament in trying to fly the Corsair.

Secrecy Shroud

As for Project Danny, they never told us much. They isolated us at Simmons Knot. Then they split us up and sent us to other locations to train with rockets, including the Tiny Tim. We did part of that training flying the F6F Hellcat and learning to release the rocket coming in at 165 and 170 miles per hour at low angles and low altitudes. They never intended for us to fly the Hellcat in combat, though. They loaded our F4Us on a carrier in Norfolk and told us we were going to Europe.

Later I learned that four squadrons belonging to MAG-51 were to be

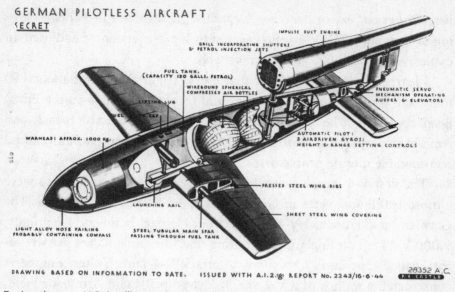

During the war, U.S. intelligence experts put together this detailed drawing of the first German "revenge weapon," the pilotless V-1 buzz bomb, or "Doodlebug." Marine Corps F4U Corsair pilots were preparing to attack V-1 launch sites, but never knew it until long after the project was cancelled.

[Norman Polmar]

equipped with the Corsair–Tiny Tim combination to attack the German submarine pens at Brest, which seemed invulnerable to high-altitude bombing. But two things happened in the summer of 1944 to change priorities. First, the Allies landed in Normandy and the U-boat pens ceased to be a problem. Second, and this is only what others tell me, the German V-1 terror weapon began hitting England. Going to Brest would have made sense, but as I saw it, the buzz bomb thing did not add up.

As it turned out, I flew the F4U-1C Corsair in combat on Okinawa with squadron VMF-311.

J.J. GEUSS We Americans called the V-1 a "buzz bomb" or "the Doodlebug." The German term *V-1* was created for domestic consumption within Germany by Joseph Goebbels's propaganda ministry at Adolf Hitler's direction. The term identified the craft as first in a series of *vergeltungswaffen,* or "revenge weapons," a response to Allied bombing of Germany. The V-1 was powered by a pulse jet engine and used an explosive warhead like that on a torpedo.

I learned long after the war that the V-1 had a range of about 150 miles and was raining down on England from launch sites on the European continent. The V-1 actually tied down hundreds of British and American antiaircraft gun crews and fighter interceptors and caused considerable morale problems.

The first V-1 struck Britain on June 12, 1944. By then, there were almost 100 launch sites in German-occupied France and Belgium. The Germans also launched V-1s by air from Heinkel bombers. Eventually, 9,000 V-1s fell on England, prompting the Allies to launch a massive effort, called Operation Crossbow, to attack V-1 launch sites. Engineers constructed a replica of a V-1 site in a swamp at Eglin Army Air Field, Florida. And, of course, they revved up the MAG-51 with the Corsair and the Tiny Tim.

After the war, we learned about a briefing that was given to General Marshall.

The Army chief remembered competition, rivalry, and flawed command relationships between soldiers and Marines during the First World War. To describe its plan for the Marines, the Navy Department sent over Comdr. Thomas H. Moorer to give the briefing to Marshall. Moorer was a patrol plane pilot who had seen combat beginning at Pearl Harbor when his PBY Catalina was blown up on the ground. He was a gruff, no-nonsense veteran who would later become chief of naval operations, but on this day he wasn't Marshall's match.

Marshall was the de facto boss of the war in Europe. He had picked the supreme commander, Gen. Dwight D. Eisenhower. As far as Marshall was concerned, the Navy and Marines could do whatever they wanted in the Pacific, but not over on the other side of the world.

Marshall arrived at the briefing late. He listened briefly, then stood and walked out. On his way to the door, he said, "As long as I'm chief of staff, there will be no Marines in Europe."

We were so close to going to Europe, our planes and equipment were loaded aboard a ship when the project was cancelled. By then, the V-2 ballistic missile had joined the V-1 buzz bomb in terror attacks on England. The V-1 and V-2 proved to be a horrible distraction to the Allies, to say nothing of killing and injuring thousands of civilians, but it was a situation that we Marines never became part of.

When we first saw the combination of the Corsair and the Tiny Tim rocket, we asked, "Is this going to work?" Firing the 11.75-inch Tiny Tim and the five-inch HVAR (high-velocity aircraft rocket) was an experience and a half. When they went off, there was just a blast of flame in front of us. None of us liked it. I worried about what would happen if an enemy round hit the Tiny Tim while we were carrying it. I'm sure the weapon would have been effective against the doodlebug launch sites, but we wondered if it might kill us first.

We fired HVARs out over the water off the gunnery range near Cherry Point. While Project Danny was still on, everybody was in hurry-up mode and they couldn't familiarize us with the rockets fast enough. It was a big hurry-up. Half of our squadron went to Quonset Point, Rhode Island, and half went to Key West, Florida, to fire more 5-inch HVARs.

After Project Danny was cancelled, we went out to China Lake, California, and launched Tiny Tim rockets using a new arrangement with the lanyard that connected the plane to the rocket. Soon after that, half our squadron went to sea on carriers. Our commanding officer, Robert Maze, the son-in-law of Adm. Arthur Radford, was lost in combat at Sakashima near Okinawa.

We went to Okinawa as replacement pilots. We had been training and testing with Danny for so long we doggone near missed World War II. VMF-511 became the first Marine carrier squadron, and those who stayed with our original squadron went aboard a carrier and spent the rest of the war at sea. The rest of us ended up in a new outfit, flying from a land base on Okinawa.

Along with Red James and Maj. Michael R. Yunck, our executive

Difficult to see in the shadows under the fuselage and wing root of this F4U Corsair, two 11.75-inch Tiny Tim air-to-ground rockets resembled naval torpedoes. For the supersecret Project Danny, which would have made Geuss and his buddies the only Marines in England, the Corsair would have carried a single Tiny Tim. This aircraft also has eight 5-inch HVAR (high velocity aircraft rockets), four under each wing, and its guns have been removed.

[J.J. Geuss]

officer, we began flying from Okinawa at a place called Yontan. Yunck became the squadron CO of VMF-311 "Hell's Belles"; Red and I became members of VMF-311.

Our new squadron was equipped with the F4U-1C model of the Corsair, which was armed with four 20-millimeter cannons instead of the machine guns we'd been familiar with. The cannons couldn't be recharged. They had a very, very slow rate of fire. Still, they were very effective in part because every third round was an armor-piercing shell. This was the first operational version of the Corsair with cannons, and it paved the way for the far more effective F4U-4B, which we used in Korea and which had almost double the firepower.

We were going to need firepower because Okinawa was the place where swarms of Japanese suicide pilots were hell-bent on bringing about a last-minute reversal of the war. They were called kamikaze. The suicide pilot was a far more effective weapon than many Americans ever realized.

In a kind of defensive ring around Okinawa, there were 12 picket stations where Navy destroyer escorts were supposed to detect the incoming kamikazes. Our primary mission was to defend against the kamikazes. An inlet on Okinawa was littered with wrecked American destroyers and destroyer escorts that got hit.

So we were going to stop these suicide pilots in our Corsairs, or so we thought. You want to hear the words *huge frustration*? We circled 24 hours a day standing guard for the kamikaze pilots, ready to intercept them and shoot them down. We always had a division of Corsairs in the air at 500 feet on patrols that lasted three to three and one-half hours. Our squadron flew during the day and was relieved by the night fighters after dark. There were other squadrons that engaged the suicide aircraft and shot some down, but we were frustrated because we never got the chance. Somehow, they were never coming when we were ready for them. We were circling and circling and never got vectored to anything. If I was on picket station seven, picket station nine would be getting all the action, and vice versa.

One rule of thumb was never fly over the escorts. There was a Corsair pilot who flew right over the picket ships and they shot him down.

I wasn't in it myself, but I recall that one of the most amazing battles with the kamikazes involved two pilots from another squadron, VMF-312, "Checkerboards," Capt. Kenneth Reusser and 1st Lt. Bob Klingman. They went after an unidentified aircraft that was leaving vapor trails over the harbor. They had to get up to 38,000 feet, the maximum ceiling for a Corsair. They got behind the twin-engine Japanese fighter, a Kawasaki Ki-45 Type 2 known to us Americans as a "Nick." Klingman had a newer Corsair that was slightly faster than Reusser's, so he drew closer to the Nick, only to find that at this extreme altitude his guns were frozen. The rear-seat gunner in the Nick looked at Klingman frantically and tried to fire his own gun but it, too, was frozen, and Klingman later said the Nick's crew was probably freezing with part of their cockpit open at that height. Anyway, Klingman closed in on the Nick and chewed up its rear fuselage with his propeller. Klingman actually hit the Nick's rear canopy, tore its gun away, and killed the gunner. The Nick spun out of control and took its crew to their deaths. Reusser and Klingman were exceedingly low on fuel and barely made it home. Klingman landed with the tips of all three of his propeller blades clipped off by about six inches each. Both Reusser and Klingman were awarded the Navy Cross. Two days later, Klingman had to bail out of a Corsair with mechanical troubles. He parachuted into the water and was on his own for a short time before being plucked to safety by a Navy destroyer.

Air to Ground

The other mission, which was much more satisfying, was close air support, dropping napalm. There was always a Marine forward air controller with a frontline battalion. We carried the napalm on the centerline. I had two 6.2-hour missions from Okinawa carrying a belly tank, a 500-pound bomb (both on the centerline), and eight 100-pound wing bombs. We would come back very short on fuel. Man, we'd feel like we were frozen in the cockpit. There was no heater in the aircraft.

We did one mission covering minesweepers off the China coast. That was a six-hour flight.

What's the hairiest thing that happened on Okinawa? Nothing was accomplished, but at about 4:30 p.m. one day, we got an urgent, urgent "Send all planes off!" They sent us up to a small island nearby with the intention of attacking some Japanese shipping. The CO, the exec, and the operations officer were away at a staff meeting up at wing headquarters. So I was the senior officer.

Sixteen of us took off. It was late in the day. It was getting darker. It was cloudy. We were on the same frequency as the night fighters. They operated alone. They warned us: "I wouldn't come in here with 16 of you." It had never been intended that a large gaggle of Corsairs would fly into combat after dark, with no navigation aids, to attack an enemy who would be difficult to find.

I made the decision to turn around. All the while, my knees were shaking. I was thinking, "I'm going to get court-martialed." We got back to Okinawa. Ships were making smoke that covered Yontan, so we couldn't see our own runway to set up a landing. The smoke was mixed with patches of heavy clouds.

There was no arrangement for an instrument letdown. I began thinking about being the junior officer in charge of 16 guys who had to bail out. Then, suddenly, there was a hole in the clouds right over the airfield. They shone a spotlight up. I figured, "Oh, my God, we can't land this way!" But we did. We landed, one by one, without incident. The CO, Mike Yunck, came running up to me. I thought he was going to court-martial me. He threw his arms around me and hugged me. He said, "I thought for sure I was going to lose 16 aircraft." Later, another guy said, "If you had gone ahead under those conditions, you would have gone by yourself."

Also in the category of hairy things that happened on Okinawa, I was in one formation where three planes blew up. They had wired the arming wires incorrectly. That was neither the first nor the last time I saw our guys killed by our own ordnance.

Yontan Airfield was way, way too crowded. They had everything there. They carved out a new airstrip called Chimu and I went there. There were occasional Jap snipers around the airfield and we didn't dare go out of our tents after dark. They cleared the snipers away after about a week.

We knew we were going to see the home islands of Japan. We did. We began flying fighter sweeps up to Kyushu, the southernmost of the main Japanese islands. Those were six-hour missions with belly tanks, so we were sweating fuel on the way back. Our targets were airfields on the southern tip of Japan. It was a real marathon going up there and back. The flying and weather conditions were extremely difficult, but we didn't see a lot in the way of Japanese defenses. By then, I think the

Corsairs stand ready on Iwo Jima. The famous Corsair fighter did not go to England to fight Germany's V-1 buzz bombs after all. Marine pilots Geuss, James, and Dworzak went to Okinawa instead. By 1945, Corsairs were fighting over Japan.

[Vought]

Japanese had decided to rely on the kamikazes—suicide pilots—as their last hope of saving their empire.

BUD DWORZAK I first flew the Corsair in July 1944 at El Centro, California. We were sent overseas in January 1945 as replacement pilots in Marine Air Group 31, or MAG-31, which included squadrons VMF-311, "Hell's Belles," and VMF-441, "Black Jacks."

We began at Roi-Namur on Kwajalein Atoll in the Marshall Islands. Col. Charles Lindbergh flew with VMF-441 as a technical advisor several months before I arrived. The pilots who flew with Lindbergh said he was a very professional, precision pilot and after each mission landed with more fuel remaining in the tank than any of the other pilots. He also redesigned the Corsair bomb racks to carry a 2,000-pound bomb on the centerline rack and a 1,000-pound bomb on each of the two pylon racks, giving the Corsair a bombload of 4,000 pounds.

In March 1945, we moved to Okinawa. At Yontan Airfield, things

Who's Who

1st Lt. (later Col.) John J. "J.J." Geuss, F4U-1C Corsair fighter pilot, VMF-311, Okinawa

1st Lt. (later Maj.) Eugene N. "Red" James, F4U-1C Corsair fighter pilot, VMF-311, Okinawa

Capt. Willis "Bud" Dworzak, F4U-1C Corsair fighter pilot, Okinawa

were rather primitive. We lived right on the airfield, on the other side of the taxiway from where our aircraft were deployed. At first we each shared a shelter half with another pilot. Later, pyramidal tents were provided, which we shared with three or four others. Sometime in May the Seabees replaced our tents with Quonset huts.

I was a long way from home. I was born in 1923 in Ashbury Park, New Jersey. I went to El Centro and studied bombing in the SBD Dauntless dive-bomber before they shifted me to the Corsair. The Marine Corps was lucky to benefit from the hard luck the Navy had with the Corsair. It started out with wet wings (prototypes) that leaked. They put a 240-gallon fuel tank right behind the engine. The tank on the fuselage did leak a little. They put pink tape over it to try to keep fuel from flying back.

We initially had F4U-1D models with six .50-caliber machine guns, but they were replaced in April with F4U-1C Corsairs with four 20-millimeter cannons. We all wanted a chance to engage the Japanese in the air, but there were fewer and fewer chances.

On May 11, 1945, I was part of a division led by Rob Raber. He wasn't as aggressive as I felt he should be. They vectored us to intercept a twin-engine Japanese aircraft that turned out to be a Mitsubishi Ki-46 Type 100 known as a "Dinah"—an armed reconnaissance aircraft that probably was sizing up our forces for kamikaze, or suicide, raids.

I dropped my belly tank because I didn't want to be burdened with that damn thing. I put up full power, left Raber behind, and went after the Jap. That's when I saw it was a Dinah. I didn't know whether he had a tail gunner. I squeezed off a few rounds and said, "Oh, son of a bitch!" My guns were not boresighted.

I was flying a newly delivered Corsair and the guns hadn't been boresighted. I could see my tracers going out all over the place instead of forming a V with the apex at the target. I thought, "He's going to get away."

I'm closing on him now. He's heading down for a bank of clouds. There are ships off to my left. One of them may have been the picket ship that was vectoring us. I didn't want this guy getting down and hitting any ships. I just held down on the trigger.

We had 200 rounds per gun. I had to put a violent input into the control system as I was overtaking him to avoid hitting him. His left wing was completely shot off by that time. He was spinning in. I was credited with the kill. A broadside from a destroyer and I got an Air Medal for that.

Japanese Suicide Pilots

The act of killing oneself to achieve success in battle has never sat well with Americans, but the act is painfully familiar to U.S. Marines and sailors who fought in the Pacific in the final phase of World War II. They withstood attacks by Japan's "special attack force," or kamikazes— military aircraft rebuilt into flying bombs with suicide pilots at the controls.

"The sky was full of them," said Al Noll, 81, of Fredericksburg, Virginia, who was a loader on a stern gun tub of tank landing ship LST 949 during the invasion of Okinawa in 1945. Noll's 40-millimeter Bofors antiaircraft cannon threw out a constant stream of flying steel that joined gunfire from hundreds of ships, "and yet they kept coming at us, like nothing was going to stop them. They had incredible determination."

In October 1944, Japan's Adm. Takijiro Onishi suggested using military planes as manned flying bombs. "They weren't nuts," said Howard Johnson, 56, of San Francisco, California, a historian who studied the era. "They believed in their course of action. They were making one last effort to save their empire."

The kamikaze ("divine wind") was the typhoon that destroyed Kublai Khan's fleet and halted his invasion of Japan in 1281. As the war drew closer to Japan, fighters and bombers were converted into flying bombs. When an aircraft exploded and killed 25 men, wounding 106, aboard the carrier USS *Randolph* (CV 15) on March 11, 1945, it was a twin-engine bomber known as a "Frances." Near the war's end, Japan developed both a small airplane and a piloted rocket bomb for suicide missions.

A popular myth is that Japan's suicide pilots were ineffective. "Just ask any sailor," said Noll.

"I was on the radar picket line off Okinawa for two months," said retired Capt. H. E. "Bucky" Walters, 83, of Springfield, Virginia. "They crashed all around us, constantly."

Walters was engineering officer on the destroyer USS *Bache* (DD 470). "On May 13, 1945, ten airplanes came after us. We shot down nine. The tenth was a Val dive-bomber that came right up our stern. He cut off the number 2 smokestack and crashed on the main deck. His explosion blew a big hole in the deck above the waterline." The *Bache* was gravely damaged and suffered 42 killed, 14 missing, and 32 wounded.

A Japanese history published in 1974 says that Japan lost 2,525 aviators—1,204 navy and 1,321 army pilots—in kamikaze attacks. The Japanese side claimed 81 Allied ships sunk and 195 damaged. Other sources give the actual figure as 34 sunk and 288 damaged. Suicide attacks caused 80 percent of American losses in the final year of the Pacific war. Kamikaze pilots sank 26 U.S. combat ships, including three escort carriers, and killed 3,000 sailors.

Chapter Five

Devil Dogs in a Dive-Bomber

BUD PAGE On the day the war ended, I was getting out of the hospital at Cherry Point, North Carolina, after medical complications from a crash in an SBD Dauntless two years earlier. For most of that time, I hadn't realized that my insides were messed up, but it became obvious when it started hurting to eat.

I had just gotten out of the hospital and was running a Corsair line and O & R shop (overhaul and repair). I learned about the Japanese surrender over the radio. Everybody knew we had dropped something, but no one knew for sure exactly what we'd dropped. They said Japan threw in the towel. People went about their business without a lot of excitement, but, for me, it was a good feeling to have survived a bad airplane crash during training, flown the Dauntless in combat, and come home in one piece. Well, I was in almost one piece. I had permanent leg and internal injuries from the crash and they have never gone away.

When we celebrated VJ Day on August 15, 1945, we were marking a victory over Japan that might not have happened without the Douglas SBD Dauntless dive-bomber.

Gunnery Sgt. Bud Page
August 15, 1945
Douglas SBD-5 Dauntless
Marine Scout Bombing
**   Squadron VMSB-331**
Majuro, Marshall Islands

Bud Page, who served with an SBD
Dauntless squadron during World
War II and flew the F3D Skyknight
in Korea.

[Bud Page]

JIM BAILEY I was coming home across the Pacific on an LST, a landing ship tank that was being used, in effect, as a troop ship. I washed my clothes, played bridge, and got to know a little about the Navy. One night at chow, the ship's captain said, "They dropped the big bomb on Japan." I said, "I know we have 2,000-pound bombs. We dropped those on Okinawa. Was this a 3,000- or 4,000-pound bomb?" The captain said, "No, this is some new bomb. It's bigger than that." He was convinced that this big bomb was going to end the war, but he didn't make an announcement or anything until a few days later on August 15, 1945, when the Japanese surrendered. Our LST dropped us off on the dock at Pearl Harbor, and we walked up to Ewa and checked in. It had all begun at Ewa when Marines like Robert Galer looked up into the sky to see Japanese planes hurtling overhead, and now it was over and we had won.

I agree that it would have been harder to achieve victory without the Dauntless dive-bomber. That SBD was very, very accurate. When Navy Dauntless pilots turned the tide at the Battle of Midway, they started their dive on the Japanese carriers, lined up their bombsights on the big red

The SBD Dauntless dive-bomber was already obsolete when the United States was drawn into World War II. Navy carrier pilots used it to attack Japanese aircraft carriers at Midway. Marines also flew the SBD, among them Bud Page, who was seriously injured in a Dauntless crash but did not allow that to prevent him from reaching the Pacific war.

[Douglas Aircraft]

meatball painted on the decks of each Japanese carrier, and dropped their bombs with uncanny accuracy. We Marines used the Dauntless to good effect, but it was the Navy at Midway that turned the tide.

The Dauntless was a delightful-handling airplane. The dive flaps opened up and you could fly it vertically. The only disappointing thing was that it was underpowered. You wanted to be downwind of the target when you were dive-bombing because if you were upwind, the wind would blow you toward the target and you'd overrun it. That would force you into a negative dive angle and you could lose control of the aircraft.

BUD PAGE I began in engineering and was a maintainer on the SBD-5 Dauntless. I'm also a pilot and spent plenty of time at the controls of aircraft in World War II, Korea, and Vietnam. I joined squadron VMSB-331 at Bogue Field, about 20 miles from Cherry Point, North Carolina, in May 1943.

At Bogue Field, we had a full complement of SBD-5 Dauntlesses, plus an SNJ Texan trainer we used to make the mail run to Cherry Point every day. They threw us into a heavy training program with two flights per day, plus some night flying and gunnery.

There wasn't much to see at Bogue Field. The only permanent structures were the mess hall, the control tower, a supply shed, and the ops buildings. Everything else was in tents or "Dallas" huts. These were 16-by-16-foot plywood huts, each with a pyramid roof. Each had a single lightbulb in the middle and screen windows protected by a plywood door that was let down during bad weather. There was a heavy influx of incoming personnel at this time and creature comforts were few.

The SBD-5 had a Wright R-1820-60 Cyclone engine, a Hamilton Standard Hydromatic propeller, and a Baker radar unit. That old radar had a hand-operated Yagi antenna on a mast under each wing. The antenna was controlled by a double-lever quadrant on the lower left side of the rear cockpit. The radar was useful only for surface search, and it was marginal at best. Except during morning and evening sector searches, we didn't use it.

The SBD had automobile-style brakes that could and did drag on occasion. This usually caused the aircraft to ground loop. This meant you were going to have a damaged Dauntless or, at best, would have to tow the aircraft back onto the hard surface out of the dirt. There was one SBD sitting next to the line tent with its left wing gone as the result of a ground loop. A new wing was lying on top of several old tires next to it, along with a new wingtip. Several of us new arrivals were given the job of putting that wing back on. No crane was available, so about 15 Marines lifted the wing up until a few of the 150 or so bolts that held it could be installed. We placed an empty 55-gallon fuel drum with old tires on top beneath the wing until we could install the rest of the bolts. We finally installed everything that is part of a wing, meaning trim tabs, control cables, electrical wiring, aileron, flaps, and dive brakes. The wingtip didn't fit, so I filed the holes to elongate them and got the screws in. We were putting an SBD-3 wingtip on an SBD-5 airplane. I asked for a torque wrench to torque all those ⅜-inch bolts but was told none was available. So I spent several hours trying to get all those bolts tightened approximately the same. Other Marines were finishing up the job of getting the aircraft ready to test. I was still worried about the torque on the bolts but told Master Sergeant Kuchinisk it was done. He promptly told me to get some flight gear and go with it on the test hop. I climbed into the backseat.

If I remember correctly, Captain Beatty was the pilot. He really rang that bird out. He blacked out both of us several times. This was in the days before G suits that protect the body from gravity forces. I asked the captain how many negative Gs he had pulled and he said, "Plenty." The next morning, I was assigned my section. A *section* in naval aviation is a formation of two planes; a *division* is two sections.

Our Dauntless dive-bombers were practicing dropping bombs on a place called Cat Island. Often, pilots were making dives of 50 to 85 degrees, which caused them to overshoot the target and to have to corkscrew to get back on target.

We lost two airplanes doing this. Luckily, the rear seats were empty on both. The SBDs collided just after peeling off for their dives. Marines in our squadron spent a couple of days wading in Bogue Sound until we recovered the remains of both pilots.

Dauntless Crash

A little later, Capt. Jack Bohning and I went on a night FCLP (field-carrier landing practice) hop. That day, the weather at Bogue was good, but there were thunderstorms in the area. The Accident Investigating Board found pilot error in the ensuing mishap, but I believe we had a wind shear, a phenomenon that was unknown then.

Anyway, as we were coming down on final approach, we ran out of airspeed, altitude, and ideas all at once. We came down short of the runway in a cluster of small pines. Jack had power on, but our SBD just fell out of the air. The left strut came partway up through the wing. We lost about 18 inches of the propeller blades.

After all this happened, the aircraft bounced back up and was airborne again. By this time, we were just along for the ride. The plane was vibrating violently. I could smell hot oil and fuel and we were falling like a rock again. We came down on the runway with the left wing low and crabbed to the left.

The right gear collapsed. We went skidding down the runway in a shower of sparks, parts, oil, and gas. Miraculously, our SBD didn't burn, but it was in a sad, sad state.

The crash crew arrived and pulled us out of the wreckage. They took us to the sick bay and "Doc" Harrington checked us over and told us to go to bed. If the SBD Dauntless hadn't been built like a battleship, we wouldn't have made it. I was to have medical problems years later, including a hospitalization just before the Japanese surrender, but that crash didn't prevent me from going to war with the squadron.

I saw that SBD in the salvage yard a week later. They were going to try to repair it, but the center section was found to be cracked through the main spar. They told me they were going to scrap it. The next weekend, it was gone.

That airplane was really tough. I had one instance, and saw others during bombing runs in the Marshall Islands, where the aircraft mushed into and bounced off the top of a coconut tree. The SBD returned to base with palm fronds shoved through the engine cowling and oil cooler door, with the bomb displacement yoke bent, with the fairings over the fuel sump lines smashed, and glass broken in the cockpit floor window. In one incident in another squadron, both crew members came back with about an inch of raw intestine hanging out. The flight surgeon shoved it back in, packed it with opium ointment, put Kotex on the wound, and grounded them for a while. I don't know what the "G" meter told that crew, but I would say their Dauntless was overstressed.

Leaving Bogue Field (with me unaware, then, that my crash had inflicted internal injuries that would haunt me later), we were assigned to Marine Air Group 31, or MAG-31, for our trip to the Pacific. The ground echelon and equipment were loaded on a train at Moorhead City and headed out for the West Coast at the end of August 1943. Our flight echelon flew to North Island near San Diego, California. Eventually, the ground echelon arrived at nearby Camp Miramar.

Off to War

The flight echelon departed aboard the escort carrier USS *Nassau*‚(CVE 16) for Pago Pago, Samoa. The ground echelon departed the West Coast on the USAT *Pueblo,* a former German tourist liner converted into a troop ship. It had very cramped quarters, and each Marine received just one meal each day plus a sandwich.

We reached Samoa and then departed for Wallis Islands, some 300 miles to the west. Wallis, a French colony, offered something for everyone. It had a mud airstrip, tents, and huts with no floors, made by the natives. It also had a large leper colony, it turned out. There was a Marine antiaircraft outfit, a Navy PV-2 Harpoon squadron, and several partial Marine squadrons of F4F Wildcats, SBD-3 and SBD-4 Dauntlesses, and F4U Corsairs.

We occupied an area previously used by the 22nd Marine Regiment. It was very dusty, hot, and humid. Water was limited. Food was mainly C rations. We were told they had elephantiasis and dengue fever there.

On November 13, 1943, we moved again. The forward echelon departed on board the USS *Mackinac* (AVP 13), a seaplane tender, for Nukufetau in the Ellice Islands. We arrived at "Nuki" on November 15 just as our aircraft were landing there. The *Mackinac* was never designed to carry the load we put on her. There was no room below decks for half the people. It rained all the way and the people on deck got wet and stayed wet.

One SBD had a mechanical problem and was stuck at Funafuti en route to Nukufetau. The Japs bombed Funafuti that night, so VMSB-331 had its first experience with shots fired in anger, so to speak. The Japs overflew Nukufetau to bomb Funafuti. On some nights, the anti-

Bud Page's SBD-5 Dauntless of squadron VMSB-331 at Nukufetau in the British-owned Ellice Islands in 1943.

[Bud Page]

aircraft fire from our people there would reflect off the bottoms of the clouds and was visible from Nukufetau.

If you want to know the truth, Nukufetau was the Garden of Eden compared to Wallis. It had no diseases and was generally cooler, although very small. We shared Nuki with the 11th Bombardment Group of the Army Air Forces, a Seabee battalion, and part of the Second Medical Battalion. We had several F4Fs that were sent up to Nuki from Funafuti that belonged, I believe, to VMF-441.

At Nuki, we finally got pneumatic tail wheels on all our SBDs. The small carrier wheels with which the Dauntlesses had been delivered from the factory were a handicap; at Wallis, they just dug ditches down the runway after a rain.

We began flying dawn and dusk patrols. At one point, we provided escort for a U.S. aircraft carrier that had been torpedoed three times and was limping to safety. VMSB-331 also participated in the search for VMF-422, which lost 21 planes at sea on a bungled formation flight into Funafuti. The search lasted from January 26 to February 4, 1944. Our squadron flew in very bad weather and we did locate one pilot, who was rescued.

Action at Tarawa

At about this time, a detachment of our planes and personnel was sent to Tarawa in the Gilbert Islands. I believe Major Beatty was in command. They were to be used for patrol purposes and for strikes if the demand arose. On one mission, VMSB-331's aircraft, along with 12 Army air force A-24s (their version of the Dauntless) and 15 Navy F6F Hellcats, staged through Makin Island to Jaluit Atoll in the Marshalls. The squadron received credit for sinking a 6,000–7,000-ton Japanese ship in the Jaluit lagoon. These planes eventually returned to Nuki.

At Nukufetau, there was a J2F Duck, an amphibian biplane, and some OS2U Kingfisher scout planes. I think they belonged to the Navy, but several of our Marine pilots decided to fly the Duck. The Duck had a very narrow landing gear and was very easy to ground loop. Everyone had a good time with it, including Jack Rostar, who damn near fell out of the window in the hull after buzzing two native girls in the lagoon. They stood up in their outrigger canoe, took off their lavalavas, which is all they wore, and waved them at the plane. I believe it was Captain Ross who landed that J2F Duck, going from one main gear to the other coming down the runway before finally getting it to settle down.

In February 1944, we moved to Majuro during the Marshall Islands invasion. The ground echelon arrived on board an LST. The aircraft arrived at Majuro by way of Apamama in the Gilberts.

Very quickly we settled into daily bombing missions, beating up the bypassed islands of Wotje, Mille, Jaluit, and Maloelap. The squadron's first target was Jaluit. Better than 40 percent of our planes received damage from antiaircraft fire, but we didn't lose any. On ensuing air strikes, VMSB-331 dropped surrender leaflets, bombs, depth charges, and, eventually, napalm. We carried two 55-gallon tanks of napalm in laminated paper tanks.

We had no air opposition after February 1944 until the Japs got a floatplane Zero operational and came over Majuro one afternoon while a large part of the fleet was at anchor in the lagoon. Flak from the island's antiaircraft guns fell around us for ten minutes. But even though

F6F Hellcats and F4U Corsairs were scrambled, they couldn't catch up with him, and he went home and landed in the lagoon at Jaluit. Staff Sergeant Hesli from our radio shop was walking down the flight line when the antiaircraft firing began. VMSB-331 had no dugouts in the flight line area. When pieces of our shrapnel began to rain down, almost everyone moved up close to the trunk of the nearest coconut tree on the low side and waited the stuff out. Hesli didn't. A piece of shell weighing about four pounds with a piece of the copper driving band still attached hit the ground about two inches in front of his foot. That prompted him to take cover.

We flew nearly 200 strikes from Majuro, and the damage to our aircraft was negligible. As I said, there were no longer any Japanese aircraft opposing us at this time. We beat down the Japanese antiaircraft fire pretty effectively.

While flying these missions, we were improving our living situation. Our camp area was very good. Nearly all tents had floors installed by the occupants. "Skeets" Collins had the water distillation plant running full blast, so we had a fair supply of fresh water. Many of our Marines had dug wells in the tent area, creating an unlimited supply of brackish water for bathing and washing clothes. Everyone now had an electric light in his tent. Food was good and we had a movie occasionally. Our squadron was operating under Task Force 57 as a unit of TG-57.4.

We had many bomb rack malfunctions. They wouldn't release. Our ordnance people redesigned them, right there in the field. At about this time, they gave us a wing rack package of two .50-caliber guns with 150 rounds of ammo each. We hung one under each wing of the Dauntless. The guns were fired electrically but they had to be charged and cleared manually on the ground. This brought the armament of the SBD up to a total of six .50-caliber machine guns firing forward. We played with these underwing packages for a while but finally gave up on them. The extra drag during flight was a concern, but the main thing was the safety problem: ground crews would have to face four hot .50-caliber machine guns that had an unknown safety factor while launching and recovering the aircraft.

Pacific Fighting

In January 1944, Japanese fighters shot down a B-24 Liberator that crashed on the lagoon side of Arno Atoll ten miles from Majuro. The Japanese beheaded the surviving crew members on the beach. The Japanese commander would have answered for this after the surrender but committed suicide before he could be brought to trial. All of our battle damage assessment (BDA) pictures were taken using a handheld camera in the rear cockpit. I took pictures of the B-24 at Arno and still have the negatives.

In April 1944, Lieutenant Ramsaur and Corporal Cardona were flying a BDA mission when they were hit by enemy machine gun fire. Ramsaur was shot through both legs. They brought the aircraft 130 miles back to Majuro and landed it with Cardona operating the rudder pedals from the rear cockpit.

We later had a Dauntless hit in the throttle quadrant that returned safely to Majuro using the mag switch to control engine rpm. We lost a total of seven aircraft due to enemy antiaircraft fire but saved all but two of the crew members. The pilot and gunner who were killed were shot down in their dive over Taroa Island, Maloelap Atoll, on May 1, 1944.

We also had a pilot and gunner shot down by antiaircraft fire at Wotje Atoll. The plane was hit and the left wing set afire at 1,700 feet altitude. He lost control and was forced to set down in the ocean, three miles offshore. They exited immediately and the plane sank in about eight seconds. They climbed into the life raft and for two hours fought a losing battle with a stiff onshore wind. They were rowing and paddling but made no headway. Orbiting aircraft tried to distract Japanese gunfire but the raft was steadily drifting ashore. The destroyer USS *Hall* (DD 583) arrived and made the dash in. The *Hall* had to go within 3,000 yards of shore to pick them up and received fire from antiaircraft and coastal defense guns. The *Hall* rescued them while under fire and they returned safely to Majuro.

In May 1944, our squadron was assigned to Task Force 59 under Army Maj. Gen. Willis Hale. During this period, we put up over 100 planes in one strike on Mille Atoll. We also provided spotter aircraft for the naval shelling of Taroa Island by two Navy destroyers.

We flew night harassment missions. We installed flame dampeners on our big exhaust stacks. They were effective but you had to watch cylinder head temperature carefully. It would zoom up to 255 degrees and start detonating while you were climbing out. Most of us just left the mixture on "auto rich." But it was still a problem.

In September 1944, the big change came when we got rid of our Dauntlesses and traded them for new F4U-1 Corsairs. The squadron was briefly redesignated VMBF-331 to indicate a "bombing fighter" outfit, but we reverted back to VMSB-331 in December 1944. The Corsair proved to be a very good dive-bomber. The best accuracy came in high-speed dives of 65 to 70 degrees. Its speed, armament, range, and load-carrying capability were all so much better than the SBD.

Bathroom Blowup

In November 1944, we were scheduled for a strike on Nauru Island, 325 miles southwest of Tarawa. This required staging from Majuro back through to Tarawa, refueling there, and stopping at Tarawa once again after the strike. We installed two 150-gallon drop tanks and a centerline bomb.

I had a corporal working for me on my aircraft, an F4U-1 Corsair painted with the side number F-41. It had rained a large amount and the F-41 was sitting in the middle of a large puddle just east of our engineering supply shed. When we hung the tanks, the breakaway fitting was leaking on the right tank and the engine wouldn't accept fuel from it. I was being called to do something else so I told the corporal to get a new seal and put it in. He did and told me the engine still would not run on the right drop tank.

I told him to put some zinc chromate paste on the fitting before installing it. When I got back to the F-41, he said he had filled up the drop tanks. I decided I had better check it out myself.

They had built a new, screened-in head—to non-Marines, that's the bathroom, the latrine—right behind our hardstand. The radio shack was right behind it.

I climbed up on the wing, put a cartridge in the starter breech, and got in the cockpit. I had the stick strapped back with the seat belt. I hit the switch and the first three propeller blades that passed in front of my eyes just burped gobs of burning gas out the stacks onto the pool of water the bird was sitting in. I didn't know that the water around me was covered with a surface of gasoline. The engine caught and started to come up to idle, but the entire airplane by this time had flames all around it, coming up over the leading edges of both wings.

By this time, the corporal was standing over by a big tree, clear of all this. I didn't know where he'd put the fire bottle. I motioned to him to pull the chocks so I could taxi it out of the flames but he shook his head, "No." So I crammed the throttle on it up to 30 inches manifold and looked out. The gasoline was blowing back behind the tail onto the new head. I just left 30 inches manifold pressure on it and thought it would blow out. Instead, the damn head started burning and rolled into the radio shack. Someone in there heard the commotion and tried to get out the door, but the windblast from my propeller was too strong for him. It blew him back inside.

The fire was out by then but the head was a wreck. I throttled back to idle and shut it down. About then, Sergeant Paul came up and told me the flight was cancelled. I went down to the line tent and was told we had to pump out and remove the drop tanks right away. The corporal then told me that the hose had been leaking badly when he was filling the tanks. That was where all the fuel had come from. I had to go explain to our commanding officer about the fire. When he heard about the head colliding with the radio shack, all he did was laugh. The squadron never made the strike on Nauru.

Bud Page and his fellow Marines heard about a new aircraft, the Fisher XP-75, which might be used in the invasion of Japan. The original version of the XP-75 used the same rear fuselage, tail unit, and landing gear as Page's familiar SBD Dauntless, although a production XP-75 would have had the squared-off tail surfaces seen here. By the time the Allies were close to Japan, the XP-75 program had proven unsuccessful. In the end, no invasion of Japan was necessary.

[Jim Hawkins]

War's End

As late as November 1944, we still had a few of the newer SBD-6 Dauntlesses around. The SBD-6 had different engines and radio gear from the SBD-5 but was the same old dependable bird.

The Army air forces and the Navy were working on a new emergency fighter, the Fisher XP-75. I saw one after the war. It was supposed to be a last-ditch project so all squadrons would have long-range fighters for the invasion of Japan. It had an SBD fuselage, an in-line engine, and one seat. The wings were flush riveted. It was ugly as sin and it turned out to be a grand failure. My guess is that the strength of the SBD airframe was their reason for developing it. The SBD was a Douglas aircraft. I spent the next two wars in other Douglas airplanes, the F3D Skyknight in Korea and, after I changed to the Air Force, the B-66 Destroyer in Vietnam. They always got me home. They did good work.

I was gone from VMSB-331 when the squadron converted to yet an-

These are Douglas SBD-5 Dauntless dive-bombers in the Pacific.

[U.S. Navy]

other airplane, the SB2C-4 Helldiver, for the final days of the war. The dropping of the two atomic bombs on Japan ended the proposed move of the squadron to Amami O Shima, a small island just south of Japan in the Ryukyu Islands. The Japanese commanders on the islands of Mille, Jaluit, Wotje, and Maloelap surrendered at Majuro. The squadron's last wartime mission was flown by an SB2C-4. By then, I was back at Cherry Point, and in and out of the hospital for belated treatment from the crash I experienced in training. I give a lot of credit to the SBD Dauntless for the victory we celebrated.

Douglas SBD-5 Dauntless

The SBD Dauntless dive-bomber was one of the great combat planes of World War II, flown in the Pacific by Navy and Marine crews who regarded the aircraft as sturdy and reliable.

"If that old bird hadn't been built like a battleship, I wouldn't be

Who's Who

Gunnery Sgt. Bud Page, SBD-5 Dauntless maintainer, squadron VMSB-331, Majuro, who also worked on the F4U-1 Corsair

1st Lt. Jim Bailey, F4U-1 Corsair pilot who also flew the SBD-5 Dauntless

here today," said Bud Page, 81, of Sumter, South Carolina, who survived a crash in the SBD in training at Cherry Point, North Carolina, in 1943.

Jack Northrop, who worked for Donald Douglas's Southern California aircraft company, designed the Dauntless in 1935 based on his earlier BT-1. Douglas Aircraft Company built 5,936 Dauntlesses between 1935 and 1944 in SBD-1 through SBD-6 models, even though the plane was obsolescent when the U.S. entered World War II.

The first SBD-1s went to Marine Corps units starting with Marine Bombing Squadron 2 VMB-2, at Ewa, Hawaii, in 1941 and VMB-1 at Quantico, Virginia, in 1941. These squadrons were renumbered as Marine Scout Bombing Squadrons VMSB-232 and VMSB-132 in 1941.

Among aircraft destroyed on the ground during the December 7, 1941, Japanese attack on Pearl Harbor were about 20 Dauntlesses of VMSB-232. Squadron pilot Capt. Richard C. Mangrum (see chapter 1) was reading the Sunday comics when he looked up to see Japanese bombers hurtling overhead. In the weeks that followed, Mangrum commanded an SBD squadron in Pacific fighting.

The Dauntless appeared on Navy carrier decks soon afterward. At the Battle of Coral Sea, May 7, 1942, Lt. Cmdr. Robert Dixon, leader of Bombing Squadron 2, used a cryptic radio message to report the sinking of the Japanese carrier *Shoho* by Dauntlesses. "Scratch one flattop," read the message.

The Dauntless's shining moment came at Midway on June 4, 1942, when 54 of the Navy dive-bombers attacked and destroyed the carriers

Akagi, *Kaga*, and *Soryu*. They also put the carrier *Hiryu* out of action. This was the Japanese carrier force that had attacked Pearl Harbor six months earlier. Midway turned the tide of the Pacific war.

In Marine Corps hands, the Dauntless was a familiar sight on Pacific islands, often in battles against Japanese units that were bypassed during the island-hopping advance toward Tokyo. The Dauntless was also used by the Army as the A-24 and by the air forces of France, Mexico, and New Zealand.

Douglas SBD-5 Dauntless

Type: 2-seat carrier-based scout bomber and dive-bomber

Power plant: one 1,200-hp Wright R-1820-60 Cyclone 9-cylinder air-cooled radial piston engine driving a 10 ft 10 in (3.30 m) 3-blade Hamilton Standard Hydromatic constant-speed propeller

Performance: maximum speed, 252 mph (406 km/h) at 10,000 ft (3048 m); initial climb rate, 1,700 ft (518 m) per minute; service ceiling, 26,100 ft (7955 m); range, 1,115 miles (1794 km) on a scouting mission

Weights: empty, 6,533 lb (2963 kg); loaded weight, 9,350 lb (4322 kg); maximum takeoff, 10,700 lb (4854 kg)

Dimensions: span, 41 ft 6½ in (12.66 m); length, 33 ft 1¼ in (10.09 m); height, 13 ft 7 in (4.14 m); wing area, 325 sq ft (30.194 sq m)

Armament: two .50-cal (12.7-mm) fixed machine guns with 360 rounds per gun in the nose and two .30-cal (7.62-mm) trainable machine guns with 2,000 rounds per gun in the rear crewman's position, option for two .50-cal (12.7-mm) fixed machine guns in a detachable, underwing rack package, plus up to 1,600 lb (726 kg) of bombs under the fuselage and 650 lb (2905 kg) of bombs under the wings

Crew: 2 (pilot and radio operator/gunner)

First flight: August 19, 1935 (BT-1); May 1, 1940 (SBD-1)

Chapter Six

Shot Down in Korea

J.J. GEUSS It was my 25th mission in Korea. I took off from Kangnung that afternoon at 2:50 p.m. on what was supposed to be a typical air-to-ground strike over North Korea. It was a rail cut. It was at Pyongyang, the North Korean capital.

I was a member of squadron VMF-312, the "Checkerboards," which was part of Marine Air Group 12, or MAG-12. Our air group commander was Col. Richard C. Mangrum, who had first seen real-life air warfare when he was a captain at Pearl Harbor (see chapter 1).

I was flying Vought F4U-4B Corsair bureau number 97486. The flight began like any other except that while we were approaching the target, my generator burned out. I left the battery switch on in order to use the radio.

There are always glitches when you fly an aircraft into combat. By now, however, the familiar Corsair fighter was so thoroughly proven and so reliable, we had enormous confidence in it. Marines used a variety of jet and propeller airplanes in Korea, but the Corsair was probably the most numerous. Although I flew jets later, in Korea I never envied Marines who were flying the F9F Panther or F3D Skyknight jet fighters or, for that matter, the twin-engine, propeller-driven F7F Tigercat or the

Capt. John J. "J.J." Geuss
October 11, 1951
Vought F4U-4B Corsair
(bureau no. 97486)
Marine Fighter Squadron
VMF-312, "Checkerboards"
K-18 Kangnung Airfield,
South Korea

John Geuss, known as J.J., sits on the wing of an F4U-4B Corsair loaded with five-inch high velocity aircraft rockets, or HVARs. The location is K-18 Kangnung airfield in South Korea in 1951.

[J.J. Geuss]

variety of helicopters and observation craft we had in Korea. For me, the Corsair defined the Marine Corps, and this particular mission was unfolding just like many. I had absolutely no clue that I was going to end up dunking my plane and myself in the Yellow Sea a long way from home. I also had no idea that a similar experience would happen to a squadron mate, Jim Bailey, who loved and appreciated the Corsair every bit as much as I did and flew it in two wars, just as I did.

My division made a high-speed approach over the target. We let down to 10,000 feet and rolled into our dive heading of 360 degrees. I was flying as "dash two," or the second aircraft, as wingman to the division leader. We were carrying bombs, rockets, and 20-millimeter ammunition and were expected to suppress antiaircraft batteries around the target, some of which were located near the North Korean airfield at Pyongyang.

At 4:05 p.m., we rolled in and hit a dive angle of 40 degrees. I fired my five-inch high-velocity aircraft rockets (HVARs) in pairs and released my 500-pound general purpose bomb directly over the North Korean airfield. When I pulled out at a speed of 320 knots, I felt two slight

In Korea, Marines flew several types of fighters, but none quite captured the imagination of Americans who wanted to fly so much as the Corsair. This example is an AU-1 model, similar to the F4U-4B flown by J.J. Geuss, Jim Bailey, and other Marines.

[U.S. Marine Corps]

bumps at about 6,000 feet. It didn't occur to me that I had been hit. I attributed the two light shocks to the air current around me.

After we pulled away from the target, we took up a heading of 240 degrees. At a predetermined rendezvous point, we found that my division was intact but that a Corsair was missing from another division. We had begun circling, intending to follow procedures for covering a downed pilot if necessary, when the missing Corsair caught up and joined formation with us. It seemed like just another mission. Later in the Korean War, we had U.S. forces on the island of Cho-do in the Yellow Sea, very far north of the 38th parallel off the coast of North Korea, but on this date Cho-do was still part of North Korea—enemy terrain. Not that I was thinking of visiting that garden spot.

After another ten minutes of heading toward home, I noticed my oil pressure was at 65 pounds. I notified my division leader, Capt. "Chappie" Chapple. It was now 5:00 p.m. At this point, Cho-do was directly west of our formation, about ten miles away. Now my oil pressure dropped to 50 pounds. I explained my situation to Chapple. I told him that I would attempt a wheels-up landing on the island.

Remember that we did not yet have troops on Cho-do. This was very far behind enemy lines, and the entire mainland of North Korea was teeming with enemy troops. More than one Corsair pilot had attempted to save a situation by setting down at or near Cho-do and the result wasn't usually pretty. I was trying to be businesslike as I prepared to cope with this emergency and put down my plane, but this was possibly the worst thing that had happened to me since I'd begun flying Corsairs in World War II. Incredibly, another member of my squadron, Jim Bailey, was going to confront a similar crisis in a few days. Like me, Jim embarked on a journey that spanned two wars before he ended up facing the prospect of a crash at Cho-do.

JIM BAILEY I guess the story of my journey to Cho-do begins before World War II when I was a kid, growing up in Norwood, Massachusetts. That's when I had my initial interest in aviation. I was in the fifth grade, and a guy had plans for balsa wood models of airplanes that you could assemble. I made some and discovered I could sell them for 25 cents. I was making models of the Boeing F4B-4, the magnificent biplane fighter that was flown by Navy and Marine pilots in the 1930s.

At age 15, I went to the airport and looked over the fence at the pilots and planes. One day, I saw a fellow with a blue shirt and dark pants. I figured he was the boss. So I climbed over the fence and asked him for a job. He said, "We don't need anybody. We can't afford to hire anybody."

I said, "I don't want money. I want to be around planes."

So I worked for nothing for a while, helping them to clean and maintain planes. One day, the guy came back to me and said, "We can't do this. This is illegal." I thought that was the end of my airport job, but then he said, "From now on we're paying you 25 cents an hour."

I was born in 1922 in Massachusetts. I was hooked on airplanes and flying before the Japanese bombed Pearl Harbor. After I began working at the airport, they let me work in the stockroom in the winter. I also helped mechanics on a Stinson Reliant, a classic plane of the 1930s, a high-wing, single-engine craft with a plush interior.

In 1941, I was a student at Northeastern University in Boston. I talked to a Professor Nightingale, who had been a naval aviator in World War I. He encouraged me. I went into the civilian pilot training program and got my private pilot's license in the J-3 Cub. In 1942, I flew a Waco UPF-7 biplane in the secondary phase of civilian pilot training, which included 40 hours of aerobatic training. By then, we were in the war.

I began naval flight training with preflight school at the University of North Carolina. That was in September 1942. Then I went to Hutchinson, Kansas, in December 1942 for primary flight training. Three months later, I went to further training.

I'm five foot nine and weigh 160 pounds. The reason I chose the Marine Corps is because, while in North Carolina, I got to know some experienced gunnery sergeants at preflight school who taught ordnance. They were gray-haired guys who could disassemble a .30-caliber machine gun and put it back together. Later, in Hutchinson, a Marine captain just back from the Pacific, Robert E. Cameron, influenced me to request the Marine Corps. I flew the Stearman N2S biplane at Hutchinson. One of my instructors was Wayne Morris, who had been an actor in western movies before the war and later became a Navy air ace in the Pacific. He was a big guy. He was a tough guy. He didn't usually show up until Tuesday because he had to sober up after a weekend. After being an instructor, he went to the fleet and flew Navy F6F Hellcats against the Japanese.

I went to Corpus Christi, Texas, for basic flight training in the twin-engine Beechcraft SNB and to fly the PBY Catalina amphibian seaplane. I got my wings in June 1943 and graduated as a PBY pilot.

Next, the Marine Corps sent me to Cherry Point, North Carolina. There I had a critical interview about my next assignment with John L. Smith, who was wearing the Medal of Honor on his uniform. I was in the outer office waiting to see him and I was nervous. I was an awkward second lieutenant and Smith was a full colonel. He was also a full-blooded Indian who had once been a cavalry officer. As a pilot, he had been on the cover of *Life* magazine. When he called me in, I knew enough to stand at attention in front of him.

He said, "Lieutenant, take that chair over there." He told a sergeant, "Get us coffee." Now, I had never drunk a cup of coffee in my life, but this time I was going to do it. He said, "You take it black, don't you?" Being a PBY Catalina pilot was not the assignment I wanted, and with that on my mind, I didn't know how I wanted the coffee, so I took it black. That's when Smith looked at me and said, "I'm going to put you in a fighter squadron." I was still an awkward young Marine but now I was a happy one. Smith gave me an assignment to squadron VMF-323, commanded by Maj. George Axtell, who later became a lieutenant general. It was at Oak Grove, an outlying field near Cherry Point.

Major Axtell said, "We've almost completed our Marine syllabus." He was referring to the 180 hours of training for new Corsair pilots that most of his Marines—but not I—had finished. He said, "You fly SNJ trainers for now and soon you'll be able to join a new squadron." So I flew trainers until I could join VMF-314. It didn't have a nickname then, but it was known in later years as the Black Knights. They formed the new squadron and the new commander that walked in the door, a major, was Cameron, whom I'd known in Hutchinson as a captain. This was a great outfit, with outstanding Marines like Frank Buckley and Mike Yunck. At first, however, I still couldn't get near an F4U. The squadron moved from Oak Grove to Mitchell Field in New Bern, North Carolina, and after a long and frustrating time with nothing to fly but the SNJ, one day there was a Corsair out on our flight line.

Corsair Baptism

That one and only Corsair at New Bern was the most formidable plane I had ever seen. It was a monster. Most of us in the squadron made our

The R5C Commando transport served Marines in World War II and Korea. One well-known Marine R5C pilot was the actor Tyrone Power. For Jim Bailey, struggling with a navigation problem in poor weather, an R5C was supposed to be the ticket to safety. But it wasn't.

[U.S. Marine Corps]

first Corsair flights in that plane, a "birdcage" F4U-1, the early model with all the problems.

Eventually, in early 1944, the squadron had a dozen Corsairs. We moved to Kingston, a larger, nearby airport with more supporting facilities. One of the interesting things that happened was that Charles Lindbergh came and lectured us on fuel management in the Corsair. He was quite a hero to us. He had been out in the Pacific, helping pilots to learn to coax greater range out of their airplanes. Distances were great in the Pacific theater, so Lindbergh's special knowledge meant a lot to us.

We completed 180 hours in F4U-1s, which included gunnery. That was it for North Carolina. We boarded a train. They had boxcars with bunks in them. We made the six- or seven-day trip to San Diego, California. While crossing the country, we weren't allowed off the train. When we arrived, we got on a bus and were taken immediately to the aircraft carrier USS *Nassau* (CVE 16) for transport to Pearl Harbor. When we arrived at Pearl, they took us to the airfield at Ewa, which became a way station for so many Marines during the war. Then we boarded R5C Commando transports and were hauled to Midway, 1,000 miles farther out in the Pacific.

The R5C was the naval version of the Army's C-46. It was a workhorse that contributed a lot to the role of Marine Air in the war and rarely received credit. It figured later in an awful incident for me at Iwo Jima. One Marine who piloted the R5C during the war was Hollywood actor Tyrone Power. He pulled his time in Marine Air cockpits just like anybody else.

HOWARD CHRISTENSON One of the Marine aviators in transport squadron VMR-253 was the late Tyrone Power. Marines with Kodak cameras often snapped pictures of him and asked for autographs.

Sometimes, First Lieutenant Power would pose willingly, but at other times he would threaten with his first lieutenant rank, jokingly. He was overly conscious of his short stature and resented posing with taller fellow Marines.

JIM BAIILEY At Midway, we were given F4U-1A Corsairs there. They had the extended tail wheel, the spoiler on the right wing, and the bubble canopy. We were at Midway for three or four months, training. This was in spring 1944, until about July. We did a lot of flying there. Midway at that time was a sub base with a protected harbor. It was home to the sub tender *Proteus* and many submarines.

On one morning patrol, I noted a submarine on the opposite side of the island from where our subs would normally be. I called the fighter director and told him I had a sub. He came back and said, "No friendlies in the area." By then the sub had made a crash dive. While I was approaching Midway to land, I watched our destroyers work the area with depth charges.

While we were at Midway, I was already a division leader, so I formed a team with four guys. We flew a practice bomb run on an outlying island. I looked back and saw my wingman's elevator tear off. The horizontal surface tore away. The airplane assumed a high angle of attack and the wings tore off. My close friend, 1st Lt. Dale Willard Baird, from Saint James, Minnesota, was killed. The leader of the second section, 1st Lt. Thurman H. "Stretch" Keller, from Boise, Idaho, ran right through the wreckage, tore his plane to pieces, and had to ditch. I later named my first child after Dale. After the accident, we examined our Corsairs and found that the rib on the elevator had detached from the trailing edge of the elevator. They were able to fix this in the field.

After Midway, they brought us back to Ewa and equipped us with F4U-1Ds. We flew down to the range at Molokai and did air-to-ground rocket training with practice versions of the five-inch high velocity aircraft rocket, or HVAR. They watched us fire at 60 degrees at 1,600 yards. Soon afterward, there was another change of aircraft and we got new F4U-1Cs with the 20-millimeter gun. That particular installation gave you a foot and a half of gun barrel sticking out of the wing and a bump in the wing to accommodate the ammo feed. The 20-millimeter was much more impressive than the .50-caliber on the earlier Corsairs.

Westward to Guam

We had 32 F4U-1Cs. We took off from Ewa and landed at Ford Island. They put those -1Cs aboard the aircraft carrier USS *Thetis Bay* (CVE 90) that was being used to transport our squadron, VMF-314. The airplanes were unloaded by crane. We arrived on Guam around March 1945. We were initially at Orote Field and then at Agana, the main field.

At Guam, we put on three drop tanks and flew to Iwo Jima. The plan was for us to stop there briefly and proceed on another long, overwater hop to our intended base at Ie Shima, a small island near Okinawa. As it turned out, a lot of things happened before we ever reached Ie Shima.

They said Iwo was secure, but there was shooting and bomb dropping going on. We were there for two nights and the Japanese bombed and strafed us both nights.

Iwo Jima was the emergency airfield for battle-damaged B-29 Superfortress bombers that were returning from Japan and couldn't make it to their bases in the Marina Islands. They would try to get to Iwo any way they could. If the island was covered by fog, they would fly on a radar vector until they were over the island and just bail out.

I will never forget the sight of the badly damaged B-29 Superfortress bombers with wounded on board landing at Iwo. I watched one of the bombers land, crumple in pieces, and run off the runway. I was concerned he might wipe out our eight Corsairs that were parked together with wings folded, but the B-29 didn't hit them. There was only one person who could walk who got out of that B-29. All the rest of the crew were dead or badly wounded.

For us, Iwo was supposed to be just a refueling stop. But when we were finally able to set forth on the long flight to Ie Shima, we had an incident that cost the lives of three brave men without the Japanese firing a shot.

This happened in April or early May 1945. There were seven of us in F4U-1C Corsairs flying formation on a twin-engine R5C Commando that was supposed to be navigating for us. Having a bigger plane as a pathfinder was a standard practice for over-water navigation when it was possible.

That day, when we took off, we were specifically briefed that there was to be no weather flying. The R5C pilot was told not to lead us into weather. We had a full load of fuel and ammo so we did not want a lot of problems. The R5C turned into a cut in the clouds and a rising cloud enveloped us. We very quickly found ourselves fighting the bad weather that was so typical for this part of the Pacific, the weather our guiding R5C had been told to avoid. We were caught in a thunderstorm.

Once we were in it, the only way out was to climb. The R5C climbed at maybe 100 knots. That was just plain too slow for a heavily loaded Corsair. He slowed his airplane down to where we could not stay with him and, one by one, our airplanes started falling out of the sky. We lost three airplanes.

That left me the senior guy in the surviving four F4U-1Cs. I told my guys, "Hold the same heading and we'll meet on the other side of the weather." The guy on the R5C didn't know what to do. I said, "We'll go back to Iwo. We'll go under the weather and we'll look for our missing men while we do it." Iwo wasn't far away, but now it was under heavy cover.

We fought our way back to Iwo beneath a thunderstorm. We never saw any sign of the three Corsair pilots who had started out that day and who simply fell from the sky. They were all first lieutenants. One was Thurman H. "Stretch" Keller, who had survived that collision and ditching back at Midway but did not survive this time. The others were Charles R. White and Lovic J. Marbury. While we were struggling through that weather and fighting to survive, 1st Lt. Marvin Maxwell Westover, from Saskatchewan, was the only one who would come up on the radio. Nobody else, including the R5C crew, would answer me. Westover had been a hockey player before the war and went back to it afterward.

I repeated my instructions, hoping the others were hearing me: "Return to Iwo Jima and we'll do it on the surface of the water and keep our eyes open for survivors." We got together on the other side, but instead of seven airplanes, there were only four. The four of us made it back to Iwo and I went immediately to the PBY Catalina rescue squadron there. They sent out a PBY, but there was nothing for the PBY to find. I think my three Corsair pilots were out of control and went straight in. The R5C got so slow that they stalled and rolled off, inverted, entering the weather below us. They went right down into a whole line of thunderstorms.

Corsair Against Japan

If we were ever going to find those guys, that was the moment. I got some criticism for trying to save our guys. It took us an extra day to arrange for us to toy the flight again. We had been scheduled to land at Naha, Okinawa, but now they told us to overfly Okinawa and go straight to Ie Shima. This time, the weather cooperated.

People remember Ie Shima as the small island where war correspondent Ernie Pyle was killed by a Japanese sniper. We were on the same airfield as an Army P-47N Thunderbolt fighter group and a Marine night fighter F6F Hellcat squadron. I didn't have a high opinion of the P-47. We could take off with plenty of runway left, but the P-47s had to strain mightily to get into the air. We were flying missions against Japan. It was about 300 nautical miles from Ie Shima to the southernmost main Japanese island of Kyushu.

On the F4U-1C the guns had to be cocked on the ground with an arming rod. That 20-millimeter cannon was very effective when it worked well, and I guess every Marine fighter pilot had a dream of shooting down an enemy plane.

I never got the chance. The closest I got to a Japanese aircraft was a near midair collision. We were coming home from escorting a PBM Mariner on a long over-water flight. We were running low on fuel and our field at Ie Shima was under attack from the air. A Japanese aircraft came straight at me, missed me, and kept going. There was no way to get on his tail.

The missions from Ie Shima to Japan were long and difficult, and the enemy was often the weather. More than once, I spent four hours in the cockpit. By the summer of 1945, the B-29s had inflicted enormous damage on the Japanese war machine, but there were still targets for us to strafe and bomb.

I flew my missions and finished my war. I flew 60 or 70 combat missions in World War II. I had no idea I might be returning to the Marine Corps or flying in a place called Korea. Like most Americans, I had other plans. Later in life, I fulfilled a lot of them, becoming a test pilot for Honeywell and participating in some key aviation and space programs as a test pilot. But first, there was Korea.

In 1946, I married a gal I'd known in high school. I went back to Northeastern. I graduated the same week the Korean War started.

I got my degree in June 1950. I got a call telling me I was on a list of people with the fighter attack military occupation specialty, or MOS. If you were one of those, they needed you. I had just bought a $10,000 house a little bit out of Boston. That was Friday. On Monday, I reported to Logan Airport and was loaded aboard an R5C Commando that took us to El Toro, California. It was a grueling overnight trip, and one of our enlisted guys passed out during the flight.

At El Toro, I was initially assigned to squadron VMF-235, which was supposed to be a carrier backup squadron. We did some carrier work and polished our gunnery. I was there for four or five months until I was picked to become a replacement in Korea. I was at Barber's Point, Hawaii, en route and was airlifted to Haneda, the Tokyo airport. From there, I went to Itami Airfield in Japan, which had been a training base for kamikazes. And from Itami, we flew into K-1 and joined-312, which had come off the light aircraft carrier USS *Bataan* (CVL 29) a month before.

I went to Korea as a replacement in VMF-312, and that, of course, is where I began flying F4U-4Bs along with J.J. Geuss. What I didn't expect was that J.J. and I were going to end up crashing our airplanes at Cho-do island off the coast of North Korea, a week apart.

J.J. GEUSS I didn't know Jim Bailey during World War II. I was on Okinawa for the last days of the war (see chapter 4). After the surrender, they sent us to Yokosuka Naval Air Station in Japan, and we practically landed with the Fourth Marines who secured the base. We lived in the quarters of Japanese naval kamikaze pilots. We were there four months. We flew over Japan looking for prisoner of war camps. There were row after row of brand new airplanes on Japan's airfields, but the Japanese didn't have a drop of gas for them.

After the war, I flew with a Reserve squadron at Glenview, Illinois. The Korean War meant a return to active duty. I was in a group of Marines who were shipped out in 1951. For me, it was a return to Japan.

We landed at Itami Airfield outside Kyoto at the end of July 1951. We were sent to K-1 Pusan West Airfield, South Korea, which was the rear echelon for Marine Aircraft Group 12, or MAG-12, under Colonel Mangrum. Our first flight wasn't against the North Koreans or Chinese. Instead, it was a flight straight back to where we'd started—typhoon evacuation, from K-1 back to Itami. We soon returned and began our war.

My first mission was on August 21, 1951, in the F4U-4B with four

20-millimeter cannons. The guns had a faster rate of fire than those we'd used in the F4U-1C on Okinawa, and you could cock and uncock them from the cockpit. For each mission, I logged my ordnance in my logbook. On that first mission I fired seven HVARs and dropped one 500-pound bomb. Someone suggested that I look at the wing when the guns were being fired. I tried it. I looked out and saw the wing bouncing up and down and I swore it was going to fall off. The force of the guns tore at the wing spar.

I flew five missions out of K-1 Pusan West until we transferred up to K-18 Kangnung. One of those five missions was a strike on a railroad tunnel. The fourth mission was a rail cut and so was the fifth. We never made more than one run on the target in most cases, but with close air support we had to keep going back.

In Korea, the antiaircraft fire was much more intense than in World War II. You would climb away and get into a cloud layer and the goddamned antiaircraft fire would follow you because they had radar on the guns. We always had four planes on the alert line ready to go. Once I was alerted to support the 27th Infantry, the "Wolfhounds," under very low cloud cover. They were taking a pounding. I picked up the target from the Mosquito, the forward air control plane. He said, "The weather's too bad. You can't get any altitude. You can't get any speed." But we had napalm and 500-pound bombs and the troops down there needed support, so we delivered our ordnance without ever getting above 200 knots of airspeed because of the weather conditions. The guy in the backseat of the Mosquito was an infantry officer. He said, "I've counted 40 KIA down there," referring to enemy killed in action after our strike.

We wanted to cover our own Marines all the time, but they wanted to use us for air support for all troops, all over the map. This was a ridiculous arrangement. It took hours for headquarters to decide how to use us.

Let's get back to the experience I began with—being the first of two squadron members to crack up an airplane at Cho-do. I was shot down on October 11, 1951. I got hit over Pyongyang in the left oil cooler. I

This is a Marine F4U Corsair that cracked up on the beach at Cho-do island many months after J.J. Geuss and Jim Bailey crashed there. This pilot suffered relatively minor damage compared to Geuss and Bailey.

[Jack Mason]

dropped 500-pound bombs on a rail cut and fired HVARs. When I fired the last pair of HVARs, I felt a bump, like something hitting the airplane. When I pulled off the target, my oil pressure started to drop. We headed out to the west coast to Cho-do Island. We alerted rescue. Four of our planes climbed to 10,000 feet to call Air-Sea Rescue. My wingman stayed with me on the way down.

Crack-Up at Cho-do

The island of Cho-do was under cloud cover. Chapple dived down to the island and discovered that the northwest tip was clear of hostile forces and had a nice beach.

My oil pressure was down to 35 pounds when I came over the beach, heading 180 degrees at 4,000 feet at 5:10 p.m. I could hear the other division of Corsairs alerting the Dumbo. That was our term for

Who's Who

Capt. (later Col.) John J. "J.J." Geuss, F4U-4B Corsair fighter pilot, VMF-312, K-18 Kangnung Air Base, South Korea

Capt. Jim Bailey, F4U-4B Corsair fighter pilot, VMF-312, K-18 Kangnung Air Base, South Korea

Howard Christenson, a Marine Air sergeant in an R5C Commando squadron

For J.J. Geuss, going down on an island off the coast of North Korea, the only hope for survival was "Dumbo," an Air Force SA-16 Albatross amphibian.

[Norman Taylor]

the Air Force Albatross amphibian that orbited off the coast of North Korea and waited for problems like mine. They were the rescue guys, but they couldn't help unless I could get down alive. Even then it wasn't certain the SA-16 would be able to land or take off.

I worried about the sand at Cho-do. I thought that if my landing gear dug into the sand, my Corsair would flip on its back. I alerted my division leader that I would make a 360-degree turn and let down to land on the beach north to south.

On the approach end was a 250-foot hill and at the other end was a

750-foot hill. This was not an ideal place to set down under any conditions. I wanted to land on the hardest sand I could find, so I tried to put her down where the beach met the water. I didn't want to be too far inland because the farther inland you go, the softer the sand is.

But when I dropped my flaps, oil poured out of the left wing root. Suddenly, my oil pressure was dropping to zero. And the shoreline of Cho-do was rushing up at me.

Chapter Seven

A Rescue Mission That Couldn't Happen

KENT SMITH I don't remember pain when the bullets hit me. I don't have a continuous-motion memory of it, either, not like a movie film. My recollections are more like snapshots. One shows skin, muscle, blood, and bone protruding from the left sleeve of my utilities. One shows someone shouting into a field radio in an infuriated voice. And in the snapshot that comes alive and comes back to haunt me all the time, my eyes snap open inside some kind of machine. I'm wrapped in a kind of cocoon. That's the terrifying part, being completely enclosed.

I didn't feel the impact from being hit by three Chinese 7.62-millimeter bullets. I didn't hear the noise from the helicopter rotors thrashing over my head. But what sticks permanently in my memory is that horrible feeling of being wrapped inside a cocoonlike enclosure the size and shape of a coffin. Half a century later, I needed a routine MRI test as part of a medical exam and I couldn't do it. I couldn't permit my body to be enclosed in a tube. I still experience that fear of being completely enclosed. It comes to me in nightmares.

I was born in 1932 in Illinois. I enlisted in the Marine Corps in Chicago in 1950. The Korean War began a few weeks later. I missed out on the Inchon invasion, but joined the First Marine Division in time for the aftermath of the November 1950 battle with Chinese regulars at the Chosin Reservoir.

I can't claim to have experienced much of it. I was on the line for about three weeks. I was plunked down on a snow-covered berm near the North Korean village of Koto-ri when they hit us in the middle of the night. I remember dodging some incoming mortar rounds, experiencing a brief lull, and then getting hit by Chinese infantry.

The literature of the era portrayed the Chinese as dope-crazed fanatics who attacked in human waves while flares exploded overhead and bugle calls whipped them into a frenzy.

That's a bunch of crap. My buddies and I will tell you. The Chinese People's Volunteers—that's their official title—were seasoned combat soldiers who had training and tactics every bit as good as our own. I never saw a flare. I never heard a goddamn bugle. I saw the Chinese, but only a few of them, coming at us in rapid, stealthy movements. The only real light was from the snow on the ground and an occasional muzzle flash. Again, a lot of this is just snapshots in my mind, like a pile of snapshots, frozen in time.

They told me later I was hit by two 7.62-millimeter bullets from an apparent Soviet-made PPSh-41 burp gun, plus a metallic object that might have been a ricochet. My platoon held its ground and our corpsmen got me back to a location a few hundred yards away where somebody was shouting into a radio. They moved me again and after dawn loaded me on a helicopter that carried me to the port city of Hungnam. That claustrophobic enclosure wrapped around me was the external stretcher litter dangling from a Marine HO3S-1 helicopter belonging to Marine Observation Squadron VMO-6. A day later, a second helicopter hauled me to the hospital ship in the Sea of Japan. I was told the ship was the USS *Repose* (AH 16), which was one of the first Navy ships to have a helicopter pad mounted in its stern.

My understanding is that we Marines were among the first to make practical use of helicopters on the battlefield.

S.Sgt. Paul Moore
1951
Sikorsky HO5S-1
Marine Observation Squadron
**   VMO-6**
Tonga-ri, South Korea

Paul Moore, seen here as a staff sergeant in 1947, served in World War II, Korea, and Vietnam. During the Korean War, Moore was a maintainer in squadron VMO-6, working on the small and cantankerous HO5S-1 helicopter. Moore was also a pilot and held flying jobs in several countries after retiring from the Marine Corps.

[Paul Moore]

PAUL MOORE I worked on the HO3S-1 helicopter a little, but mostly on its intended replacement, the HO5S-1. Both were lifesavers in Korea and both represented a quantum leap forward. The Marine Corps understood from day one that the helicopter was not just a new invention but was a way of revolutionizing warfare. When I was going through helicopter-maintenance school just before the Korean War, the other service branches were still treating the helicopter like a newfangled gadget. The Marines were seeing it as a tool that would directly support combat troops.

I arrived in Korea to see guys working their hearts out to keep helicopters in the air, and pilots doing everything in their power to use them to help the troops. My squadron, VMO-6, had a mixture of fixed-wing airplanes and helicopters, and our officers were working hard to develop the best tactics to use both to support our guys on the ground.

What Happened

Marines took to helicopters from the very beginning.

The Army was unprepared in Korea, played catch-up during the late 1950s and early 1960s, and then got it right in Vietnam.

This is a Sikorsky HO3S-1 helicopter of Paul Moore's squadron, VM O-6, which operated both fixed-wing and rotary-wing aircraft to support ground troops in Korea. Many Americans remember the HO5S-1 as the helicopter flown by the Mickey Rooney character in the movie *The Bridges at Toko-ri*.

[U.S. Marine Corps]

The Marines had it right at the start. With help from the Navy, which handled procurement for the Corps, Marines were among the first to use choppers to rescue people in combat and to transport troops to and from the battlefield.

During the Korean fighting from 1950 to 1953, many Marines flew the HO3S-1, the same rickety craft known to the Air Force as the H-5.

To many Americans, the HO3S-1 helicopter is familiar only because Mickey Rooney flew it in Hollywood's version of James Michener's novel *The Bridges at Toko-ri*. In the film's climax, downed fighter pilot William Holden and HO3S-1 helicopter pilot Rooney die in a rice paddy in a realistic portrayal of a rescue that went wrong.

Real life was grimmer than the movies. On July 3, 1951, Navy Lt. (j.g.) John M. Koelsch took off in an HO3S-1 helicopter belonging to HIM from the rescue ship LST 799 in Wonsan Harbor. Koelsch and crewman, AM3 (Aviation Medic 3rd Class) George M. Neal, attempted to rescue Capt. James V. Wilkins, a Marine pilot shot down behind enemy lines 35 miles south of Wonsan.

Navy and Marine Corsair fighters flew escort as Koelsch reached the rescue area. Because of solid clouds beneath him, he was forced to descend into harm's way without the Corsairs. He took his helicopter down in a perilous descent through clouds into mountainous terrain defended by Chinese infantrymen.

Under heavy fire, Koelsch persisted, hovered above Wilkins, and lowered a rescue sling. But a furious burst of gunfire tore into the helicopter and it plunged to earth.

Koelsch discovered that Wilkins' arms and legs were so severely burned that he was unable to walk. Koelsch and Neal fashioned a crude litter and carried the wounded Marine toward the coast. For nine incredible days, Koelsch's trio evaded Chinese troops but they were finally captured. As a prisoner of war, Koelsch continued his valorous actions and inspired fellow prisoners until he finally succumbed to dysentery and starvation in the hands of the enemy. He was awarded the Medal of Honor posthumously.

Marine Rescues

On the ground in Korea, squadron VMO-6 barely had time to get settled with its initial half dozen HO3S-1 helicopters, plus OY-1 Sentinel observation planes, when it was thrown into action following the September 1950 Inchon invasion. On September 29, 1950, North Korean troops shot down one of the OY-1s near Uijongbu, an outskirt north of Seoul, which they still occupied. Members of VMO-6 learned that the observer aboard the OY-1 had perished but that the pilot was intact. First Lieutenant Arthur R. Bancroft won a coin toss with another experienced HO3S-1 pilot and launched to attempt the rescue, fully aware that he was flying into hundreds of North Korean guns. Leading a two-helicopter formation with the loser of the bet, 1st Lt. Lloyd Engelhardt, in trail, Bancroft was descending to the pick-up site when bursts of fire touched off its fuel and transformed his HO3S-1 into a blazing torch. Engelhardt directed fighters into the area. They determined that there was no sign of the OY-1 pilot and that Bancroft had been killed.

When the Chinese People's Volunteers entered the Korean War in

November 1950 and engulfed Marines at the Chosin Reservoir, the HO3S-1 was tested, along with pilots and ground crews, as never before. Chinese antiaircraft fire was everywhere, often revealing itself in the form of muzzle flashes and tracers that appeared, deceptively, to be in slow motion.

The Chosin fighting took place amid one of the harshest Korean winters in memory. The high altitude, powerful winds howling down from Siberia, and often horrendous weather prompted some Marines to question whether helicopters would be able to operate at all. On one HO3S-1 mission a few miles southeast of the reservoir, Capt. Eugene Pope had to bring his HO3S-1 back to a landing after only a few minutes aloft because subfreezing temperatures had made the cyclic and collective controls top stiff to respond to the pilot's touch. It turned out that some of the lubricant used to keep the helicopter functioning had, in fact, frozen.

On November 5, 1950, Pope was aloft again, hauling supplies, when powerful winds literally grabbed his HO3S-1 and slammed it against a snow-covered slope. Pope climbed out unhurt, but the helicopter was a write-off.

When six Chinese divisions swarmed down on two regiments of Marines at Chosin, surviving HO3S-1s of VMO-6 flew all kinds of missions, including hauling the commander of the First Marine Division, Lt. Gen. Oliver P. Smith, over the battlefield for a close-up look at the fighting. According to the Marines' own official history, on a single day VMO-6 logged 40 sorties (one reconnaissance, 16 transport, and 23 medical evacuations). The helicopters flew out 50 seriously wounded men to the hospital ship offshore and to other destinations and brought in valuable supplies including radio batteries and medicine.

Pvt. Kent Smith was one of dozens of ground-pounding Marines who learned about the HO3S-1 and its cocoonlike external litters. The cost of saving fellow Americans was high. First Lieutenant Robert A. Longstaff rescued a downed Navy pilot and airlifted him to the escort carrier USS *Sicily* (CVE 118). But on December 3, 1950, while Longstaff was trying to rescue a critically wounded Marine at the

Chosin Reservoir, Chinese ground fire found his HO3S-1 and brought it down. Longstaff became the second Marine helicopter pilot to be killed in action.

During the Chosin battle, HO3S-1 pilot 1st Lt. Wallace D. Blatt became a participant in a dramatic and tragic event that focused on two Navy carrier-based F4U-4 Corsair pilots who were supporting the embattled Marines at the reservoir. Blatt was at a forward location not far from the reservoir, working with his ground crew to keep the HO3S-1 airworthy in spite of subfreezing temperatures and a host of minor mechanical problems. Blatt was launched on a rescue mission and then called back when told he would need a fire extinguisher and a crash ax. When he launched a second time, Blatt was about to become part of a drama that involved two Navy pilots.

Medal of Honor Mission

The two could not have been more different. One was married, one single. One had a rural Mississippi upbringing, the other a comfortable New England background. One was black. One was white.

On December 4, 1950, F4U-4 Corsair pilot Jesse L. Brown was flying in support of Marines at Chosin when Chinese gunfire ripped into his plane.

Brown was the first Negro—the term in use then—to complete naval aviator training and is recognized today as the Navy's first African American pilot. He was a section leader in squadron VF-32, "Swordsmen," flying from the carrier USS *Leyte* (CV 32).

Badly out of control and coughing gouts of smoke, Brown's Corsair made a belly landing on snow and ice. Though Brown spoke clearly on the radio while going down, once on the ground he was silent. His wrecked plane sputtered and smoked.

It was late in the day and, although Blatt's HO3S-1 rescue helicopter was approaching the scene, it appeared that nightfall might arrive first. Lieutenant (j.g.) Thomas Hudner, Brown's wingman, decided not to wait for Blatt. Hudner got rid of his napalm bombs and belly tank, fired off his rockets, and put his own Corsair into a tight, carrier-style approach with wheels down.

He landed in the snow.

No one had ever done anything like that in a Corsair before. And as Hudner had known when he touched down, his own plane was too badly wrecked to ever take off. But Hudner wasn't even thinking about the fact that he'd volunteered to maroon himself behind the lines in North Korea, surrounded by Chinese troops.

"Jesse had barely survived the crash," Hudner said later, "but his aircraft had been crumpled in the landing and he was pinned in his cockpit." Brown was near death, his badly mangled leg stuck in the twisted fuselage.

"The canopy of his aircraft was open but he was gravely injured and wedged inside, unable to move," said Hudner.

Struggling to suppress the fire in the burning Corsair, Hudner began packing snow around its smoking cowling. He had to use one hand to balance himself, so had only one hand to attempt to snuff the blaze and attempt a rescue. "There was no way to get traction to pull." Although Chinese troops were racing toward the scene from about a mile away, HO3S-1 pilot Blatt made a risky landing. Blatt now had an ax, but it proved useless in extricating Brown.

"We were running out of daylight, Jesse was obviously dying, and we could find no way to get him free," Hudner recalled. Because the HO3S-1 could not navigate at night, Hudner knew that if he and Blatt did not leave, there would be three bodies in the Korean snow instead of one.

"We had no choice but to leave him. I was crushed. But there was absolutely nothing we could do." Brown and Hudner had met when serving at Naval Air Station Quonset Point, Rhode Island. Despite his lower rank, Brown had greater flying experience and flew as section leader with Hudner on his wing.

The two men did not socialize, but they knew each other well and enjoyed great mutual respect.

Brown died quietly. Hudner and Blatt escaped in the HO3S-1 with night and Chinese troops closing in. It was an extraordinary feat of helicopter flying by the Marine, and it prevented Hudner from becoming a prisoner of war. Because the crash site was far behind Chinese lines and there was no hope of retrieving the slain pilot's remains, VF-32 returned to the site a few days later and torched it with napalm.

Jesse Leroy Brown was born in 1926 in Hattiesburg, Mississippi, enlisted in the Naval Reserve in 1946, and became a naval aviator in October 1948. He flew the F9F Panther jet fighter before transitioning to the prop-driven Corsair. He wrote daily letters to his wife, Daisy, and year-old daughter, Pamela. He was awarded the Distinguished Flying Cross for his Korean War combat service. The destroyer escort USS *Jesse L. Brown* (DE 1089), later classified as a frigate (FFT 1089), was named in his honor.

Thomas Jerome Hudner was born in 1924 in Fall River, Massachusetts, where his father ran Hudner's Markets, a chain of grocery stores. He was graduated from Phillips Academy in 1943 and the Naval Academy in 1946. He served aboard the cruiser *Helena* and became a naval aviator in August 1949. For his unsuccessful effort to save his section leader, Hudner was awarded the Medal of Honor by President Harry S Truman on April 13, 1951, the first Navy member to receive the award during the Korean War. He retired as a Navy captain in 1973. He believes recognition should go to helicopter pilot Blatt, who came to the scene "at great peril."

Over the years, Hudner has maintained an aw-shucks attitude about the nation's highest award for valor. "I once tried to clean it with Brasso but that didn't work very well." In 1998, Hudner misplaced the medal during an appearance in Boston. A local resident found it and returned it to him.

Blatt was awarded the Navy Cross for his role in the attempt to save Navy pilot Brown but, like Hudner, was frustrated that the men came away empty-handed.

Robert E. Galer, who was at Pearl Harbor (see chapter 1) and soon afterward at Guadalcanal where he was awarded the Medal of Honor, became, like infantryman Kent Smith, an early beneficiary of the tech-

Robert E. Galer, who witnessed the attack on Pearl Harbor and was awarded the Medal of Honor for action on Guadalcanal, was shot down in Korea while at the controls of an AU-1 Corsair. Galer became one the first Marines to be rescued by a helicopter when an HO3S-1 piloted by E. J. McCutcheon came to his rescue behind enemy lines.

[U.S. Marine Corps]

nological advances offered by the helicopter. In Korea, Galer was a colonel and commanded Marine Aircraft Group 12, or MAG-12. On August 5, 1952, Galer led a flight of 31 warplanes against targets in mountainous North Korea, near the harbor city of Wonsan.

Galer was rolling in on his target at the controls of an AU-1 Corsair, the "attack" version of the famous fighter, which had originally been called the F4U-6 (see chapter 8). He was in a sharp bank when gunfire ripped into his Corsair. He knew instantly the plane was crippled. Galer threw back the canopy and parachuted to earth, landing only feet from where his Corsair smashed into the ground. Galer sprinted away from the plane, which seemed likely to draw Chinese troops, and found that his survival radio was working. Other Corsairs circled overhead and called an HO3S-1 helicopter piloted by 1st Lt. E. J. McCutcheon.

McCutcheon cursed, cobbled, and coaxed the rickety HO3S-1 and brought the helicopter to a point where its turning rotor blades were less than ten feet from the slope where Galer was trying to evade capture. Galer triggered a smoke flare to alert rescuers to his location. At the

The Sikorsky HO5S-1 never quite replaced its Marine cousin, the HO3S-1, but it also saved many Marines who otherwise might have died from combat wounds. To Paul Moore and other Marines of squadron VMO-6, maintaining the small, cantankerous, and underpowered HO5S-1 was a constant challenge.

[U.S. Marine Corps]

right instant, he dashed out to the helicopter and grabbed a lowered rescue sling. McCutcheon lifted off and turned east, dodging antiaircraft fire. The HO3S-1 skimmed over patches of fog and hauled one of Marine Air's most famous aviators to safety.

By the time McCutcheon rescued Galer, the familiar HO3S-1 helicopter was beginning to give way to a new helicopter intended to replace it, the HO5S-1. Mechanic Paul Moore spent a brief period working on AD-4 Skyraider attack bombers before being assigned to squadron VMO-6 and the newer HO5S-1.

PAUL MOORE The HO5S-1 was intended as the replacement for the HO3S-1 and HTL-3, both of which had carrier stretchers on both sides above the skids. The Army helicopters seen in the movie and television drama *M*A*S*H* were H-13 models, which are identical to the HTL-3, and they were really not quite adequate for the job.

We removed the copilot's seat from the left side of the HO5S-1 nose canopy. With the seat gone, we could insert two stretchers, one above the other. A rear seat behind the pilot (on the right side of the aircraft) could accommodate a corpsman to tend the wounded en route to the hospital ship offshore. Most MASH wounded arrived by ground ambulance, especially those who were less seriously wounded, but sometimes the HO5S-1 was the difference between being wounded and being killed.

The HO5S-1 was used to fly observers from the First Marine Aircraft Wing and senior ground commanders for their planning missions. It was also used for fire control. Rescue missions were sometimes flown for patrols when they were isolated or caught in the vicious tides along the rivers.

Maintenance was fairly simple with the six-cylinder horizontally opposed engine sitting upright with the prop shaft end turning a spring-loaded clutch inside a Chrysler brake drum (the same as on a Chrysler car). There were no servos, so there were no avionics and hydraulics loads. The helicopter was underpowered, and in summer sometimes a run down the dirt strip helped it to become airborne. Once in flight, it was a smooth helicopter. On coming in for a hover and landing, once committed it had to land. One grunt attempted to direct a landing HO5S-1 on a rice paddy. The pilot could not avert the landing and chopped off his head and the rifle slung on his back. The rotors were low on the HO5S-1 and several incidents with the tail rotor resulted in fatalities. A medic and a First Marine Division colonel were killed when they exited the rear seat and ran aft into the tail rotor. So it was an excellent helicopter in some ways, but there were problems.

Paul Moore

Paul Moore is a pilot. He is also a Marine who enjoyed a full career in Marine aviation. Yet he was never a pilot with the Marine Corps.

Moore, 80, of Kurtistown, Hawaii, is a retired master sergeant. After his retirement, the name of his rank has changed to gunnery sergeant. "I loved aviation from childhood," Moore said, but he became a pilot only in the civilian world.

Moore enlisted in April 1942 and was accepted for the Navy's en-

Who's Who

Pvt. (later SSgt.) Kent Smith, Marine infantryman, First Marine Division, wounded and evacuated by HO3S-1 helicopter

Col. (later Brig. Gen.) Robert E. Galer, AU-1 Corsair Pilot and Medal of Honor recipient (see chapter 1), shot down in Korea and rescued by HO3S-1 helicopter

S.Sgt. (later MSgt.) Paul Moore, crew chief and mechanic on HO5S-1 helicopter in Korea

listed flight training program. Before he could complete pilot training, the service solicited overseas volunteers with a promise that pilot training would come later. Moore became an aircraft maintainer.

In July 1944, the Marines sent Moore to Turtle Bay, New Hebrides, in the South Pacific as a maintainer with Marine Torpedo Bombing Squadron VMTB-232, the "Red Devils," equipped with TBM-3 Avengers.

"James Michener, who wrote *South Pacific,* was there as a Navy supply officer," Moore said. "We lived in tents near the coral airstrip. As crew chiefs, we went out every day and preflighted the aircraft, unfolded the wings, and ran them up. Each of us was required to fly [as a crew member] four hours a month because we were on flight orders. In those days, flight pay was 50 percent of your basic pay, which for me as a corporal was $38."

Moore and his squadron shifted locations as the war moved toward Japan. During the 1945 battle for Okinawa, "I got blown over an embankment by an exploding eight-inch gun round from a Japanese gun on the island." Moore finished the war as a staff sergeant on the flightline at Kadena, Okinawa, in charge of four Avengers. Briefly out of the Corps in the postwar era, he took flying lessons on the GI Bill.

When the Korean War began in 1950, Moore was one of the Marine Corps' first helicopter maintainers. Still, the Corps sent him to a base in Korea to maintain the fixed-wing AD Skyraider. "I said, 'Well, hell, I have never even seen a Skyraider,' and they said, 'We're really short of

Skyraider guys,' so I worked on it for six months." Then, in Tonga-ri, South Korea, he joined Marine Observation Squadron VMO-6, maintaining the HO5S-1 helicopter, as well as the OE-1 Bird Dog liaison plane.

Although the HO3S-1, which rescued Smith and Galer, was better known, Moore believes the HO5S-1 was a pioneer in Marine helicopter aviation, setting the standard for today's medevac choppers. "It didn't have a lot of power or a lot of range," he said, "but it rescued dozens of Marines." The Corps operated 79 HO5S-1s in Korea.

Moore held assignments in Marine helicopter aviation in the 1950s and 1960s. He joined Marine Air Group 16 on Okinawa in 1962 and had a role in shipping UH-34D Seahorse helicopters to Da Nang, South Vietnam, where the U.S. presence was in its early stages. Moore retired from active duty in October 1963. By that time, he had accrued hundreds of air hours as a civilian pilot.

Moore's post-Marine work as a civilian includes flying as a helicopter test pilot as a member of an advisory team for the Air Force in Vietnam (1964–1968), flying SH-3D helicopters for the Malaysian Air Force (1969–1971), and serving as a technical representative to the Marine Corps on the CH-53 helicopter (1973–1987), a job which included being on the scene for the evacuation of Saigon in April 1975. He later worked on Wessex helicopters in Egypt (1991–1994).

"I had the good fortune to enjoy a great many different experiences," Moore said—including service in three wars.

Sikorsky HO3S-1

The Marines received their first helicopters in February 1948, when two factory-fresh Sikorsky HO3S-1s joined squadron HMX-1 at Quantico, Virginia. They were figured for four seats inside a narrow, "greenhouse" cabin with a three-blade, 49-foot rotor whirling overhead. The HO3S-1 was identical to the Air Force's R-5, which was renamed the H-5 in mid-1948, and for some reason neither ever had a popular nickname. The HO3S-1 was popular with troops nonetheless. As reported in

HO5S-1 crew chief Staff Sgt. (later, Gunnery Sgt.) Paul Moore stands next to his helicopter at A-9 airfield in Korea in summer 1952. The right-hand windshield of the 1 helicopter is broken, the result of a collision with a duck.

[Paul Moore]

the Marine Corps' own official history, the service's first operational use of a helicopter occurred when a Quantico-based HO3S-1 led a salvage party to an amphibious jeep mired in a nearby swamp. In May 1948, the squadron began operating HO3S-1s from the escort carrier USS *Palau* (CVE 122), demonstrating that helicopters could haul assault troops in an amphibious operation.

The Navy, which handles Marine Corps aircraft procurement, eventually acquired 88 HO3S-1s for itself and for the Marine Corps. They were considered identical to the Air Force's H-5F. They became a familiar sight along the rugged ridgelines of Korea, where they often flew with external litters to carry wounded Marines. The Marines also operated another, lesser-known Sikorsky product, the HO5S-1, which never flew in any other service branch. Many of the Corps's pilots and maintainers were trained in every type of helicopter in service, and flew and maintained them interchangeably.

Sikorsky HO5S-1

The HO5S-1 was the replacement for the HO3S-1. At least, that was the plan. One Marine calls the Sikorsky HO5S-1, "the forgotten helicopter from 'the Forgotten War.' " It was based on the Sikorsky's civilian S-52 and was almost identical to the Army H-18. It was supposed to replace not only the ubiquitous and popular HO3S-1 helicopter but small fixed-wing airplanes as well. But the HO5S-1 never lived up to these expectations.

Still, hundreds of ground-pounding Marines owe their lives to the HO5S-1, which flew medical evacuation missions in Korea from 1950 to 1953.

The small HO5S-1 had the distinction of being the first U.S. helicopter with all-metal rotor blades. The civilian S-52 prototype made its initial flight at Stratford on February 12, 1947. A somewhat larger version

---

Sikorsky HO3S-1 helicopter (H-5)

Type: 2- to 4-seat combat rescue and utility helicopter

Power plant: one 450-hp Pratt & Whitney R-985-AN-1/5 Wasp Junior radial, fan-cooled piston engine driving 49-ft (14.94-m), 3-blade main rotor

Performance: maximum speed, 103 mph (166 km/h); cruising speed, 75 mph (122 km/h); climb to 5,900 ft (1800 m), estimate 7 minutes; service ceiling, 11,000 ft (3352 m); maximum duration, estimate 4 hours; range, estimate 180 mi (305 km)

Weights: empty, 8,788 lb (1820 kg); normal takeoff weight, 4,400 lb (1995 kg); gross weight, 4,985 lb (2263 kg)

Dimensions: main rotor diameter, 49 ft (14.94 m); length overall (rotors turning), 57 ft 1 in (17.40 m); fuselage length, 40 ft 11 in (12.47 m); height, 12 ft 11 in (3.94 m); wheel track, 12 ft (3.60 m); main rotor disc area, 1,810 sq ft (168 sq m)

Armament: none

Crew: 1 pilot, 1 medic

First flight: August 18, 1943 (XR-5)

---

with a maximum of four seats was sold to the Marine Corps. This aircraft had a 245-horsepower Franklin O-425-1 engine and a rotor diameter of 33 feet. The first of these was delivered to squadron HMX-1 at Quantico, Virginia.

Today, HMX-1 provides VIP transportation for the president. In the 1950s, the squadron's job was development and flight test. It drew the job of preparing the HO5S-1 for battle.

In Korea, the HO5S-1 replace the Bell HTL-3, which had wooden rotor blades and carried two litters in external pods, those cocoonlike enclosures that could seem claustrophobic to a wounded Marine. The HO3S-1 also had the external pod, but the HO5S-1 carried its litters internally. The HO5S-1 offered slightly higher speed and slightly greater range. The HO5S-1 also could carry two stretchers, but they were inside on the left side, with the pilot—as is typical in helicopters—seated on the right.

"It was a pretty little bird but it was underpowered," said Paul Moore, who was a line chief with squadron VMO-6 in Korea when the HO5S-1 arrived. "It had the same engine as the HTL-3, which was inadequate. We called it 'six-cylinder horribly opposed,' rather than 'horizontally opposed.'"

Carrying the wounded internally produced a grim and unintended consequence. "When you hauled wounded, you got blood all over the place, unlike with the HTL-3," remembered Moore. "The blood would run down to the bottom of the damn fuselage, and within days it would have a terrible odor. You never could get it out of there."

The HO5S-1 had the advantage of being stable on the ground, thanks to its low center of gravity and four-wheel landing gear. A unique feature was a hinged, two-piece observation bubble enclosing the nose of the aircraft. When the left side of the bubble was raised into the open position, two stretcherborne patients could be loaded aboard or removed from the helicopter.

Retired Capt. Wallace D. Bracken, 72, of Penn Valley, California, joined VMO-6 after the squadron had returned to Camp Pendleton. He first flew an HO5S-1 on October 12, 1955, at a time when pilots stayed current in both helicopters and fixed-wing airplanes like the Cessna OE-1. "It was routine to switch back and forth, so you had to keep up your flying skills," Bracken said.

"The HO5S-1 was stable and about as reliable as any helicopter in those days," Bracken said. "It was horribly underpowered. That made it a good experience for a new, fresh-caught helicopter pilot, who learns to plan a flight based on fuel load, weights and balances, and so on."

The HO5S-1 was plagued by performance problems and structural defects that limited its career. The Marine Corps retired its last HO5S-1 in 1959.

Sikorsky HO5S-1 helicopter (H-18)

Type: 2- to 4-seat combat rescue and utility helicopter.

Power plant: one 245-hp Franklin O-425-1 engine

Performance: maximum speed, 115 mph (185 km/h); cruising speed, 90 mph (144 km/h); climb to 5,900 ft (1800 m), estimate 7 minutes; service ceiling, 12,400 ft (3780 m); maximum duration, estimate 3 hours; range, 190 m (305 km/h) at 1,500 ft (457 m)

Weights: empty, 2,000 lb (907 kg); normal takeoff weight, 2,555 lb (1158 kg); gross weight, 2,750 lb (1247 kg)

Dimensions: main rotor diameter, 33 ft (10.05 m); height, 8 ft 8 in (2.63 m); tail rotor diameter, 6 ft 4 in (1.93 m)

Armament: none

Crew: 1 pilot, 1 medic

First flight: February 12, 1947 (S-52); 1949 (HO5S-1)

Chapter Eight

Crisis in a Corsair Cockpit

J.J. GEUSS My letdown for an emergency landing at Cho-do was well under way when I saw oil pouring out of the left wing root, coming from the left oil cooler. This first indication of a full-blown oil leak came at 1,000 feet on final approach with flaps down. Oil was flowing under the flap. Now oil pressure dropped to 25 pounds.

I cleared the hill at the north end of the beach by several hundred feet at an airspeed of 140 knots. My F4U-4B Corsair hit just at the edge of the beach and kept skidding for 600 feet as if on a greased surface. The sand was very hard surfaced. The forward motion of the Corsair was almost stopped when the plane skidded right and went out into water. When the aircraft came to a full and final halt, it was partially submerged in water about 18 inches deep. The time was 5:15 p.m.

I heard them calling the Dumbo again. I made one radio transmission saying I was in good shape. Then, according to squadron SOP, or standard operating procedures, I gave the circling Corsairs the proper visual signals to tell them I was all right.

About a dozen Korean men gathered on the beach and headed toward my plane. I motioned them back and invited one to step forward. He identified himself as a policeman of the Haeju prefecture and said

Capt. John J. Geuss hauls his gear out to the SA-16 Albatross rescue plane, while residents of the North Korean island of Cho-do look on. His wrecked Corsair is behind him.

[U.S. Marine Corps]

his name was Rhee Khe-Wook. In broken English and sign language, he indicated he wanted to help me. He took my parachute to shore and returned to carry me ashore piggyback. I kept the Koreans back from me as much as possible, fearing the circling planes might fire. At no time did it occur to me that the Koreans didn't have the best of intentions—but these were North Koreans, remember. It was my understanding that there were North Korean guerillas on the island, but I did not see any people who looked military.

By this time, several hundred people had gathered. It had been my personal observation while covering downed pilots that if Koreans were unfriendly, they would stay out of sight and fire from cover, especially with covering planes buzzing the downed aircraft. These people were the enemy but they were not acting like the enemy.

Twenty minutes after my landing, the SA-16 landed but got hung up on a sandbar about 30 feet from shore in two feet of water. I had to get myself wet anyway, for the water was too deep for the Korean to carry me out. So I walked out of the surf toward the Albatross.

I climbed into the SA-16. About 15 minutes behind him was the he-

Geuss's crashed Corsair at Cho-do.

licopter coming belatedly to perform a rescue that was no longer needed. The SA-16 pilot was apologizing for the time it had taken him to get out of being hung up on that sandbar. Fortunately, despite the fact that waves could reach 28 feet in that part of the Yellow Sea, he was able to take off and haul me out of North Korean territory. The SA-16 took me to K-16 Yoi-do Airfield on the Han River just south of Seoul, and later a TBM Avenger being used as a transport carried me back to our home base at K-18.

If you were shot down and recovered, you were supposed to get a staff job for the rest of your tour. When I was shot down, it was my 25th mission. So I'm expecting to be relieved of flying and the colonel says, "Too bad, J.J. There's a new directive. You're going to have to keep flying." They did give me a week of R & R, that's rest and recuperation leave, and my next mission was on October 26, 1951, after they plucked Jim Bailey from those same waters around Cho-do.

I flew my last mission in Korea January 18, 1952. I finished my tour as a staff officer at K-18 and departed in April 1952. During my final week, they moved the air group over to K-8. Brig. Gen. Jay Hubbard always had something good to say about us reservists. We were taking

The Geuss crash scene, including the SA-16 Albatross rescue plane and the crashed F4U-4B Corsair.

[U.S. Marine Corps]

their money and were expected to do our job. Over 50 percent of the pilots in the air wing were reservists.

JIM BAILEY We were assigned to hit the rail facilities at Sunchon in northwestern North Korea. I was flying with squadron VMF-312, the "Checkerboards," from K-18 Kangnung Airfield, South Korea. It was October 16, 1951. That may have been the only day in the entire war when a squadron lost three Corsairs attacking a single target.

To back up for just a second, before Johnny Geuss or I joined the squadron, VMF-312 was operating from the light aircraft carrier USS *Bataan* (CVL 29). During its time on the carrier, the squadron's mission was to escort friendly ships and blockade enemy craft on the west coast of Korea. The squadron flew many close-support missions on the Korean west coast. On April 4, 1951, the squadron's commanding officer, Maj. Donald P. Frame, was killed when antiaircraft fire hit his Corsair and started a fire in his cockpit. Frame had difficulty bailing out and his parachute opened immediately, causing him to hit the tail of the aircraft. He was later rescued but died in the helicopter en route to Seoul. When the squadron finished its deployment on the ship, it had flown 4,945 combat hours and made 1,920 carrier landings. Thereafter, the Checkerboards deployed to K-18 and that's when I flew that mission to Sunchon.

It was our second combat mission of the day. Earlier that day we had hit a bridge and the associated rail facilities. When we got back, we reported a lot of guns on the ridgeline above the bridge. Now, we were going back to that valley to hit the bridge again.

There were eight Corsairs in the fight, four to work the bridge and four to break the track at Sunchon where the rail line came from the northwest. There were supposed to be 800 freight cars bottled up in that area. This was part of something called Operation Strangle, at least that's what the Air Force called it. B-29 Superfortresses were supposed to take care of the marshalling yard but they couldn't hit the tracks, so it was our job to hit the tracks. A railroad track is a very difficult target to hit with any kind of precision. To hit it, you have to be up close and personal. Even then, the enemy often can repair and reconstruct a section of rail line almost overnight, so you've got to be both accurate and thorough.

It was unquestionably a mistake to hit the same target from the same direction for a second time on the same day. When they told me we were going back in the afternoon, I suggested that we assign two Corsairs to attack the gun positions. They said no. So we went directly west to Sunchon for the second time that day and ran into a flak trap. Another division pulled off to the south and flew away but ours flew into the middle of everything.

Of the four airplanes in our division, one was shot down in flames. That was 1st Lt. Ralph H. Thomas. A second made a crash landing on a roadway near the target area. That was 2nd Lt. Carl R. Lundquist. He climbed out of his Corsair and had enemy all around him. A second lieutenant named Baker stayed around and tried to protect Carl. Baker got hit so bad his aircraft was a "strike" when he limped home to our base, so I guess you could say the North Koreans got all four airplanes in our division. Carl became a prisoner of war and was badly treated by the North Koreans. That was a tough day, and it was unnecessary.

I left the target area at probably 100 feet of altitude. I was able to climb out of there and get up to 4,000 feet, but it was clear that I wasn't going to make it home. At that moment, I remembered a name of a geographic spot on the map. Johnny Geuss had landed on the beach at Cho-do five days earlier and because of that I knew the name of that island. I needed a place name for the Dumbo, the Air Force SA-16 Albatross rescue amphibian. Thanks to John, I had a place name that I could pass along.

Fight for Survival

I passed within 20 miles of Pyongyang. I told the Dumbo I didn't think I could make the island. The ground fire that hit my plane apparently had destroyed one oil cooler. The Corsair has two oil coolers and you can shut one off and operate if you know where the leak is, but I didn't know where the leak was. Part of my windscreen had taken what I thought was a 12.7, and I had taken some rounds in the tail. I didn't know how long I could stay airborne.

I ended up ditching about 15 miles north of Cho-do. The airplane settled into the water at a 60-degree angle. I stood up at the edge of the cockpit. I climbed over the windshield, inflated the raft, and got in. The waves were about nine feet and there were a lot of whitecaps, so it was pretty rough. I could see the Dumbo coming but didn't know if he could touch down in these waves.

The first flare I got out was inoperative. I reached to pull the pin and it was busted. Finally, I got a flare lit and was making smoke.

When I looked at the Dumbo, he was in a 90-degree turn, going away from me. He told me later he was leaving because he didn't expect me to survive the landing in that rough water. When he saw my smoke, he changed his mind and came to get me. He got a line out and pulled it across me and pulled me in to the Albatross. I got aboard and went up and talked to him.

The pilot of the SA-16 was Air Force Capt. Charles Fisher. When I climbed aboard the Dumbo, they cut my raft loose. I said, "Why did you do that? It'll be floating around and they'll see it." Somebody said, "Oh, yeah. You're right." An Air Force guy pulled out a .45 and fired at the raft to fill it full of holes. But he couldn't seem to hit it from the plane.

We had to taxi downwind of the island to get sea conditions that permitted a takeoff. I wanted to give Fisher a gift for pulling me out if the water, so I gave him my .38.

But he wasn't ready to quit for the day. That Dumbo pilot, Fisher, really had guts. He said, "I understand you have another guy down," referring to Carl, who had landed his Corsair in the middle of the enemy.

I said, "Yes."

He said, "There's a lake near where he went down. I'll land there."

I said, "You can't go in there. You don't understand. There are too many enemy troops around." While we were having this conversation inside the Albatross, Carl had almost certainly been captured already.

I couldn't help but think about Charles R. White, who had been lost in that World War II incident near Iwo Jima when we flew into a thunderstorm with an R5C and our planes started dropping out of the sky. White was engaged to a girl. She refused to give up hope. I had some contact with her. I knew his plane dropped out of the sky and he went straight in, but she wouldn't stop hoping. This was one time when hope wasn't going to help.

Albatross Aloft

We tried two takeoffs and couldn't get off. So we had to taxi to the downwind aside of Cho-do island and it was dark and we were finally able to take off.

Fisher's SA-16 Albatross hauled me out of North Korea and took me to K-16, just as one of these Dumbos had done with Johnny Geuss a week earlier. There was a big difference, however. Unlike John, I didn't get a ride home quite so easily.

There was an R4D Skytrain, the Marines' version of the DC-3 Gooney Bird, that traveled from base to base in Korea, hauling people and mail. Lugging my water-soaked parachute—yes, I still had it and brought it back with me—I tried to get on that R4D to get a ride home to our base at K-18. They said, "If you don't have any travel orders, you can't get on this plane."

I said, "Of course, I don't have any travel orders. I was shot down over North Korea."

They said, "No orders, no ride. No exceptions."

I stood around with my wet parachute until another plane came along and they hauled me home.

Remember that I had urged we assign Corsairs to attack the gun sites around our target. That wasn't done, and we lost three Corsairs that day—four, if you count the one that returned to its base too badly damaged to fly again. I felt this wouldn't have happened if we'd assigned some of our planes to the dedicated flak suppression mission.

So I had a discussion with Marine Air Group 12, or MAG-12, commander Col. Richard C. Mangrum. I told him we were going to have to use flak suppression. He listened carefully. He nodded.

"You've lost two tent mates," Mangrum said. He meant F4U-4B pilots Thomas and Lundquist, who had gone down near the target. "You don't need to think about flak suppression now. I'm going to ground you for five days. Then you come back and we'll talk about it."

During those five days in nonflying status, I worked in the tower at K-18. One day, a Corsair turned the pattern on final approach and the pilot made the routine radio call to confirm that his landing gear was down. But it wasn't. He was coming in with his gear up.

One of our guys wanted to warn him by firing a flare. But in his haste, the guy fired the flare while he was still indoors. It created an awful mess, all around us. And at about that point, the Corsair pilot put his wheels down.

After five days, Colonel Mangrum said, "We will use bombs with airburst VT fuses to suppress antiaircraft guns from now on."

RED JAMES I served with VMF-312, the "Checkerboards," in Korea from October 1952 to April 1953. During my time, we took the cannon-armed F4U-4B aboard our jeep carrier, the USS *Badoeng Strait* (CVE 116). We were on the west coast near the island of Paengnyong-do, or PY-do for short.

My first hop in Korea was on October 31, 1952, in bureau number 97436, an F4U-4B. It was a TARCAP, or target combat air patrol mission, lasting 2.1 hours. My notes from that mission show 20 enemy troops killed in action and 30 wounded in action. For me, it was the first of 101 missions in Korea. Needless to say, I never had any idea I was going to be in Korea at all. I thought it was over when I came home from Okinawa in 1945.

I got out after World War II and finished college at the University of Detroit with a degree in business. I had been at West Virginia Wesleyan in 1940 and 1941. I finished college in Detroit. I flew in the organized Reserves at Grossville, Michigan, from 1946 to 1949. The regulars under President Harry S Truman and Defense Secretary Louis Johnson didn't have enough gas to sustain everyday operations at any reasonable level, but the Reserves did. I could go over to Grossville and climb into a Corsair and fly anytime, which is one reason I logged a lot of hours in the Corsair. In September 1949, I moved to the central valley in California and was selling automobiles until November 1951. Like a lot of us World War II veterans, I was still subject to being called back up for duty.

The Marine Corps kept sending me greetings and I didn't reply. I had two children, ages three and one. That didn't matter. In November 1951, they sent me orders and I had to put on my Marine uniform again.

I checked in at El Toro, California, and was assigned to squadron VMF-235 at Kaneohe Bay, Hawaii. This was the first outfit at the base after Kaneohe made the shift from being a naval air station to being a Marine Corps air station, but we weren't there long. They brought us back to the States for maneuvers at Kodiak. After we arrived, the maneuvers were cancelled due to an oil strike in May or June 1952. So we went back to Kaneohe. We practiced carrier landings and navigation.

In July, they sent us back to El Toro to become an F9F-2 Panther

Capt. Jim Bailey
October 16, 1951
Vought F4U-4B Corsair
Marine Fighter Squadron
VMF-312, "Checkerboards"
K-18 Kangnung Airfield,
South Korea

Capt. (later Maj.) Eugene N. "Red" James of squadron VMF-312, the "Checkerboards," poses on the wing of his F4U-4B Corsair fighter in Korea in 1953.

[U.S. Marine Corps]

outfit. The Panther was the straight-wing jet fighter built by Grumman that was flown by Navy and Marine pilots in Korea. I was the operations officer and scheduled myself in the F9F-2 twice. On my first flight, the landing indicator did not indicate the gear was down. I flew past the tower and they said, "They appear to be down." I landed and everything was all right. At some point, the Marine Corps decided that my many hours in the Corsair were more important than my limited experience in the Panther, and that's when I found myself heading for the Far East instead of flying jets.

When I arrived in Japan to learn about my assignment, the officer said to us, "I've got good news and bad news." First he told me the good part: "You get to choose whether you want land based or carrier based."

There was no hesitation. I remembered shaving out of a helmet on Okinawa and using a sleeping bag during World War II. I said, "I'll take the carrier because they've got napkins, tablecloths, and showers every day."

We said, "What's the bad news?"

He said, "I know that when the war started some of your buddies came over here and flew 35 missions, or 50 missions, and went home.

I'm sorry to tell you, you're going to have to fly 100 missions before you go home."

My F4U-4B in Korea was a lot more stable than my F4U-1C on Okinawa. It had four blades. It had good acceleration. They still had the device on the leading edge of the wing that made both wings stall at the same time. I felt very comfortable handling that airplane in the low-speed, low-altitude environment around the carrier.

I would come upwind, make my U-turn, come back on final approach, judge the approximate distance, and be the height of the island on the carrier. I would have full rpms and come in at about 93 knots, which is 6 or 7 knots above stalling speed. That airplane just performed beautifully. When I got close to the landing signal officer, or LSO, I would have the right height and could judge by that. The LSO gave you a cut and you had to see what attitude the deck had. The attitude of the carrier deck was a matter of life and death once you were committed to landing. There were a lot of swells in the Yellow Sea. A 585-feet ship responded a lot to those swells. You had to hit your airplane on the deck on three points or the high wheel would be driven through the wing.

Once in a while, we would have icy decks. It was terrible. Your brakes weren't effective. On an icy deck at idle rpms, you were getting some forward progress. One time, my left wheel got right on top of the edge of the carrier, right at the point where the F4U-4B was going to go over the side. I undid my safety harness. If a Corsair goes over the side, the plane hits the water on its back, so I had made up my mind: I would throw myself out of the cockpit first. That might have been a mistake, but I didn't go into the water. We had one guy go into the Yellow Sea when the ring broke off the catapult. The captain swerved the ship. The carrier ran over him but he missed the carrier's propellers and he survived.

Landing on a carrier sometimes got your attention more than being over target. When you're looking down at the carrier from the sky, it looks very small. That was a postage stamp out there and we had to get aboard that postage stamp. Every landing on one of those jeep carriers was an adventure. Every one.

On November 27, 1951, I made a wheels-down landing in bureau number 81912. I got shot up at Chinampo and landed at "Bloodstone," which was the radio call sign for the island of Paengnyong-do, or PY-do for short, in the Yellow Sea south of Cho-do.

At PY-do, oil completely covered my windshield. I pulled out to the right and told the rest of the flight to go on in. I proceeded south along the water, intending to make a water landing. As I went back past Paengnyong-do, the beach was exposed and I had the thought to land there. I went in wheels down. It was like landing at Daytona Beach. A British mechanic there discovered that a bullet had hit my sump pump. He said it was cleaned up, so I decided to try to get out of there and fly back to my ship. I poured the power to it for takeoff. I didn't realize the tide had come in and I didn't have much beach to take off from. I took off in a very short distance. I returned to the carrier.

It turned out the pilot of the next group behind me was the commanding officer, Colonel Cameron. I warned him and others about the dangers involved in landing at PY-do. Still, a guy in the next flight landed wheels down and flipped and burned.

On another mission, I had a problem and the possibility of another such emergency landing crossed my mind once more. I had oil on the windshield again. I had my mind made up: I wasn't going to PY-do. I was going to divert to K-6 Pyongtaek Airfield in South Korea, but then I flew through a rainstorm and that cleaned the windshield.

On another mission, we saw this gook leading an ox toward the Yellow Sea. The guy I was flying with made a turn and put his guns on him. The guy slapped the ox and started running toward the Yellow Sea. My leader tightened his turn and didn't have the power to do it, so he flew his Corsair into the ground. He flew into the ground and bounced and continued flying. He was Capt. Jerry Jerominsky. He got back to the carrier with no gas tank. He'd been flying so low he returned to the carrier with weeds in his rocket launchers. He knew he'd made a mistake.

I put the power on and fired a 20-millimeter at the ox and not a one of those rounds hit him. He must have jumped 20 feet into the air but he wasn't hit. We came back from that mission with ordnance hanging under the wing. Returning with ordnance was dangerous, especially high-velocity aircraft rockets, or HVARs.

At the end of my tour, I sneaked in one more mission than the expected total, to reach 101. I didn't intend to remain in the Marine Corps forever, but I extended for two years and went to Whiting Field, Florida, to instruct in the SNJ Texan trainer. I extended for one additional year at Whiting and retired from the Reserves. On my birthday, June 2, 1957, I was officially retired from the Marine Corps.

In Korea, I sometimes wondered if everything we were doing was a waste of time and money, especially bombing and strafing animals and rail lines. I'm not sure we actually did very much damage to North Korea.

Vought F4U-4B Corsair

The Corsair proved itself as one of the great fighters long before the Navy introduced the F4U-4 model, first flown on April 19, 1944. The F4U-4 incorporated numerous improvements based on combat experience and was greeted with enthusiasm by pilots. The Navy officially accepted its first production F4U-4 on October 31, 1944, and airplane buffs immediately spotted a quick way to distinguish these and later models from the earlier Corsairs. The F4U-4 introduced a four-blade propeller instead of a three-blade one.

The F4U-4 also had a more powerful engine, a chin scoop under the engine cowling, and a redesigned cockpit with a "blown" canopy (named for the shape of its glass) to improve comfort and pilot visibility. A few F4U-4 models reached Okinawa and flew missions against Japan during the final days of World War II, but most saw service in the postwar and Korean War eras. Included among the 2,357 airplanes manufactured until August 1947 in the F4U-4 series were 297 F4U-4B fighters armed not with machine guns but with four 20-milimeter cannons. Marines who had previously flown the cannon-armed F4U-1C (see chapter 4) found the new cannons on the F4U-4B to be more reliable and deadlier.

Who's Who

Capt. (later Col.) John J. "J.J." Geuss, F4U-4B Corsair fighter pilot, VMF-312, Korea

Capt. (later Maj.) Eugene N. "Red" James, F4U-4B Corsair fighter pilot, VMF-312, Korea

Capt. Jim Bailey, F4U-4B Corsair fighter pilot, VMF-312, Korea

During the Korean War, Marines flew several types of fighters, including twin-engine, propeller-driven F7F Tigercats, jet F9F Panthers, and jet F3D Skyknight night fighters. There was also a subsequent version of the Corsair called the F4U-5. But sailors and Marines say no warplane ever received the wide acceptance of the F4U-4. They said this about every kind of F4U-4 Corsair, including F4U-4s with machine guns and the F4U-4Bs with cannons.

Marine Corsair pilots operated from the decks of escort carriers off the west coast of Korea and from land bases like K-18 at Kangnung, South Korea. Squadron VMF-312, the "Checkerboards," flew straight F4U-4s during one cruise at sea but swapped these planes for F4U-4B models when flying on land. Maj. William J. Sambito described the reason for the swap-out process in the official history of the squadron: "The 20-millimeter cannons were more difficult to load, especially on a crowded carrier deck, and since the ammunition was explosive, it had to be kept in a special locker while .50-caliber [machine gun] rounds could be stored in ready lockers below decks." According to the recollections of pilots like Red James, the concern over 20-millimeter ammunition on the carrier did not last. F4U-4Bs went aboard ship by 1952.

Although the F4U-4 series, which included the F4U-4B, was the best-known Corsair, there was yet another version of the famous fighter that also saw Korea duty with the Marines. In fact, it served exclusively with the Marines.

The theory behind the final U.S. version of the Corsair was that Korea was different, requiring constant close air support at low level where gunfire was intense. "Antiaircraft fire in Korea was often more intense than in World War II," said pilot Jim Bailey. "The Corsair was tough but we always knew you could take hits to the oil coolers or to other vulnerable parts of the aircraft."

At the same time, Korea did not pose a need for a highly maneuverable, air-to-air combat fighter, at least not in the latter stages of the war. There simply was no Japanese Zero in Korea.

To fill the need for a plane optimized for close air support, the Marine Corps began receiving a different kind of Corsair—not a "thoroughbred" but a "workhorse," as one veteran said it.

The new version was first called the F4U-6. But experts decided that it was not a "fighter" but an attack plane. It became the AU-1. It first flew on January 31, 1952, but it didn't fly nearly as fast or as high as an F4U-4.

The familiar external oil coolers of the F4U-4 were moved inboard to reduce vulnerability, and the aircraft was given new layers of armor for protection against hostile fire. Fully loaded for combat, an AU-1 could weigh 19,398 pounds, or about 20 percent more than a fully loaded F4U-4. It could also carry about 20 percent more ordnance. A typical load consisted of two 1,000 pound bombs under the fuselage and six 500-pound bombs on the outer wing racks. In Korea, some AU-1s carried ten 5-inch HVARs.

Because of the extra armor and weapons load, the AU-1 was rated at only 238 miles per hour at medium altitude with a service ceiling of less than 20,000 feet. In contrast, an F4U could reach 446 miles per hour and 37,000 feet.

Despite the intentional tradeoff of performance for armor, Marines loved the AU-1 because it could take punishment and dish it out.

According to a Web site devoted to the history of Marine Fighter Squadron VMF-323, the AU-1 "was strictly a low-altitude aircraft with a two-speed supercharger, versus the two-stage, two-speed supercharger in the F4U-4. It had more power at the lower altitudes, but was a 'dog' up high." Twelve AU-1s reached the squadron in Korea in 1952.

Even with its armor, the AU-1 was not invulnerable. On August 5,

Corsair of squadron VMF-312, the "Checkerboards."

[U.S. Marine Corps]

Vought F4U-4B Corsair

Type: single-seat carrier- and land-based fighter

Power plant: one 2,450-hp (1828 kW) Pratt & Whitney R-2800-18W or -42W Double Wasp 18-cylinder radial engine driving a 13 ft 2 in (4.01 m) 4-blade Hydromatic propeller

Performance: maximum speed, 446 mph (713 km/h) at 19,900 ft (6065 m); 360 mph (575 km/h) at sea level; initial climb rate, 3,100 ft (944 m) per minute; service ceiling, 39,000 ft (11887 m); range, 1,005 miles (1606 km)

Weights: empty, 8,982 (4074 kg); loaded, 14,670 lb (6654 kg)

Dimensions: span, 41 ft (12.49 m); length, 33 ft 8 in (10.36 m); height, 14 ft 1 in (4.12 m); wing area, 314 sq ft (29.17 sq m)

Armament: four 20-mm M3 (T31) cannons with 4 ammunition boxes, 2 per gun, in each outer panel, supplying 220 rounds of ammunition per gun; up to 5,000 lb (2267 kg) of fuel, napalm, bombs, or rockets

Crew: 1 (pilot)

First flight: May 29, 1940 (XF4U-1); April 19, 1944 (F4U-4)

1952, Col. Robert E. Galer was leading 31 warplanes to a target near Wonsan, North Korea, when gunfire ripped into his AU-1. Galer had witnessed the Japanese attack on Pearl Harbor and had earned the Medal of Honor on Guadalcanal (as an F4F Wildcat pilot). Although his AU-1 went down, Galer bailed out, was rescued by a helicopter (see chapter 9), and later retired as a brigadier general.

After fighting in Korea ended in July 1953, the Marine Corps quickly made the transition to jets. A few F4U-4 and AU-1 Corsairs remained in service briefly, but the last was retired in 1957.

Chapter Nine

Helicopter Haul in a Forgotten War

What Happened

In January 1951, Lt. Col. George W. Herring took command of the first helicopter transportation unit in any branch of the armed forces. There had never been anything quite like squadron HMR-161.

Herring was one of about a dozen officers who pioneered the idea of using the helicopter to carry combat troops into battle, giving Marines a speed and mobility the enemy might not be able to match and freeing them from what one flier called "the tyranny of terrain."

As a major, Herring had commanded the First Marine Raider Battalion during World War II and had become an aviator only after the war, when helicopters first began to appear. Together with executive officer Maj. William P. Mitchell, Herring put together Marine Helicopter Transport Squadron HMR-161 at Tustin, California. "There was very little time to turn this into a combat-ready outfit," one Marine remembered. "We were going to be the first to use helicopters to lift Marines onto the battlefield, and while we were training, our guys were going eyeball to eyeball with the Chinese in Korea." Except for Herring, every pilot in the squadron had flown fighters in World War II.

Korea was a slog. it was a mountainous country with all of the extremes of terrain, climate, and weather. Without HRS helicopters, the Marines would never have achieved the kind of mobility that enabled them to win battles. This recent picture of the Korean War Memorial in Washington, D. C, suggests the harshness of the Korean War.

[William T. Rando]

Equipped with the Sikorsky HRS-1 helicopter, the aircraft known to civilians as the S-55 and as the H-19 in the Army and Air Force, Herring had only a few months to stand up the squadron. In August 1951, Herring's helicopters and Marines began boarding the aircraft carrier USS *Sitkoh Bay* (CVE 86) at San Diego, California, with orders for Korea. Within weeks, the squadron's glossy blue HRS-1s were operating at K-18 airfield at Kangnung, on the east coast of South Korea, as part of the First Marine Aircraft Wing.

The Marines already had a squadron of smaller helicopters in Korea. Squadron VMO-6 (see chapter 7) was busy performing utility flights, target spotting, and medical evacuation duties. Marines from that squadron helped Herring and his HRS-1 crews get settled in just as the Korean summer began to fade and Marines looked ahead to their second winter of heavy fighting.

Not surprisingly, a lot of Marines gathered around simply to look at an HRS-1 and to ask to climb inside or to fly in it. Squadron members found themselves talking to some Marines who had never before seen any helicopter close up. Certainly none had seen a craft the size of the HRS-1. It was all new and different, and the significance of the big blue

These are examples of the world's first transport helicopter, the Marine Corps HRS-1. These were the first helicopters that went to squadron HMR-161 and pioneered helicopter operations in Korea.

[Sikorsky Aircraft]

aircraft was going to take time to sink in. Helicopter pilots and crew chiefs were suddenly giving guided tours of their unusual flying machine.

FRANK HASS I had a similar experience as a crew chief on the HRS-1 in the second Marine Corps squadron, HMM-163, which was formed at Santa Ana, California, in 1951. We took one of the aircraft down to Camp Pendleton and suddenly everybody wanted to look at it and touch it. I was just a buck sergeant and I was surrounded by a whole bunch of colonels. I thought, "Gee, I'm doing this! It's really great that I'm doing this. What an experience!"

I'm also a pilot, although not a helicopter pilot, so I was glad when I had a chance to fly it for about ten minutes. I spent about three minutes making the HRS-1 go this way and that before I seemed to get the hang of it. I had read that the HRS-1 is difficult to handle. You have to anticipate where the helicopter is going and stay on top of the situation, but once you become accustomed to it, handling the HRS-1 really isn't that hard.

I had great opportunities. I had two years of regular duty and four years in the Reserve.

I didn't start out to become a crew chief. I was born in 1928 in West

A Sikorsky HRS-2 helicopter of Marine Helicopter Transport Squadron 161, or VMR-161, lifts off on a mission. The HRS-2 model was introduced late in the Korean War, replacing the nearly identical HRS-1. Both were underpowered, but still managed to make history as the first helicopters to haul troops into battle.

[Jack Plumly]

Virginia. I went into the Marine Corps in 1946, right after the war. I did two years in the Marines, got out, and went to college for a year. Like a lot of people, I was recalled to active duty when the Korean War came along. They sent me to maintenance school at Millington, Tennessee, near Memphis, and then I was assigned to Santa Ana, where the two blimp hangars were.

The duties of a crew chief were still evolving, but in general you were expected to know the aircraft and keep it flying. The HRS-1 had some complications that you needed to know about. A crew chief should be able to check all of the places that need to be lubricated: You have reservoirs for fluid in the aircraft and you need to know where they are and how they work. You ought to recognize if there's a dent in the side of the aircraft. You should know when the tires are low. If the pilot says, "Hey, there's something wrong," you should be able to find it and fix it.

Whenever you deal with a new aircraft, the company that builds it prepares a maintenance program to train mechanics. They take a great deal of effort to train you on systems. I didn't go to Sikorsky for training but others did, and I got my training from people in the squadron who had used the manufacturer's help to become very familiar with the aircraft.

Basically, the HRS-1 was a medium-lift helicopter—although it seemed much larger in those days—capable of hauling 19 people or 12 people or four litter cases. It was designed for the Wright R-1820 engine, which put out about 1,200 horsepower, but our HRS-1s were delivered with the Pratt & Whitney R-1340 Wasp, which was also used in the famous T-6 Texan trainer, and so it was underpowered.

We had a case or two where the front of the engine itself, where the driveshaft went through, was not strong enough for the load, and on several occasions that case that holds the driveshaft would break. When that happened, you got a crash. Otherwise, I don't think there was a better flying machine than the HRS-1.

Up front, it had two clamshell doors that opened out to give you easy access to the engine. For the most part, it was relatively easy to work on. Everything was right out in the front. The engine was World War II technology, but the basic concept of the helicopter was very sound. It was very practical.

What Happened

In Korea, as the HRS-1s of Herring's squadron HMR-161 began flying, Herring's bosses were watching closely. They wanted to see whether his squadron could make its transport helicopters an integral part of an air-ground combat team rather than an appendage without a clear mission. The Marines intended the first Korean deployment of HMR-161 as a test of the helicopter in support of land warfare, not of the Corps's signature role in amphibious assault. The test confronting Herring would have been little different if he had been in the Army, although, at this point, the Army was still many months away from having its own version of the HRS-1 in the field. Ships designed to carry helicopters were not yet available, and it was only later that HMR-161 operated from Navy ships off the Korean coast.

After setting up a base camp at K-18, the squadron was assigned to auxiliary field X-83 in the eastern Punch Bowl region of Korea, supporting the First Marine Regiment. It was a place with a single crude building, tents, no running water, and electricity provided by generator. Looking up at the slopes around them, Marines now had an appreciation of the mountainous terrain of Korea, to say nothing of the powerful and unpredictable winds that whipped down the mountain passes all the way from Siberia. The Punch Bowl was an extinct volcano surrounded by other craggy hills and slopes. Marines were clearing Chinese troops out of a series of hills nearby that were 600 to 700 meters in height, exactly the kind of terrain where a lift from a helicopter might make a big difference.

As the portly blue HRS-1s began flying, Marines were reminded more than ever that Korea confronted them with the full array of challenges related to weather, terrain, and operating conditions. The Korean Peninsula offered the full range of seasons, from subzero winters to blistering summers, all of it spread across a mosaic of craggy ridges and sprawling paddy fields. Helicopters dislike heat and high altitude, and no helicopter disliked them more than the underpowered HRS-1. On one of the early trial flights from airfield X-83, a fully loaded HRS-1 huffed and puffed, straining to clear a mountaintop, and couldn't get over it. The pilot settled down on a slope, the HRS-1 coming to a halt at what looked like a precarious angle. Neither men nor machine were harmed, but it was a reminder that Chinese bullets weren't the only threat.

Operation Windmill

The HRS-1 might have had a tendency to become a little shaky at high temperatures or near mountain peaks, but it offered a new way to haul bullets and beans to embattled troops. In the official Marine Corps his-

The HRS-1 seated two pilots, side-by-side, above and in front of a cargo or troop compartment with a sliding door, from which a cameraman is aiming a motion-picture camera here. The large cargo compartment held a great deal in terms of volume, but much less when measured by weight.

[U.S. Marine Corps]

tory of the era (*Whirlybirds: U.S. Marine Helicopters in Korea*, by Lt. Col. Ronald J. Brown), a battalion commander of the First Marine Regiment described the situation that confronted Herring and his helicopter crews:

"We were attacking from Hill 673 toward Hill 749," said Lt. Col. Franklin B. Nihart. "Our supply and evacuation route consisted of foot trails. The only way to keep supplies moving . . . was by using Korean Service Corps porters. . . . [They] could not keep up with the logistical demands imposed by heavy casualties and high ammunition expenditure, [so] HMR-161 was called to fill the . . . gap."

Another minor mishap that left an HRS-1 temporarily marooned on

This Marine Corps HRS-3 is an example of the final version of the transport helicopter that pioneered operations in Korea.

[U.S. Marine Corps]

a slope did not deter preparations to put the helicopters to good use. On September 12, 1951, HMR-161 indoctrinated the Marines of the First Shore Party Battalion in the techniques of loading and giving landing instructions to the transport helicopters. The next day, as final preparations were made for the first serious use of the helicopters, the Marines sorted supplies into 800-pound (362-kilogram) loads. At 3:50 p.m. on September 13, seven HRS-1s lifted with supplies suspended below each aircraft to fly a seven-mile route to supply the Second Battalion, First Marines.

So began the squadron's first action, Operation Windmill I, on September 13, 1951. The squadron flew 28 sorties and its fat, bright blue HRS-1s hauled about 19,000 pounds (8618 kilograms) of supplies to a Marine battalion holding a hilltop in the middle of the Punch Bowl area fighting. While flying these supply runs, Herring's HRS-1s also evacuated 84 casualties. Operation Windmill I consisted of 28 flights for a total of 14.1 flight hours. The numbers are modest but nothing like it had ever been attempted before.

At the same time, Herring's squadron began a Marine tradition of using transport helicopters to rescue the wounded: Unlike the Army, the Marine Corps has never employed dedicated "dust off" helicopters for the medical evacuation mission. Wounded Marines are brought off the battlefield by the same helicopters that carry men, machines, and material into the fight. In HMR-161, there apparently were no assigned litters, medical evacuation supplies, or Navy corpsmen. Still, some of the wounded hauled out by Herring's helicopters reached a field medical facility less than an hour after being hit. Korea was the first American war in which significant numbers of seriously wounded men were saved because of the speed and success of medical evacuation. The helicopter was the reason.

Herring's squadron was quickly asked to take on a follow-up aerial supply mission, dubbed Operation Windmill II. On September 19, 1951, ten HRS-1s hauled more than 12,000 pounds (5443 kilograms) of cargo. One of their destinations was Hill 812, as devoid of foliage as the surface of the moon and crisscrossed by fortified slit trenches. Pilots reminded each other that this was not a place where they wanted to run into trouble. Crew chiefs suddenly enjoyed new and visible respect.

From the beginning, the Marines intended to use the HRS-1 to haul men as well as supplies. In fact, they viewed hauling troops into battle as the primary mission of the HRS-1. But it quickly became apparent that the HRS-1 had some disappointing characteristics. Although sturdy and tough, with the engine out front where it served as a kind of unintended armor to protect the pilots from flying bullets, the HRS-1 just didn't have the oomph. The R-1340-57 Wasp engine, which was supposed to deliver 600 horsepower, was, under most realistic conditions, good for only 500 or less. The HRS-1 was designed to carry up to 15 combat Marines with all their gear, and in comfortable stateside settings had routinely carried 12, but in the practical conditions of altitude, climate, and weather that prevailed in Korea, it could rarely carry more than five men or 800 pounds (362 kilograms) of cargo. When evacuating wounded, the helicopter was supposed to be able to handle three to five casualties but, under the harsh conditions that obtained in Korea, three was usually an optimistic maximum. Marine pilots had difficulty hovering the straining HRS-1 at mountain elevations greater than 2,000 feet (609 meters), and the squadron lost one of its helicopters on a rescue mission when the HRS-1 simply didn't have enough power to climb over a tree stump on high ground. One forwarding operating location for the HRS-1 was already at about 500 feet (152 meters) elevation and the HRS-1 had difficulty remaining stable even while hovering in ground effect.

Nevertheless, HMR-161 went ahead with Operation Summit. The squadron's mission was to haul a Marine reconnaissance company to the peak of Hill 884, an important observation post overlooking the Chinese, where the Marines would replace a South Korean unit. After delays due in part to high winds and generally bad weather, and after operations were halted by a thick fog, Summit kicked off on September 21, 1951. Eventually, 12 helicopters made the 14-mile (22-kilometer) flight and hauled 224 men. The first Marines on the scene descended from hovering HRS-1s, hand over hand, down knotted ropes to the ground. After they set up a security perimeter, some of the Marines bounded out of the HRS-1s on the ground. Soon afterward, the HRS-1s were laying telephone lines for the Marines as they settled into their positions.

As always in Korea where extremes were routine, the weather was as much an adversary as the Chinese. In early morning, the area around the Marines' airstrip and the valleys beneath the Korean ridges were thick with clinging gray soup. In spite of the dense fog, HMR-161 hauled 224 fully equipped Marines to Hill 884. The HRS-1s also carried 17,772 pounds (8061 kilograms) of cargo. The operation consisted of 65 flights, included 31.2 total flight hours, and took four hours.

Operation Blackbird

On September 27, 1951, Herring's squadron carried out the first night troop lift of combat Marines in Operation Blackbird. On paper, it was a "training" effort, since there were no Chinese troops in the immediate area, and for once the weather cooperated, but HRS-1 pilots and crews still saw it as a challenge. The HRS-1s lifted 200 Marines of E Company, Second Battalion, First Marines to the Punch Bowl, on a night

Who's Who

Lt. Col. George W. Herring, HRS-1 pilot, commander, squadron HMR-161, Korea

Sgt. Frank Hass, HRS-1 crew chief, squadron HMM-163, California

with no moonlight, in two hours and ten minutes. In the essay, "The Marine Helicopter and the Korean War," Maj. Rodney R. Propst wrote that Operation Blackbird was not an unqualified success but that many lessons were learned. Propst quoted the Marines' official report:

> Night troop lifts in mountainous terrain are feasible provided a daylight reconnaissance of the landing zone together with the avenues of approach and retirement can be effected. Present equipment indicates that under present conditions in Korea these night lifts should be limited to movements within friendly territory.

Operation Blackbird was the only large-scale night lift of combat Marines in the Korean War, an era long before the arrival of night-vision goggles and other tools intended to permit operations in the dark. Even in Vietnam a dozen years later, helicopters were not yet able to carry out an assault during the nocturnal hours.

In other missions, HRS-1s proved to be versatile and resilient. Operation Pronto proved that HMR-161 was capable of fast response when the helicopters moved 662 troops and 10,000 pounds of supplies in just 3¾ hours after orders were issued. Operation Bushbeater and Operation Houseburner were antiguerrilla actions that marked the first exchange of fire between helicopter-borne forces and enemy troops on the ground.

The HRS-1 had been in the combat zone for a year when the improved model finally became available. In October 1952, HMR-161 received its first HRS-2, a new model of the familiar big blue helicopter, now with a redesigned tail boom intended to create greater clearance beneath the main rotor and to prevent the main blades from slapping the boom during a hard landing. Sadly, although the HRS-2 boasted many minor improvements, it retained the Wasp engine that Marine pilots and crew chiefs insisted was inadequate. Only in the post-Korea era would Marines have an opportunity to fly the HRS-3, with the larger engine for which the aircraft had been designed.

One Marine source indicates that 17 HRS-1 and HRS-2 helicopters were lost in action during Korean fighting. Numerous times, one of the helicopters sustained battle damage but brought its Marines home before expiring. After one sortie, a crew counted nearly 100 small arms hits on one of the blue helicopters.

By the time of the July 27, 1953, cease-fire in Korea, HMR-161 had accumulated 16,538 flight hours in the HRS-1/2 on 18,607 sorties, operating on rare occasion from carriers. The helicopters were credited with more than 60,000 individual troop movements. Marines found the HRS-1 tough and durable, but underpowered—far from effective on hot days around Korea's jagged mountain peaks.

Sikorsky HRS-1/2 Transport Helicopter

The new helicopter taking shape on drawing boards at Sikorsky's Stratford, Connecticut, plant in the late 1940s was bigger than anything that had been attempted up to that time. It would carry more than just an extra crewman or a rescue litter. It would handle a payload of up to ten passengers, eight hospital litters, or 5,000 pounds (2267 kilograms) of freight in a large fuselage that sat on a wheeled landing gear or on amphibious floats.

With its engine in the nose, mounted so that the driveshaft sloped up to the base of the rotor pylon, the new helicopter made good use of lightweight materials. Marine Air, seeing that the new helicopter would be able to fly missions up to a radius of 210 miles, took an immediate interest. But first came five test ships for the Air Force, called YH-19s,

Marine Corps HRS-1 helicopter.

[U.S. Marine Corps]

the *Y* prefix signifying a service-test mission. The first YH-19 completed its maiden flight on November 10, 1949.

The YH-19's 600-horsepower Pratt & Whitney R-1340 Wasp radial air-cooled piston engine was the same proven power plant used in the North American T-6 Texan trainer. The engine was mounted at an angle in the nose of the fuselage, with the novel driveshaft arrangement already described. Large, sideways-opening clamshell doors made maintenance easy. Maintainers could complete an engine change in two hours.

The Marine Corps liked the sturdy, unattractive, and somewhat underpowered helicopter, which they called the HRS. In Korea, the Marines flew troops into combat via helicopter more than a year before the Army did. During the Korean War, pilots and crews of Marine Air paved the way for helicopter tactics later used in Vietnam.

For some reason, the HRS never acquired a popular nickname. At the time, planes like the Corsair, Tigercat, and Panther were deemed worthy of names, while mere helicopters had to settle for alphabet soup: The *H* meant helicopter, the *R* signified a transport, and the *S* identified the builder, Sikorsky. The first version of the HRS was designated HRS-1, the second HRS-2, and so on.

The HRS was the Marine Corps's name for an aircraft its builder,

Sikorsky, called the S-55. It was the H-19 to the Army and Air Force, and the HO4S to the Navy. The Marines eventually acquired 240 of the helicopters, including 60 HRS-1, 91 HRS-2, and 89 HRS-3 models.

A rounded, portly aircraft with a big cargo door and a roomy compartment for people or supplies, the HRS was an advanced helicopter for its era and reflected the dramatic advances in aviation that followed World War II. There were times when Marines were consternated by its need for more power but they always appreciated its toughness.

The first aircraft in the series made its initial flight on November 10, 1949. The Marine Corps placed its initial order for production HRS helicopters on August 2, 1950. The Korean War had started the previous month. Marine leaders moved quickly to form units that could operate the new helicopters on the battlefield.

Marine squadron HMX-1 at Quantico, Virginia, took delivery of the first HRS-1 models on April 2, 1951. Almost immediately, the helicopters were crated and shipped to Korea.

While the Marines were preparing to use the HRS-1 for combat troop transport, the Air Force was employing the same helicopter on behind-the-lines rescue missions, including some rescuing Marine Air pilots. Two Air Force models joined the Third Air Rescue Squadron at Wolmi-do, Korea, on March 23, 1951, and participated in numerous rescues before one of the helicopters was transferred to Central Intelligence Agency duties. There, in black paint and devoid of markings, it flew clandestine missions for the CIA, including a mission aimed at retrieving a crashed enemy MiG-15 jet fighter for evaluation.

By then, of course, the Marines were making everyday use of their HRS-1s. As noted in this chapter, the first use of helicopters to carry combat troops to an objective was recorded on September 13, 1951, when HRS-1s of squadron HMR-161 hauled Marines across a seven-mile contested zone to a Korean hilltop being assaulted by Chinese troops. HRS-1s flew 28 sorties and evacuated 84 casualties.

Another Korea operation that involved the HRS-1 was Operation Ripple in 1952. Marines tried a new tactic with their ground rocket launcher—firing barrages at the enemy and then quickly relocating via helicopter before the enemy could zero in on their firing positions. Incredibly, it was not until the following year—January 1953—that the Army began using its version of the HRS on the Korean battlefield.

For a period of time, the Marines and the Air Force were working simultaneously, and with an unusual degree of cooperation, to develop the new transport helicopter, while the Army lagged. In 1951, the Air Force ordered 50 production H-19A models. The Navy and Coast Guard ordered a version called the HO4S-1. Next came the H-19B version with a new power plant, the 700-horsepower Wright R-1300-3. Sikorsky built 270. By then, Marine HRS-1s were rolling off the line beside their counterparts from the other services.

The Air Force's equivalents to the HRS-1, known as the H-19A and H-19B, went to the 3rd and 2157th Air Rescue Squadrons in 1952. In its rescue role, the H-19 was equipped with a hydraulic hoist mounted on the starboard fuselage just above the door. A number of combat rescues were achieved in Korea, including the celebrated save on April 12, 1952, of the ranking ace of the war, 16-kill Capt. Joseph McConnell.

In Korea, Air Force and CIA H-19s dropped allied agents behind enemy lines and recovered them. Despite the helicopter's limited navigation suite, some of these missions were carried out at night. A dangerous cloak-and-dagger mission took place in summer 1952 when Capt. Joseph Cooper and Capt. Russell Winnegar of the 581st Resupply Squadron flew an H-19A into enemy territory with a small party of South Koreans to recover a crashed MiG-15 fighter. The MiG was the first to fall into allied hands and was evaluated by American scientists.

The Third Air Rescue Squadron had detachments scattered throughout Japan and Korea. By the time of the July 27, 1953, Korean armistice, the squadron had received over 1,000 personal citations—more than any other Air Force unit.

The Marines never stopped making their own records with the HRS-1, HRS-2, and HRS-3 helicopters. After the July 27, 1953, Korean armistice, an HRS-2 established time-to-climb and weight-hauling records that remained unbroken for almost a decade.

An HRS-2 was the first helicopter to use the helipad at the Pentagon building on November 2, 1955. Another HRS-2 retrieved the instrument capsule from a *Discovery III* satellite on August 4, 1960—the first time an object that had been in orbit was recovered.

Altogether, these helicopters served with nine Marine transport (HMR) squadrons, plus HMX-1, which was then a test unit. When the Pentagon overhauled its system for naming aircraft in 1962, several dozen HRS-3 helicopters were still in Marine units. They were redesignated CH-19E. With the new name, some were used as recovery craft during the *Mercury* manned space program.

The HRS-1 and HRS-2 models were powered by a 550-horsepower

Sikorsky HRS-1/2 helicopter (H-19)

Type: 2-place transport helicopter driving a 3-blade, 53 ft (16.15 m) main rotor

Power plant: one 600-hp (482-kW) Pratt & Whitney R-1340-57 Wasp or one 800-hp (682 kW) Wright R-1300-3 air-cooled, radial piston engine driving a 53-ft (16.15-m) three-blade main rotor

Performance: maximum speed, 112 mph (180 km/h) at sea level; cruising speed, 91 mph (146 km/h); service ceiling, 28,000 ft (85334 m); range, 360 miles (579 km); combat radius, estimate 100 mi (161 km); endurance, estimate 5 hr 20 min

Weights: empty, 5,250 lb (2381 kg); normal takeoff weight, 6,200 lb (2812 kg); maximum takeoff, 7,900 lb (3583 kg)

Dimensions: main rotor diameter, 53 ft (16.15 m); length overall, rotors turning, 56 ft 8½ in (17.27 m); length, 42 ft 3 in (12.88 m); height, 13 ft 4 in (4.06 m); tail rotor diameter, 8 ft 8 in (2.64 m); main rotor disc area, 2,206 sq ft (209.94 sq m)

Payload: 10 to 12 armed troops or 4 hospital litters

Armament: none

Crew: 2 pilots, plus typically 1 flight mechanic

First flight: November 10, 1949 (YH-19)

Pratt & Whitney R-1340 Wasp radial engine. The HRS-3 (CH-19E) used a 700-horsepower Wright R-1300.

A Korean War–era HRS-1 and a post-Korea HRS-3 are both part of the Marine Corps's museum collection at Quantico, Virginia, today. The National Museum of Naval Aviation at Pensacola, Florida, has an HRS-3.

The Army introduced the H-19 long after the Air Force did. The Coast Guard and Navy operated other versions. The H-19 was given the popular name Chickasaw by the Army when that service began naming helicopters for Native American nations in the late 1950s. During the Korean War era, these popular names were not yet in use.

Chapter Ten

Air Duel over MiG Alley

What Happened

The weather was marginal on July 11, 1953, when Maj. John F. Bolt, a Marine Corps officer serving an exchange tour with the 51st Fighter Interceptor Wing, shot down his fifth and sixth MiGs to become the 37th American air ace of the Korean War.

Bolt was one of several Marine pilots pulling exchange duty with the 51st. He had six kills from World War II and had logged 89 combat missions in the F9F-2 Panther with squadron VMF-115, "Able Eagles," before shifting to the Sabre. He and his wingman, 1st. Lt. Jerry Carlile, were near the Yalu, at about 20,000 feet, when they found two MiGs down on the deck. Bolt and Carlile closed in, more in danger of running into each other's streams of .50-caliber bullets than anything else. The MiGs were essentially sitting ducks. Bolt's gun camera footage confirmed that he shot down two of them, bringing his total to 12 enemy aircraft, six in World War II and six in Korea.

It wasn't that easy every time. By 1953, some of the MiG pilots belonged to the second-string team. But some were extremely aggressive, right up to the end.

Maj. John "Jack" Bolt
July 11, 1953
North American F-86F Sabre
39th Fighter Interceptor
   Squadron, "Cobras"
51st Fighter Interceptor Wing,
   "Checkerboards"
K-13 Suwon Air Base,
   South Korea

John Bolt, known as Jack, was the
only Marine Corps pilot—in fact,
the only naval aviator—to become
an air ace in two wars. In Korea, he
flew the F-86 Sabre with the 39th
Fighter Interceptor Squadron, the
"Cobras." He shot down six Soviet-
built MiG-15 jet fighters.

[Robert Bolt]

Bolt's second war in the air came to an end three weeks after those
aerial victories when the Korean armistice was signed. Bolt had begun
his tour of duty near the end of Korea fighting, yet became, among other
distinctions, the only naval aviator to become an ace in two wars.

DEAN ABBOTT I was Bolt's wingman on one of his kills. On that mission, he got within three shiplengths of his prey and was pouring all of
his six .50-caliber guns into the MiG's tailpipe.

The MiG pilot ejected. His canopy sailed over both of us. The MiG
pilot came down between us and fell right through the hail of gunfire
Bolt was pouring into that MiG. He lit up like a Christmas tree, and, for
the first time in my life, instead of seeing an aircraft being shot down, I
saw a guy die.

I flew home with my heart in the pit of my stomach. On landing, I
walked over to Bolt's Sabre. He was filling out the required entries in the
Dash One, the pilot's manual. I said, "Major Bolt, I have seen a lot of
MiGs shot down, but this is the first time I have ever seen a MiG pilot
die. How do you feel about that?" Without stopping his writing he told

me, without even looking at me, "He won't be up to fight us tomorrow, will he?" There was nothing mean-spirited in his tone. It was simply businesslike.

I walked back to my aircraft and thought, "Well, young Abbott, maybe I am learning my trade."

JOHN BOLT I don't know if there was such a thing as a typical mission. We flew with a minimum of four aircraft. That's a "division" to Marines but a "flight" to the Air Force.

Our F-86 Sabres took off in twos. As soon as we were airborne, as flight leader I throttled back, very quickly, so three and four could catch up. Then I advanced my throttle until somebody started dropping back. At that point, I reduced power slightly and locked the throttle. We'd climb at 400 knots to altitude. We cruised into the area. And we would normally set up a patrol along the Yalu River. The MiGs were at Chinese airfields like Antung, right across the river.

We always tried to stay together. We wanted to maintain flight integrity with two aircraft high and two low. Number one and three were the leaders, and two and four were the wingmen. We worked very hard on tactics. We had excellent air discipline. That's probably the third reason that we did as well as we did: the people who were shot down, who came out of prison camp later, were people who invariably had been separated from their wingmen while locked on a MiG. In this game, at this time, you could not clear yourself. You could not work on your gunnery problem alone. It was totally impossible. You had to have that wingman clearing you all the time. Never take your eyes off the target. A guy I knew came out of prison camp. I said, "What happened?" He said, "Well, I didn't watch my wingman, but I was locked onto this guy, I had him cold, and . . ." He wasn't clearing himself and became a target.

A mission was an hour and 20 minutes. If we became engaged, we had to drop our tanks. That limited our time in the area. We tried to leave MiG Alley with a thousand pounds of fuel. Many times, we didn't have that much fuel. Fortunately, we had tailwinds from the northwest,

The North American F-86F Sabre was a thoroughbred, pilots said, and it held its own in the long aerial campaign against the Soviet-built MiG-15 in Korea. This F-86F belongs to the 51st Fighter Interceptor Wing, the parent outfit of Marine exchange officer John Bolt's squadron.

[Jim Sullivan]

coming out of Manchuria. We figured that if we could get from the Yalu River south as far as Pyongyang, it would be safe to glide part of the rest of the way. If you shut down at 35,000 feet over Pyongyang at 250 knots, you could arrive over Suwon at 10,000 feet. Then we would restart the engine. That would give you enough fuel to make a power landing. Sometimes it wouldn't restart and you could usually make a dead-stick landing if there weren't too many other pilots making dead-stick landings.

The enemy didn't have to think about fuel starvation. He didn't have to worry about handling a long flight at high altitude. He was always fighting over his own territory. He picked the time and place of the fight, or tried to. The MiGs were usually only a few minutes away from their own bases when they were battling us. They were not going to be captured if they had to bail out.

We did not know, then, that some of the pilots were Soviet. Early in the Korean War, all of the MiG-15 pilots coming up from bases across the Yalu were Soviets. But by 1953, a lot of them were North Koreans. The general feeling was that although some could be very aggressive, most were not up to our level of training and skill. Some of the North Korean pilots felt that the safest thing to do when a Sabre was behind you was to hunker down behind the armor plate until the MiG was on fire and then eject, get out. There was one dogfight in which an enemy pilot took to his parachute before anyone fired at him. We felt very good about our leadership and wondered about theirs.

What did they think, coming up against us, even with a great many advantages? Long after the Korean War, I sat down with another F-86 ace, Bill Lilley, and we talked about what we knew about the MiG pilots and what we didn't. Bill and I agreed that some of their pilots were very good, but that some of their leaders weren't. Bill suggested that maybe their top officers didn't fully understand what they had going for them.

Bill said something like, "If I had been an enemy officer talking to his pilots, I would have emphasized the advantages that they had. The MiG flew higher than we did. Our service ceiling was around 40,000 feet (12384 meters). We could get to 45,000, but if you got up there, you just were hanging in the air. You couldn't do any violent maneuvering."

There was a very good reason for going as high as we could. Above a certain altitude, you no longer left vapor trails, or contrails, those long white plumes that told the enemy exactly where you were. At some times of year in Korea, you could get above the contrails and not leave those telltale white tracks. If we could, we climbed above the contrail level, sort of hiding up there, waiting for them to come across the river, hoping they came by lower than we were.

The MiG-15 had a much higher service ceiling. In our conversation long after the war, Bill Lilley remembered seeing them at 50,000 feet (15480 meters). We never got up to fight them at 50,000. But they could fly comfortably, in formation, at 50,000 feet. I've been at 45,000 (13932 meters) and had four MiGs, line abreast, come down out of an azure sky. Four planes, line abreast, all shooting at you. Their altitude advantage could be translated into an airspeed advantage.

At the end of the day, our aircraft was better (even though it couldn't fly higher), our equipment was better, our training was better, and we had excellent leadership.

This is a gun-camera photo of a MiG-15 being attacked by Bolt's squadron near the Yalu River between Korea and China. The MiG-15 could fly higher than the F-86, which offered an advantage at the start of a fight, but the F-86 pilots had better tactics, training, and leadership.

[U.S. Air Force]

JAMES MacALPINE Jack Bolt and I were in the 39th squadron, "Cobras." Jack went through the Air Force's gunnery center at Nellis Air Force Base, Nevada. When he arrived in Korea, the Marines told him to get a job. He went up to the Fourth Fighter Interceptor Wing and they wouldn't even talk to him. He went to the 51st Fighter Interceptor Wing and talked to Air Force Col. John Mitchell, and Mitchell said, "Yes, I want you."

Bolt was a hell of a flier. He just made the airplane do what he wanted it to do. He was a very proficient flier. For a couple of missions, he went up with Capt. Joe McConnell, the top ace of the Korean War, as wingman, and then he became a flight leader. He thought McConnell was shooting from way out of range. Then he learned that McConnell was trying to get the guy to turn so he could close on him.

Bolt's hero was Greg Boyington, the great Marine aviator of World War II. He had the same aggressive spirit as Boyington. Bolt's nickname was the Duke of Mukden. We called him that because he would go all the way to the Great Wall of China to shoot down a MiG.

Bolt said that only 10 percent of the people were shooters and the others just went up to MiG Alley to look around. He came to us as a captain and was a major before he left. We were getting mostly second smokes and junior lieutenants, so a captain was God. In the 39th squadron at that time, we also had Canadian and British exchange officers who were flight leaders. Jack Bolt became a flight leader, so out of the four flights in our Air Force wing, an Air Force guy led only one.

Another Marine, not quite as well known as Bolt, was John Glenn in our sister squadron, the 25th. Glenn got three MiGs before the Korean War ended.

Along with all of his other attributes, Jack Bolt was quite a singer. He was also a hard charger. When he went up in the air, you knew someone was going to get killed. One of Bolt's wingmen was Archie Shaw. Archie had not been north of the Yalu River until he went with Bolt.

Bolt's favorite wingman was Jerry Carlile. Jerry kept him clear. I was up in the air when Bolt was flying, but I was tail end Charlie. So I looked up to Bolt but I can't say we knew each other well. Like I said, he was God.

DEAN ABBOTT Joe McConnell was sent home right after becoming the top jet ace and his replacement as D Flight leader in the 39th squadron was another Marine exchange officer, Maj. Jack Bolt, who arrived in our wing along with John Glenn. In those last six weeks of the Korean War, Jack Bolt shot down six MiGs to become the only aviator to become an ace in World War II and Korea.

Bolt seemed to have the ability to think ahead of what the MiG pilots were going to do. He was awarded the Navy Cross for one of his final missions in Korea, and it was well deserved. He was one of the great leaders I've seen in my lifetime.

Bolt was a perfect gentleman. He never mentioned to us in D Flight that he had been a part of Pappy Boyington's Black Sheep Squadron in the Pacific in World War II and had been credited with six Zero kills. I only learned about that many years later at a reunion of the 39th in Orlando in 2000, when he attended and showed his gun camera films.

Lt. Col. George I. Ruddell, the 39th squadron commander at that time and also an air ace, was instrumental in getting Bolt into the 39th.

This is a North American F-86 Sabre in flight.

[U.S. Air Force]

I know that Bolt made trips up to the Fourth Wing at Seoul to talk to Jim Jabara and Pete Fernandez, and he said that they told him that they frequently went across the Yalu, which American pilots weren't supposed to do. I know that Bolt did, too, but not on the one I described, the one where I saw a MiG pilot die.

Bolt told us at our reunion in Orlando that Lieutenant Colonel Ruddell called him into his quarters and begged Bolt to take him across, which he did, probably for the first time. On that mission Bolt got Ruddell on the tail of a MiG who dove from 40,000 feet down to the surface, but Ruddell, who was behind the MiG during the dive, failed to turn on his windshield and canopy heat and they froze up on him. So Bolt took control and shot that MiG down.

I know all the above, having heard it from Bolt at a reunion in Orlando four years ago. He showed us his gun camera film of some of his kills, including the one I was on, and he brought with him cartoons that I had drawn at that time of Ruddell with a frosted canopy and Marine Jack Bolt shooting down the MiG instead of Ruddell. I had forgotten all about them, but Bolt still had them. It was common knowledge, which we young guys knew but didn't pass on. In our circle, Ruddell was called Cousin Weak-Eyes. He was guided into every kill he got.

The first time I flew with Ruddell as his number two, Joe McConnell got me aside and told me that I wouldn't be able to stay with him as Ruddell had had the "rats" removed from the tailpipe of his Sabre, named *MiG Mad Mavis,* which gave that jet more power, thus speed, but caused a higher tailpipe temperature that lessened the engine life. Joe told me to stay with him by flying higher, and then when he turned, to cut him off in the turn and get back on his wing.

I found that my Sabre was able to stay with Ruddell's (it had just come out of periodic maintenance), but all I knew was what Joe had told me so I stacked high on his wing, expecting he would start to pull ahead and I could convert altitude into airspeed to stay with him. It never happened. After we landed, Ruddell complained to McConnell that I didn't fly proper formation and told him to personally give me two training sorties to teach me proper formation position. Joe just rolled his eyes and wrote off two training missions, which we never flew.

On a later mission as Ruddell's wingman, I called, "Bogeys at twelve o'clock level." He replied, "Where are they?" I responded, "They're at 12 o'clock level and they are bandits and two of them are firing!" He replied, "I don't have them." I said, "Cobra, break left NOW! I'm taking a bounce! They've gone to our six o'clock." Halfway around my turn he said, "Cobra Two, I've lost you." I just reversed my turn and got back on his wing, as did the rest of the four-ship formation. That was the end of that contact with the MiGs.

What Happened

When retired Lt. Col. John "Jack" Bolt, 83, died of leukemia at Tampa, Florida, on September 8, 2004, the nation lost one of its true heroes—the only Marine to become a fighter ace in two wars.

Born in Laurens, South Carolina, in 1921, Bolt studied at the University of Florida for two years. In summer 1941, he joined the Marine Corps Reserve to train as a pilot and earn money for college. By then, according to a high school friend, retired Air Force Col. James L. "Mac" McWhorter, 83, Bolt had been "powerfully motivated" by an

Who's Who

Maj. (later Lt. Col.) John "Jack" Bolt, Marine exchange officer, F-86F Sabre pilot with the 39th Fighter Interceptor Squadron, "Cobras"

1st Lt. (later Lt. Col.) James MacAlpine, Air Force F-86F Sabre pilot, 39th Fighter Interceptor Squadron, "Cobras"

1st Lt. (later Col.) Dean Abbott, Air Force F-86F Sabre pilot, 39th Fighter Interceptor Squadron, "Cobras"

English teacher at Seminole High School in New Smyrna, Margaret Lawson.

"In later years when everyone talked about what a gentleman Jack was, he always credited her," said McWhorter in a telephone interview. "When Jack became an attorney in New Smyrna, Florida, he created a fund for the school's teacher-of-the-year award in her honor."

Bolt flew the F4U Corsair in the South Pacific with Marine Fighting Squadron VMF-214, the famous Black Sheep squadron commanded by Lt. Col. Gregory "Pappy" Boyington. He called the Corsair "the plane every young man wanted to fly," in an interview several years ago.

Bolt flew it better than most, completing 94 missions, shooting down six Japanese Zero fighters, and becoming an air ace. He also led a highly successful strafing mission against Japanese ships and barges.

One war later, Bolt was a major serving an exchange tour with the Air Force in 1953, flying the F-86 Sabre with the 39th Fighter Interceptor Squadron, the "Cobras," in Korea. He was so low key, most of his fellow airmen did not know of his ace status.

Bolt shot down six MiGs in Korea, raising his total number of aerial victories to a dozen. In addition, he was awarded the Navy Cross for a heroic action in July 1953 when he led F-86s, low on fuel, in an attack on four MiGs and personally downed two of them.

After retiring from the Marine Corps in 1962, at the age of 47, he enrolled in the University of Florida law school where, not coincidentally, his son also was a student. While studying, father and son played handball regularly enough to win the law league handball tournament several years in a row. For two years after graduation Bolt served as an associate dean at the University of Florida law school and then entered private practice in New Smyrna Beach. Bolt practiced law for over 20 years and became a leading lawyer and beloved member of that close-knit beach community, serving for many years as attorney for the local utilities commission until retiring in 1991.

Bolt was an active sportsman and scuba diver. At the time of his death, he was in Tampa escaping from Hurricane Frances. Bolt and his wife Dottie were married for 60 years and have a son and daughter and two grandchildren.

North American F-86F Sabre

On October 1, 1947, test pilot George Welch made the first flight of a new fighter, the North American XP-86, at Muroc, California. Welch, a World War II air ace, nudged the XP-86 up against the sound barrier days before another test pilot, Capt. Charles E. Yeager, made the first documented supersonic flight on October 14 in the Bell XS-1 rocket plane. Yeager's flight also occurred at Muroc—named in reverse for the Corum brothers, who settled in the region—site of today's Edwards Air Force Base.

The early production aircraft (the *P* for pursuit was changed to *F* for fighter in 1948 and it became the F-86) had an increased empty weight of 10,077 pounds (4571 kilograms), or some 347 pounds (157 kilograms) more than the XP-86 prototype. With its more powerful engine, the fighter challenged the world airspeed record, 650.796 miles per hour (1047.352 kilometers per hour), set by the straight-wing Douglas D-558 Skystreak on August 25, 1947. The Skystreak was a specialized aircraft optimized for the high-speed effort. The F-86A-1, in contrast, was very close to a fully operational warplane.

Maj. Robert L. Johnson made the speed record attempt September 5, 1948, in an early F-86A-1. With an audience of no fewer than

This is an F-86 Sabre taxiing out to fly a combat mission in North Korea.

[Robert F. Dorr]

80,000, the only time a vast public gathering observed such an effort, Johnson flew his fully loaded F-86A on six passes over the measured course. The audience saw the new fighter fly faster than ever before, reaching an average speed of 669.480 miles per hour (1077.420 kilometers per hour). Unfortunately, technical glitches prevented the effort from being properly recorded and registered. Another attempt was mounted in the privacy of Muroc Air Base, and on September 15, 1948, Johnson achieved a record of 670.981 miles per hour (1079.836 kilometers per hour). This time, the achievement was fully sanctioned.

Also in late 1948, North American began to turn out the F-86A-5 version, or company model NA-161, with slightly more powerful J47-GE-7 and J47-GE-13 engines.

In the 1949 Thompson Trophy Race, Capt. Bruce Cunningham won the jet division of the contest flying an F-86A-5 in ten laps of a 15-mile (25-kilometer) circular course around seven pylons for 150 miles (241 kilometers). Cunningham was credited with an elapsed time of 15:21.23 minutes, or an average speed of 586.173 miles per hour (943.352 kilometers per hour).

Welch's plane evolved into a beautiful and beloved combat aircraft that proved to be the right solution at the right moment when Soviet-built MiG-15s filled the skies over Korea. No other U.S. fighter was capable of standing up to the swift, swept-wing, cannon-armed MiG when it appeared in December 1950.

The F-86 did almost everything right. Its General Electric J47 turbojet engine was effective at a time when early jet engines were notorious for being unreliable and even dangerous. Most Air Force and Navy fighters still had straight wings (the F-84 Thunderjet and F9F Panther were Korean War examples), but the Sabre, like its MiG nemesis, benefited from German technological advances in wing sweep.

With six .50-caliber machine guns, the Sabre was less heavily armed than the cannon-equipped MiG, but the Sabre was also a testimony to the simple truth that the American fighter pilot of 1950 was the best the world had ever seen. The older ones, like Marine Air exchange pilot John Bolt, were World War II veterans. The younger pilots were graduates of advanced jet gunnery training at Nellis Air Force Base, Nevada. In early Sabres, the A-1CM gunsight was coupled with an AN/APG-30 radar installed in the upper lip of the nose intake. Although almost useless at low altitude because of ground clutter, the radar could be slaved to the sight for effective tracking of an aerial target. F-86A-5 airplanes retrofitted with A-1CM sight were redesignated F-86A-6 when they retained AN/APG-5C radar, and F-86A-7 when retrofitted with AN/APG-30.

After the 554th and last F-86A model was delivered in December 1950, a number of F-86A Sabres were converted to RF-86A reconnaissance aircraft.

The first flight of the F-86E-1 Sabre or company NA-170 was made by George Welch on September 23, 1950. The "all-flying tail" and the irreversible hydraulic systems introduced in the F-86E are considered one of the most important advances of the era. At Wright Field, Ohio, World War II ace and test pilot Maj. Clarence E. "Bud" Anderson flew the early version of the "all-flying tail" and discovered that it didn't feel right. The maneuverability and artificial "feel" were sluggish, awkward, and perhaps dangerous. North American and the Air Force worked together on changing and improving the F-86E's key features until the problems were resolved and the F-86E became, in Anderson's words, "a world beater."

Sixty F-86E-1 models were followed by 51 F-86E-5s, which differed only in minor panel switches. The designation F-86E-6 went to a batch of 60 Canadair-built CL-13 Sabre Mark 2 fighters built in Canada for the USAF. The designation F-86E-1 went to the first 132 examples of the company NA-172, which were powered by J47-GE-13 only because planned -27 models of the engine were not yet available; in short, the aircraft was an F-86F with an F-86E engine. The F-86E-10 also introduced a new flat windscreen and modified instrument panel.

Subsequently, out of this order, 93 aircraft that were to have been delivered on the NA-172 contract as F-86F-15s reverted to the -27 engine because of further power plant delays and were given the out-of-order designation F-86E-15.

The 6-3 wing has appeared on several Sabre versions but is associated with the definitive F-86F Sabre, or company NA-172, the first of which was flown on March 19, 1952, by James Pearce (although early F-86Fs lacked the wing). As we shall see, the combination of an all-flying tail and 6-3 wing was absolutely vital to the outcome of that distant Asian war.

F-86Fs manufactured in Columbus, Ohio, combined with those manufactured in Los Angeles, reached a total of 1,539.

The F-86F was the first Sabre widely used in the fighter-bomber role and the last used in the Korean War. One pilot commented, "The flight characteristics of the F-86F are excellent for the fighter-bomber role. It is a stable bombing platform and permits any dive angle up to vertical without danger of control difficulties or effects from compressibility. The speed brakes have proved effective and necessary for tactics which are desired. It is believed that use of steeper dive angles and higher entry altitudes will decrease vulnerability to AAA fire." Typically, a fighter-bomber F-86F carried 500-pound (227-kilogram) and 1,000-pound (454-kilogram) GP, or general-purpose, bombs with conical fins and 120-gallon Class I fuel tanks.

Fighting MiGs along the Yalu, Bolt became part of a campaign that began on December 17, 1950, when Air Force Lt. Col. Bruce Hinton shot down the first MiG-15 to be claimed by an F-86. The Americans overcame disadvantages—most models of the MiG could fly higher, an important asset in combat—and maintained the edge.

Though it was not well known at the time, experienced Russian pilots were flying MiGs in Korea. Yet even after exaggerated wartime claims were revised downward, Sabre pilots like Hinton and Bolt achieved a seven-to-one victory edge over the MiG-15, the best such score of any aerial campaign in history.

The slugfest between the F-86 Sabre and the MiG-15 from December 1950 to July 1953 had a unique purity among aerial campaigns. It was a pure air-to-air effort on both sides, a contest between fighters and fighter pilots unaffected by other factors. When it began, the F-86A Sabre with a still-unreliable engine could not fly as high as the MiG and was outperformed in other areas from time to time. By the time it ended, the improved MiG-15s remained a formidable foe, but the much-improved hard-wing F-86F (following the F-86E and the slat-wing F-86F) was in every respect the better fighter.

So how did the two fighters fare? Two days after the war ended, Fifth Air Force news reported 818 MiGs downed for a loss of 58 Sabres, a 13.79-to-1 kill ratio.

However, in the *USAF Statistical Digest* for the year 1953, the number of Sabres downed became 78. This came from a reevaluation of certain "unknown" losses to that of destroyed in air-to-air combat. At the same time, MiG kills were reduced from 818 to 792 shot down by the F-86 alone. This is the normal ratio attributed to Korea of 10:1 in favor of the F-86.

But the actual ratio is closer to 14:1, if not higher. Soviet records reveal that Soviet-piloted MiGs went down at a ratio of 4:1. The same archive lists Chinese losses to F-86s at 8:1. That's a total of at least 12:1 with no figures for losses of North Korean MiGs, of which there were many.

Since 1953, almost everyone has been taking the 5th AF credits list apart, as no one wanted to believe it. A Coronet Harvest report titled

Saber (misspelled as on report) *Measures Charlie* (spelling original) was reputed to say the kill ratio was 7:1. In fact, the Sabre Charlie Measures report has absolutely no actual ratios in it, as it is a projection of losses based on a 1000-sortie record. And based on those figures, the ratio would have ended up being 21:1!

Sabre versus MiG was a unique campaign. Sabre pilots like John Bolt faced many disadvantages. They fought far from home while the enemy fought close to home. But they flew what became eventually a better aircraft and were more inclined to seize the initiative than their adversaries.

North American F-86F Sabre

Type: single-seat fighter and fighter-bomber

Power plant: one 5,910-lb (2681 kg) thrust General Electric J47-GE-27 turbojet engine

Performance: maximum speed, 695 mph (1118 km/h) at 40,000 ft (12192 m); initial rate of climb (clean), 9,300 ft (2835 m) per minute; service ceiling, 48,000 ft (14630 m); range (with tanks), 1,270 mi (2044 km)

Weights: empty, 10,890 lb (4940 kg); loaded, 20,357 lb (9234 kg)

Dimensions: span, 37 ft 1⅖ in (11.31 m); length, 37 ft 6½ in (11.44 m); height, 14 ft 8¾ in (4.47 m); wing area, 288 sq ft (26.76 m)

Armament: six Browning M3 .50-cal (12.7-mm) machine guns with a rate of fire of 1,100 rounds per minute and ammunition supply of 1,802 rounds, or 300 rounds per gun; two 1,000-lb (454-kg) bombs or two 200-US gal (755-lit) fuel tanks

Crew: 1 (pilot)

First flight: October 1, 1947 (XP-86); May 20, 1948 (F-86A); September 23, 1950 (F-86E); May 19, 1952 (F-86F)

Chapter Eleven

"I Ain't No Marine Officer. I'm a Corporal."

Just after midnight on November 2, 1952, an F3D Skyknight flown by Maj. William T. Stratton and M.Sgt. Hans Holind made radar contact high over North Korea with an enemy Yakovlev Yak-15 jet fighter.

The Skyknight was a portly, twin-engine jet with straight wings, an air-to-air radar unit, and a crew of two, pilot and radar operator. Operating the Skyknight as a night fighter, they had the job of preventing enemy warplanes from attacking B-29 Superfortress bombers and from making night raids on U.S. bases. In the spacious, side-by-side cockpit of their F3D that night, Stratton and Holind were among the most experienced crews in the Marine Corps. They handled the initial detection and approach toward the Yak without visual contact.

That changed when they drew closer. Stratton saw the orange glow of exhaust from the Yak. Using radar up to now, he took over the attack visually and closed in behind the flickering light.

Stratton fired three short bursts of 20-millimeter cannon fire. The Yak went down in flames. The Marine Skyknight crew flew through smoke and debris.

This was history's first jet-versus-jet aerial victory at night. A week

This is a Marine Corps F3D-2 Skyknight like the aircraft flown by Bud Page and Mule Holmberg.

[U.S. Marine Corps]

---

later on November 8, 1952, F3D pilot Cap. O. R. Davis repeated the feat by shooting down a MiG-15 northwest of Pyongyang.

As part of the response, on May 26, 1952, Marines of squadron VMF (N)-513, "Flying Nightmares," commanded by Col. Peter D. Lambrecht, began flying at Kunsan, South Korea.

Lambrecht was killed in action in August. Col. Homer G. Hutchinson took the helm.

On December 10, 1952, the VMF (N)-513 crew of 1st Lt. Joseph A. Corvi and Sgt. Dan George shot down a Polikarpov Po-2 night intruder without ever seeing it, using radar only. The Po-2 was an aircraft that the U.S. press always underestimated: although it was a slow biplane and was often perceived as a "nuisance" or a "heckler," it could, in fact, inflict serious damage as it did on one occasion when a single Po-2 destroyed half a dozen U.S. aircraft on the ground.

This is a Marine Corps F3D-2 Skyknight of Mule Holmberg's squadron, VMF (N)-513.

[U.S. Marine Corps]

Of course, every crew wanted to bag a MiG. The Soviet-built MiG-15 was a cutting-edge threat in Korea and not easy to defeat, even at night with the advantage of radar. Another F3D crew, Maj. Jack Dunn and M.Sgt. Lawrence Fortin, shot down a MiG-15 on January 12, 1953.

On January 28, Capt. James R. Weaver's F3D claimed another MiG, and three days later, Lt. Col. Robert F. Conley claimed the sixth and final Skyknight aerial victory of the Korean War. Conley had just taken command of VMF (N)-513 from Hutchinson, and his MiG also counted as the tenth and final aerial kill for all Marine night fighters (F4U Corsair, F7F Tigercat, and F3D Skyknight).

The F3D Skyknight went on to a long career. The F3D nomenclature was changed to F-10 in 1962 (the F3D-2Q model then in service became the EF-10B), and the Skyknight went on to serve the Marine Corps as an electronics intelligence platform in Vietnam. The Marine Corps has an EF-10B Skyknight at Quantico, Virginia, ready for display at the National Museum of the Marine Corps.

BUD PAGE Some Marines say we never lost a B-29 while flying missions to support the bombers. That's not correct. I lost one to a MiG in November 1952. The target was a gold ore processing plant close to the Yalu River. Every B-29 in Japan and Okinawa was on the raid. We were consistently having problems with the Air Force meeting us at the coast at the right time for these missions, which were guided by a system called Shoran. We even installed another radio in the F3D so we could talk to them.

This night was one of their early arrivals. As we crossed the Haeju peninsula, we could see all the antiaircraft fire. We went full throttle into the area. One of our F3Ds was on the Yellow Sea side of the bomber stream and we were on the east, or land, side. Their bomb run was being made to the northeast.

I got about ten B-29s strung out on my main radar unit, throttled back, and made our run to the target. My APS-28 tail radar was inoperable but everything else on the F3D was working, including the main radar.

The main radar was the AN/APS-21. The gun-laying radar was called the AN/APS-26. And then there was the thing in the tail. In the book, *Night Fighters over Korea,* written with E. T. Wooldridge, the late Capt. Gerald G. O'Rourke describes it: "The real pride of the F3D radar system, aside from the solidly good APS-21, was the small APS-28 tail warning set," O'Rourke writes. "It was a direct descendant of the reliable old APS-19 forward-looking search sets used in the Corsairs and the F2H-2N Banshees. To modify this set to work rearward, it was extensively repackaged, the range presentation was deliberately limited to only a four-mile region, and almost all of its controls and operations were made fully automatic." O'Rourke also wrote that the system worked better in theory than it did in real life.

That was the situation that night as we continued our job of escorting bombers over North Korea. We reversed our course, went back, and picked up the second bunch of B-29s and began taking them through the target area.

About then, all hell broke loose. Midway in my second string was a B-29 with every exterior light on the aircraft burning. We ran up to within 50 feet of his tail and told him to turn his lights off. He talked to me but didn't turn the lights off. By then, about 30 North Korean searchlights had zeroed in on him. All of the antiaircraft fire suddenly quit all around us. I told my pilot, Lt. Col. Robert F. Conley, a MiG was going to make a pass.

We dropped back under the tail of the B-29 again, still telling him to get his lights out. He still didn't turn them out. We sat there for about a minute and a half and then made a 360-degree turn without making contact with anything other than more B-29s. We slid back under his tail again and were talking with him when fireballs about the size of a bushel basket came across our right wing and went into the right wing root and number three engine of the B-29. Fire erupted immediately. I spotted the MiG on his way out of his pass. The other F3D on the west side exploded him with a 40-round burst of 20-millimeter fire at about 200 yards.

The B-29 could have made it to Cho-do Island less than 50 miles south and bellied in on the beach or in the shallow water. He elected to try to get back to Okinawa. He was losing altitude slowly. The fire was still burning but was confined to the engine that had been hit. We stayed off his right wing at about four o'clock and half a mile away until he crashed in a valley northeast of Pyongyang. His lights were still on when he made contact with the ground. His reasoning for trying to get south was that none of his crew had worn cold-weather survival gear and some were even wearing dress shoes. We saw no one bail out.

The B-29 was carrying secret electronic countermeasures equipment. It hadn't burned on impact. The Joint Operations Center told us to strafe and burn it. I called and refused because some crew members could still be in the aircraft. Automatic weapons fire was getting pretty bad around us by then, so we climbed back up and went to escort the remainder of the B-29s through their bomb run. Except for antiaircraft fire, which was heavy to intense, it was routine. That MiG may have gotten through because of my tail radar: after that, no one ever went north again when the tail radar wasn't working.

On another night escort mission, B-29s were bombing between the Yalu and Chinampo river deltas. They were supposed to break right after dropping bombs and head south off the west coast of North Korea. Antiaircraft fire was extremely bad in this area and several nights previously we had been blown onto our back at nearly 38,000 feet. The B-29s seldom got above 28,000 feet, given the weight of their bombload, so the 120-millimeter antiaircraft guns were really working on them.

One of the B-29s I had on my scope got hit at the coast-in point. He was burning pretty badly, too. We were at 24,000 feet and he was about two miles ahead and 2,000 feet above us. Instead of breaking right to go home, he broke left toward China. We went with him because of the MiG threat, although no MiGs showed up. His path took him to the "fence," where he took more heavy antiaircraft fire and his plane came apart. About 40 searchlights were on him and us. It appeared to us that the wreckage of the B-29 fell into China. We started climbing and got out of there, and the searchlights stalked us. I could read my maps from the lights at that altitude. The lights could really mess up your night vision.

During my time with the Marine F3D Skyknight in Korea, we had some contact with the Air Force, which was operating their equivalent night fighter, the F-94, with the 319th Fighter Interceptor Squadron. We got a small exchange program going with the F-94 outfit. Two of our guys went up and checked out in the F-94. They weren't impressed with any part of the program. It had limited range, limited radar, and poor all-weather capability all around. It did climb a little faster in afterburner but you ran out of fuel very quickly. The F-94 outfit finally claimed credit for shooting down a "Bed Check Charlie," a Polikarpov Po-2 night heckler. If they got it, they flew through it. They found the wreckage of the F-94 north of Seoul. They never found the Po-2.

I had my own experience with a Po-2. One night, the west side of Korea was all socked in so we cruised over towards Hamhung on the east coast. The weather was pretty good over there. Just west of Hamhung, we let down to look things over a bit closer. I made radar contact with a slow bird of some sort. We were badly overshooting him so we dropped wheels and flaps and put the boards (dive brakes) out. He evidently knew of our presence because he let down into a valley.

The ground was white with snow and a full moon was out with a few puffy clouds partially obscuring it now and then. We got a visual on it and it was a Po-2 flying about 60 knots. The radar was useless down there, jumping to the hills on both sides of the valley.

When we got slow enough to fire, the nose was so high we couldn't get the guns on him. We had no altitude to trade off. Twice we passed him close enough to see the red lights in his cockpit. The second time, the joker was shooting at us with a burp gun. He made a left turn up another valley and we never found him again. There was no way he could have gotten out of that valley. Anyway, we didn't get that Po-2.

MULE HOLMBERG I went after a Po-2 once. Shortly after the cease-fire on July 27, 1953, I joined squadron VMF (N)-513 at K-6 Pyongtaek. We used the radio call sign FLIGHTTRAIN. This was in 1954. We were still manning strip alerts, sitting on hot pads, and doing combat air patrols. I got one intercept on a Po-2 and my pilot wouldn't fire on him. He said we didn't have a positive ID. I made nine runs on this son of a bitch. The first five runs, he was a bogey, meaning an unidentified aircraft, and the last four he was a bandit, meaning an enemy aircraft. The rear gunner in this open-cockpit biplane carried a burp gun and for bombing he tossed out mortar shells. When we were making a run on him, I saw the wink of his burp gun.

Let me back up to describe how I got to be an enlisted radar operator in Korea, and, years later, a radar intercept officer in Vietnam. I was born in 1933 in Minnesota and enlisted in the Marine Corps in July 1951. After boot camp, I did well on dah-dit-dah Morse code stuff and ended up with a 6600 Military Occupational Specialty, or MOS, which is basic avionics. I became a striker, which is the term for a Morse code apprentice, up at El Toro, California, with squadron VMT-2. I was in the fighter section at VMT-2 working on Corsairs. The fighter section was reorganized as squadron VFMT-10 and got F8F Bearcat fighters. The Korean War was on, of course, and they were performing a training mission getting the Reserves spun up to go to war: Reserve pilots being recalled for Korea duty would get three hops in an SNJ Texan trainer to get their flying experience back, and then they'd put them straight into an F4U Corsair. That worked okay for a while, but when they changed to the F8F Bearcat, that process became a lot more difficult. When a guy strapped into an F8F, it came with a boatload of torque.

In January 1952, now a private first class, I shipped out on the *William S. Wiegle,* a lovely cruise ship of the Military Sea Transportation Service, or MSTS, to Yokohama, Japan. We went up to Itami and I was then transported across the water to K-3 Pohang Airfield in Korea. So, yes, I was in Korea while the war was going on.

I arrived at K-3 and joined squadron VMF-311, the "Tomcats." They had a WL tail code on their aircraft, and the story was it meant "whiskey lovers." They had F9F-2 Panthers. I was there for four or five months and was transferred to squadron VMF-115, the "Silver Eagles." They had F9F-4 Panthers. I remember seeing some F3D-2 Skyknights come through and was very impressed by them. The F9F-4s got grounded because they were having big-time engine problems, but that didn't affect me directly because I worked on the radios.

While I was in a Panther squadron, we had a pilot named Drury who came back from a mission with a hung bomb. It was a 500-pounder. We heard he was coming in with this thing, and, like idiots, we got up on an old bomb emplacement where the view was good and stood there to watch his airplane land. That was really dumb.

He lands. The bomb comes off the rack. It won't tumble because it's got a three-foot daisy cutter fuse sticking out the front. I say to this Marine next to me, "That thing is going to blow."

It did. It went off. There was this detonation. Stuff was flying everywhere; Drury's plane looked like a sieve. Drury was hunkered down behind the armor plate in his airplane and somehow he survived the blast. He ended up over by the side of the runway.

SSgt. Eugene S. "Mule" Holmberg
1954
Douglas F3D-2 Skyknight
FLIGHTTRAIN 24
Marine Night Fighter Squadron VMF (N)-513, "Flying Night-mares"
K-6 Pyongtaek Airfield, Korea

Staff Sgt. Eugene S. "Mule" Holmberg (center), radar operator on an F3D-2 Skyknight, at K-6 Pyongtaek airfield, South Korea, in 1954.

[Eugene S. "Mule" Holmberg]

The blast hit us and we went horizontally back about five feet. Luckily enough, shrapnel hit none of us. But we didn't climb up there to look at hung bombs anymore.

Late in my tour in Korea, I went to visit VMF (N)-513, spent a month there, and returned to K-3. During that month, I saw how neat things were for the radar operators in the F3D-2 and I said to myself, "I'd like to do that."

JOHN VERDE The F9F Panther was a first-generation, straight-wing jet fighter. Like all of the early jets, it was underpowered and not always reliable, so it had to strain to get off the runway with a bombload in the heat of the Korean summer. Still, the F9F had its attributes. It was another product of the Grumman Iron Works, which built them tough. We could go up to the Yalu River with a couple of 500-pound bombs, deliver them, and have enough fuel left to be available to fight if the MiGs came up. But I won't kid you. The Panther was frequently down with mechanical problems and it wasn't a dogfighter like the MiG-15 or the F-86 Sabre.

MULE HOLMBERG I left Korea in November 1952. Back in the States, I was assigned in December to VMF (N)-542 after coming back on the *Anderson*, a Navy-run ship. We were kept at Itami for a week and com-

The WL on the tail was chosen at random and didn't really stand for "Whiskey Lovers," but pilot John Verde and radio repairman Mule Holmberg thought the term appropriate. The aircraft is a Grumman F9F-2B Panther of squadron VMF-311, the "Tomcats," at K-3 Pohang airfield, South Korea. It is being towed over metal Marston matting by a Cle-Track aircraft tug.

[U.S. Marine Corps]

ing home turned out to be a month-long event. Now I'm in-542, I'm back at El Toro, and I've made corporal and sergeant overseas, so now I'm a sergeant in the radio shop.

They invited me to test for staff sergeant. Not long after that I learned from a list in the *Navy Times* that I'd made staff. I said, "Wow!" Soon after that came even better news: I received orders for airborne intercept operator, or AIO, school at Cherry Point, North Carolina. I was in the first class to go through with the F3D-2. Until then, AIO trainees had flown in the prop-driven F7F Tigercat and used prop-driven planes as simulated targets. I showed up for the flight physical and an old Navy captain looked at me, all six feet, six and a half inches of me, and said, "Aren't you too tall?" I reached into my anal cavity and pulled out a big lie. "They just changed the rules on height," I said. It worked. I went to VMF (N)-531, which was equipped with F3D-2 Skyknights, and became a crew member on that great airplane. AIO was the designation of the Marine radar operators who flew in F3Ds and F7F Tigercats. We were officially designated NAO(R), which means naval air observer, radar.

I went back to Korea and joined VMF (N)-513, "Flying Night-mares," at K-6 Pyongtaek Airfield. We also had a hot pad at K-2 Taegu Airfield where we sometimes stood alert when they were repaving the runway at Pohang.

This was in 1954. We were still doing combat air patrols. We were still manning strip alerts and flying below a demarcation line known as Line Fox. We were flying combat air patrols on both the east and west coasts of Korea. During one of those, I got my one intercept on a Po-2, and the rear gunner had a burp gun.

At about this time, the other side introduced the MiG-17 fighter, which was a big improvement over their MiG-15 and was much faster than our F3D-2, which was never known for its blinding speed. To fight the MiG-17 at night, the brass came up with a project called Mad Dog, which was top secret. In fact, it was so secret, we weren't supposed to use the name out loud, so when talking to each other we called it "Pissed-Off Canine." The purpose of the program was to combine the F-86 Sabre (which couldn't see at night) with the F3D-2 Skyknight (which was too slow to maneuver with the MiG). The plan was to team up with an Air Force F-86 Sabre out of K-55 Osan Airfield and do it in such a way that our two planes would fly north while creating only a single blip on the enemy's radar.

The key was for us to pick up the F-86 at Osan and fly together with him so the enemy's radar operators would think it was just one airplane. So we would head over to Osan, align ourselves on the runway, and call a five-mile final, at which time the F-86 would start his engine. A couple of minutes later, we would call a one-mile final and he would begin his takeoff roll. He would climb out while we were overhead and tuck him-self under us, so that there was only one radar blip. We would fly north that way. Despite the disparity in speed between the two planes, we could get up to the intercept point without the bad guys realizing there were two of us. Under Mad Dog—Pissed-Off Canine, that is—as soon as we got to the intercept point, we would cut the F-86 loose and he would go in and get the MiG. We flew two or three of these hunter-killer missions, but we never actually engaged a MiG-17.

The F3D-2 could fly slower than the Air Force's F-94. When we were making intercepts on the bad guys, we could go a little slower and we had track-while-scan radar, which the F-94 didn't. We also had a lock-on radar separate from our search radar. We used to tell the Westinghouse guy they made ice-free refrigerators, thrust-free engines, and blip-free radar.

That Po-2 wasn't the only bad guy I saw during that tense period in Korea right after the cease-fire.

Another time, we were launched against a submarine detected by a ground control intercept (GCI) station located off the coast of Korea. "Try to identify it," they said.

We were smoking along down at an altitude of just 300 feet. It turned out to be two submarines. They were bad guys. "Well, go down and lower your landing gear and landing lights and take a look at them." I thought, "How can we go lower than 300 feet?" Besides, on the F3D-2 we didn't have landing lights. We had taxi lights. My pilot said, "Maybe I can put my taxi light on it." He did, and that's when we were sure it was two submarines. They were kind of sitting in the water there, forming an *L* shape.

We were trying to get a destroyer to intercept them. The only thing we could do was strafe. But there were multiple layers of clouds up, and we didn't think a strafing run on our radar was a good plan. And we had never practiced air-to-surface shooting. So we went over to where the friendly destroyer was, in the hope of guiding him to the submarines, and he started shooting at us. That didn't seem like a good situation, so we went back to the submarines. After our second pass overhead at about 500 feet, one of them decided to submerge. We never learned anything else about what was going on there.

Another time when we were launched from a hot-pad alert, we had an encounter with what I thought was a MiG-9, a straight-wing Soviet fighter. I think we flew that mission from Taegu, which was predominantly an Air Force base. We loved being at an Air Force base. The Air Force guys thought we were officers and addressed us as "lieutenants." And of course at an Air Force base, they have nurses. The nurses were supposed to be off limits to us enlisted men, but we were "lieutenants," remember. At least we were for a while. But one night at the club in Taegu, one of our guys got drunk and said, "Lady, I ain't no Marine officer. I'm a corporal, USMC." After that, we couldn't go to the club or to the nurses' quarters, but they could come to ours, down at the end of the Taegu runway.

From Korea, I went to Cherry Point, then back to Japan. I was at Atsugi, Japan, from 1957 to 1958 in the same squadron that was now called VMF (AW)-513. The N for night fighter became AW in 1956, even though they had been called "all-weather squadrons" from 1948. We had the F3D-2M Skyknight and were operational with the Sparrow. I fired a missile on a practice shoot near Okinawa that took out the outer six to eight feet of an F6F Hellcat target drone.

After that, I went back to El Toro. I married a lady I'd met in Japan. I married Janice Martin in 1958 after meeting her in Japan where she was an Army civilian running craft shops. We have a son, Carl, who lives in Maui.

As a senior staff sergeant, I went to navigator school at Cherry Point. They were overloaded with staff NCOs. I was carrying a 99.5 average up until my final when I made a nine-mile error in celestial navigation. You were allowed five. They flunked me on the test and I was out of the nav program.

I went back to El Toro and was assigned to MACS-9 as a crew chief. I had a guy working for me named Oswald. He figured he should be a lieutenant and he was a private. He'd had problems overseas when stationed at Atsugi. He was studying Russian. A couple of old AIOs agreed with me that he was not working out well at all. He was resentful. He felt demeaned having to do things that privates do. "What do you really want to do?" I asked him. "I'd like to be a translator," he said. He passed the written but flunked the spoken. He was not dependable, so we said, "You're out of here." We didn't know it then, but before he joined the outfit, he had gone down to the Russian embassy in Mexico City and offered to be a captain in their military.

We gave him a hardship discharge. We took him to the gate and dumped his stuff beside him. A week and a half later his mother called

Who's Who

Gunnery Sgt. Bud Page, F3D-2 Skyknight radar operator

SSgt. (later Capt.) Eugene S. "Mule" Holmberg, F3D-2 Skyknight radar operator

1st Lt (later Col.) John Verde, F9F-2B Panther pilot

up and said, "Where's my son?" I said, "I'm sorry, ma'am. We don't deliver." Soon afterward he showed up at the American Embassy and threw his American passport into the marine security guard's face. But that was after he left us and I never saw Lee Harvey Oswald again.

I did become a backseater in the F-4 Phantom II, though, and went to Vietnam. But that gets ahead of the story.

Douglas F3D-2 Skynight

Air combat successes at night in Korea meant vindication for the whale-shaped F3D Skyknight, a portly plane developed in response to a 1946 Navy requirement for a night fighter and accused by detractors of being ugly, ungainly, and underpowered. During the early 1950s, most of the publicity went to the better-known Marine Air jets like the F2H Banshee and F9F Panther, but it was the big, fat, slow, twin-engine, two-seat F3D Skyknight that got the kills in Korea.

The first Skyknight, the XF3D-1 prototype, made its initial flight on March 23, 1948, at Muroc, California. The F3D entered service in 1950 with Navy composite squadron VC-3 and Marine Air's VMF (N)-542, "Flying Tigers."

The Skyknight was the result of a Navy requirement for a turbojet-powered, carrier-based night fighter. In the book, *Night Fighters over Korea,* written with E. T. Wooldridge, the late retired Capt. Gerald G. O'Rourke describes the Skyknight from a pilot's perspective:

A transport-type cockpit flared into the nose, just above a huge semiglobal radome [radar dome]. To get in, you climbed up the engine nacelle onto the high wing, walked forward atop the fuselage, slid back a flat square glass door, and dropped down into a spacious cavern that seemed more like a control room than a cockpit. Once you were in the left seat, the view forward and to port was fine, but astern there was just a metal bulkhead. To starboard there was the space for the [radar operator] and all the radar controls, a distant console, and a high sill. Visibility then was similar to that of a transport, as was the high wing.

Douglas Aircraft Company built 268 Skyknights at its El Segundo, California, plant between 1948 and 1957, including 3 XF3D-1, 28 F3D-1, and 237 F3D-2 models.

The Navy's use of the Skyknight drew so little notice that a re-

---

Douglas F3D-2 Skyknight

Type: 2-seat carrier or land-based night and all-weather fighter

Power plant: two 3,400-lb (1542-kg) thrust Westinghouse J34-W-36/36A turbojet engines

Performance: maximum speed, 565 mph (909 km/h) at 20,000 ft (6095 m); cruising speed, 390 mph (628 km/h); initial climb rate, 4,000 ft (1220 m) per minute; service ceiling, 38,200 ft (11645 m); range, 1,200 miles (1931 km)

Weights: empty, 18,160 lb (8237 kg); maximum takeoff, 26,850 lb (12179 kg)

Dimensions: span, 50 ft (15.24 m); length, 45 ft 6 in (13.97 m); height, 16 ft (4.88 m); wing area, 400 sq ft (37.16 sq m)

Armament: 4 fixed, forward-firing 20-mm cannons with 200 rounds per gun

Crew: 2 (pilot and radar operator)

First flight: March 23, 1948 (XF3D-1); February 13, 1950 (F3D-1); February 14, 1951 (F3D-2)

This is a Marine Corps F3D-2 Skyknight of Mule Holmberg's squadron, VMF (N)-513.

[U.S. Marine Corps]

spected reference book, *U.S. Navy Aircraft since 1911*, by Gordon Swanborough and Peter M. Bowers states—erroneously—that "operational use of the F3D-2 was exclusively by Marine squadrons." During the Korean War, Marine Skyknights shot down six enemy aircraft. But the Marines had company. By the end of the war, Navy Composite Squadron VC-4, which included O'Rourke among others, also participated in the fighting.

Contrary to plans, the Skyknight operated aboard aircraft carriers only very briefly. However, the Navy used specialized versions to test missiles and radar units and to train night fighter crews. When the F4H-1 Phantom II fighter (later called the F-4) was introduced in 1960, the Navy initially trained its crews aboard a modified Skyknight model called the F3D-2T2.

When the Pentagon system for naming airplanes was overhauled in 1962, the F3D series became the F-10 series. The Navy retired most of its Skyknights soon afterward, but a Marine Corps version used for electronic countermeasures and intelligence gathering, the EF-10B, flew combat missions in Vietnam.

Today, an F3D Skyknight is part of the collection of the National Museum of Naval Aviation at Pensacola, Florida.

Chapter Twelve

"Dog" Mission from Da Nang

WARREN R. SMITH I joined on a 120-day delay program on May 10, 1960. I entered the Marines on active duty on September 7, 1960, and went to boot camp.

We got there in Vietnam, I believe, on the last day of January 1964, or the first day of February. We actually tried a couple of times to get down there. We were on final approach in a C-130 when the government changed hands. We had to take a wave-off, fly to the Philippines, refuel, go back to Okinawa, get up the next morning at about 4:30 a.m., and make the trip all over again after they told us the government had fallen into the right hands.

In 1964, it was an election year. Johnson was in office and Goldwater was the challenger. The emphasis was to try to get out of Vietnam, at least from Johnson's standpoint. Part of that process was that we went there with a multirole mission, which included training South Vietnamese pilots and crew members to fly the UH-34D. Along with that, we flew support missions, both assault and medevac for the South Vietnamese Army, and we were the major support and sometimes the only support for the Army Special Forces based in the I Corps area that ran from Pleiku to the Vietnamese border. Those were primarily located on hill-

Corporal Warren R. Smith
July 1964
Sikorsky UH-34D Seahorse
Marine Medium Helicopter
  Squadron HMM-364,
  "Purple Foxes"
Da Nang, South Vietnam

Corporal Warren R. Smith, UH-34D
crew chief, at Da Nang, South Vietnam, in 1964. The sandbags were
"because there were a lot of snipers
outside the airfield" even in an era
when the U.S. presence in the war
was small. Smith wears a ball cap,
mottled camouflage flight suit, and
his personal Model 1938 German
Luger pistol, which he still owns
today.

[Warren R. Smith]

tops, strategically. A lot of times there were no roads in and out of their facilities. The only way they got supplied was by trail or by helicopter. We were constantly flying supplies in and out of Army Special Forces camps.

My squadron was Marine Medium Helicopter Squadron HMM-364. The "medium" designator is based on the weight a squadron carries: "Medium" means 20,000 pounds of useful load. We were flying UH-34D Sikorsky helicopters. At that time we really didn't have a nickname, although later on we took on the designation Purple Foxes. Because we had the code letters YK painted on the tail, we referred to ourselves as Yankee Kilo.

The UH-34D had a nine-cylinder, 1,820–cubic inch Pratt & Whitney radial engine. When we were pulling a max load off the ground, we'd be running at about 2,800 or 2,900 rpm and pulling 54 inches of manifold pressure. We would have about 1,800 pounds of fuel in the belly in multiple tanks. The aft tanks were a very, very light neoprene, which had pumps that would send fuel to the front tanks, which would hold about 160 gallons, and those were bulletproof tanks or self-sealing tanks. They were multilayered with a compound in the center that would react to, I believe, oxygen or air if it got a bullet hole in it, so you would always pump fuel forward so that you would have the juice to get home or out of the bad area where you're taking the fire.

The regular noncombat crew on UH-34D was a pilot, copilot, and crew chief with the pilot on the right side so he could see where the hoist was in relation to the person being rescued. This hoist could be operated by both the pilot and crew chief and was mounted right over the cargo door.

Underneath the aircraft was a cargo sling for external cargo lifts. There was what was called a "hell hole" in the floor of the cargo section so the crew chief could open and view these hookups. It had both a manual and an automatic release. The auto release was used on rapid movements in and out of a landing zone. The hook would release as soon as the cargo touched the ground and took the weight off the hook. External loads were used when the cargo was too bulky or heavy to get inside the cabin. It was also faster to move a lot of cargo when it was prestaged in cargo nets with crews to hook up.

The UH-34D may have been officially the Seahorse, but we never really called it that. I think that was more of a Navy term. In the U.S. Marine Corps, the helicopters were referred to as Dogs due to the *D* designation.

They were pretty strong aircraft. In the late years of the war, they were used a lot as medevacs because they could take a lot of hits and still get out. They could carry about 12 passengers. That would be Americans. We could take many more Vietnamese because they were sometimes half the weight of Americans. Sometimes that was a problem. I remember going in on medevacs where there was a lot of fear in an outpost. We would be going in there to pick up wounded or a few dead and the plane would get mobbed. It would fill up so fast we couldn't take off because we had too many people. We couldn't throw them out fast enough to be able to get off the ground without help. We actually took all the seats out of the plane because we found that sometimes when we went into hot zones with the seats down and South Vietnamese troops buckled into them,

When the Marines sent their first UH-34D helicopters into action, the war in Vietnam was still small and romantic, at least in the eyes of some Americans. Squadron HMM-362, seen here, was first to operate the UH-34D in Vietnam beginning in 1962, and was replaced by HMM-364, beginning in 1964.

[U.S. Marine Corps]

they wouldn't get out of the plane. And it was very difficult to throw them out if they were held in the seat by a seat belt.

So we stripped the plane clean. We made them sit on the floor where they had nothing to hold onto. When it was time for them to go, they had to go. That probably worked out better for us, too, when we were hauling cargo and animals. But those South Vietnamese soldiers were pretty done in from generations of war and they weren't about to jump out into a rice paddy that could be raked with gunfire. A lot of times you'd have to hover over riverbeds because they were natural spots in the jungle area where you could bring a helicopter right in, but you couldn't set right down, and if the South Vietnamese troops looked out the door and saw you were hovering at four or five feet, they wouldn't want to get out. They would look down and not want to jump from the helicopter. A lot of times, we helped them.

When people were shooting at us, we didn't want to stay on the ground for more than a few seconds. We actually developed a good system of getting in and out of landing zones, which involved moving quickly when we were below 1,000 feet. When we were going to and from a landing zone, we'd try to stay above 2,000 feet, which would keep us out of range of small-caliber shooters. Also, that was just about the right place for 70 or so degrees of temperature. We didn't have air conditioning, so we'd fly up to where it was comfortable, temperature-wise, and also out of gunfire range.

In Vietnam, we took the doors off and flew without doors. On a stateside flight in a UH-34D, I actually lost a door coming off an aircraft carrier flying toward Santa Ana, California, off the coast. The vibration and the wind would actually get behind the door, rip it off, and send it straight through the rotor blades. That's a four-foot-by-four-foot piece of metal. It could really damage you. And it was an unsettling ride when you were missing parts of your rotor blades, so we just thought it was better to leave the door off and then we didn't have to worry about it.

I was a corporal E-4 and a crew chief and gunner on one of the helicopters. When I went to Vietnam, I was near the end of my four years in the Marine Corps. I extended three months to go overseas with my squadron. I was too short to make the overseas tour, and I wanted to do that for the experience. Besides, I was in a CH-37 squadron, which I hated. That was a terrible aircraft. The CH-37 had two Pratt & Whitney 2800 engines, which were mounted diagonally from the rotor head. We hated it. When we were in that squadron, it was right next to -364, and my friend and I would go over to -364 and work on the UH-34Ds because we liked them better.

When you flew the UH-34D in combat, you had a pilot, a copilot, a crew chief, and a first mechanic on each plane. The crew chief was also a mechanic. You had responsibility basically for all of the mechanical aspects of the aircraft, plus you were in charge in the cabin section and everything that was going on down there was your responsibility. You had to keep the pilot advised of aircraft around you. You had to advise him about the landing zones, if there were any restrictions, if you were getting into trees. You had to tell him where you were drawing gunfire. You also had the responsibility to suppress gunfire if you could.

Originally, the Marine Corps didn't consider the UH-34D in need of armament due to the famous close-air-support capabilities of our fighter-bombers. But, of course, we didn't have Marine fighter-bombers in Vietnam in 1964. Besides, it soon became clear, anyway, that the helicopters needed to be armed.

We had an M60 machine gun in the open cargo doorway, the crew chief did, and out of the other side, the side window, the first mechanic used an AR-15. We developed our own machine gun mount for the M60. We started with an M14 rifle out of the side window, but we found that the brand-new M-14 that we took to Vietnam climbed like a homesick angel as soon as you put it on automatic and wanted to blow your rotor blades off. We were always thinking we might blow our own rotor blades off. The side window had a wind baffle added to the front edge of the window to move slipstream away from the gunner. The rear window didn't work, as it actually sucked exhaust fumes from the engine into the cabin section of the aircraft.

The Army Special Forces at the time were trying out the AR-15 .223-caliber automatic rifle that was a predecessor of the M16. They let us use some of them because we were a very close-knit team over there. The AR-15 didn't have any of the jamming problems that came later. It was a fine weapon. It had a cyclic rate about three times what the M60 was. I know, when we'd fly out over the water to test our guns, we'd cut loose with the M60 and we could put rounds of the AR-15 in between the water spurts of the M60. The biggest problem we had was hitting our tires or our strut supports. Again, we were always hitting our own aircraft with our fire.

We never used the .50-caliber M2, or "Ma Deuce," machine guns on board, but the tandem-rotor CH-46 Sea Knight helicopters that came later were armed with two .50-caliber M2s on each side.

At that time, the Marine Corps didn't yet look at their helicopters as being assault aircraft. There was quite a bit of controversy with the com-

The UH-34D had its engine in the nose, where it served unintentionally but very effectively as armor against Viet Cong small-arms fire. The helicopter was supposed to be named the Sea Horse, but Marines commonly called it the "Dog," a term derived from the letter suffix in its designation. In Vietnam, it was unusual to fly with the fuselage doors closed.

[Sikorsky]

mandant of the Marine Corps and the aviation units as to what the role of the helicopter was going to be. It was generally looked at in the Marine Corps as a logistics function and not an assault function. It became very apparent to us that you don't fly into hot landing zones when you don't have close air support. But we didn't have close air support other than an Army unit stationed with us that had Huey gunships.

The Army had UH-1B Hueys and used the call sign DRAGON. They had armed their helicopters. They would carry four M60s and four canisters of twenty-four 2.75-inch rockets, which would keep a lot of the enemy's heads down if you got into a really hot zone. Occasionally, if your timing was right, you could catch a T-28 or a few A-1 Skyraiders for close support, but that was always a little more difficult because you had to coordinate it through the Air Force or through the South Vietnamese.

In 1964, no one knew then how big Vietnam was going to get. There were only about 400 Marines in the whole country. There were maybe a total of 20,000 Army and Air Force. We didn't have any fighters that could support us like a regular Marine landing battalion would have. That came later. We were there primarily to provide training and also to help get the Army Special Forces troops out of harm's way as much as we could.

There was an incident that I remember that especially caused adrenaline to flow. An Army Special Forces base had been under fire for quite a while. It was getting late in the afternoon. They radioed that they didn't think they could make it through the night unless they could be resupplied with ammunition because they were running low on ammo.

We hustled on out of Da Nang and grabbed what we could get: we had, I believe, three UH-34Ds and a couple of Army Hueys that went with us for gun support. We flew down to Hoa Ai to pick up some ammunition.

We flew from there back into the mountains into an area they called the Arizona Territory. As we were flying along, I saw tracers coming up. As we got close to this base, we couldn't raise any radio contact with them. We kept trying. We must have had the wrong frequency. But everybody kept trying to raise this base and pretty soon the word went out: "Does anybody know any French?" We thought maybe there's somebody who speaks French down there and is listening to the radio. None of us had apparently done real well in French. We didn't raise them.

As we got closer, we could see the tracers and some of the ground fire at this particular base. They were taking quite a bit of heat. In fact, I spotted a stream of tracers coming up behind one of our choppers. We spread our formation out as wide as we could as we flew into this area so that we could find the base. It was under attack, and about the time I saw the stream of tracers come up behind one of the other choppers in our formation, we saw the base.

It's kind of funny, seeing tracers. We hadn't seen a lot of tracers so far. It was pretty much Viet Cong at that time. They were local fighters. They didn't have a lot of the automatic weaponry that they got later when the North Vietnamese started coming down. We were getting single-shot fire or repeating fire from an AK-47, which wouldn't have tracers in it, but belted ammunition a lot of times had tracers in it so they could see where the bullets were going. I think every fifth or seventh round was a tracer, which looked like a little firefly coming up.

In fact, once we saw how much fire was hitting this one base, we decided on this operating procedure: We brought two Hueys as wingmen on each side of the lead UH-34D, just in front of it, and they laid down machine gun and rocket fire to keep down the heads of all those people who were surrounding the Special Forces base. They then circled around and kept their heads down while the -34 landed in the middle of the compound.

Most of these compounds were pretty much all the same: They had a blockhouse in the center. They had firing pits. They had barbed wire around the perimeter. They were fairly small bases. They had a landing zone in the center.

I was flying cover above with the other two Hueys. The second chopper in our flight went in. He was able to get in and drop off ammo and get out. But on the exit from the compound, one of the Hueys took a round in the fuel tank and was spraying fuel out the back of the plane. They were concerned that they might torch the leaking fuel with their exhaust. So about a mile from the Special Forces base, they set down on a sandbar right next to a river, with a village looking them in the face. No sooner had their skids hit the deck than all of a sudden gunfire from everywhere was hitting us. In fact, as I looked out the door, I saw all of these tracers coming up, filling the skies. I said to myself, "God, that's just like all of those movies you saw about World War II where all the kamikazes were coming down and all of the ships were shooting and filling the skies full of gunfire." It was almost mesmerizing. The pilot called down and said, "Smith, are you going to send any of that stuff back to them?"

That kind of woke me up and got my trigger finger going. I found that once you picked up on a tracer you could generally follow it back with bursts and you could see where the source was. You followed them back and they went silent, and then you picked up another stream of tracers and followed them back. That's how you found out where they were shooting from and how you could knock them out, which was hard to do.

Crewchief Warren R. Smith snapped this "fire drill" photo at Da Nang in 1964 to show how a UH-34D helicopter arrived "in country"—partially dismantled inside the bowels of an Air Force C-124 Globemaster transport.

[Warren R. Smith]

This was kind of a terrifying experience because we had all these planes flying in a very small area. We had one on the deck and, basically, three of us flying around up above. We were interlocking our fire and then leaning out of the doorway when firing the machine gun, worried about crossing over into our own stream. So we started to get really concerned about hitting some of our own planes. We went down. The UH-34D that had actually gone in to the outpost to drop the ammunition off now had to rescue the four-man crew of the Huey that was on the ground. They dropped down and the guys who were on that Huey scrambled into the UH-34D and they took off.

They got off the ground and we realized that they had gone out of the area so quickly, because of all of the gunfire, that they had left the four M60 machine guns and all the ammunition on the Huey. That would be a prize possession for all the guys who were shooting at us. Remember, the Viet Cong were not that well equipped then. They were using just about any weapon from World War I or World War II onward. They used to take drainage pipes and make mortars out of them. They had small factories scattered around in the jungle that made armaments. So now we're flying around thinking maybe we should try to torch that Huey, as in burn it up. Then the Viet Cong wouldn't get those guns.

Generally when we had a plane down, we would get South Vietnamese Army Rangers in to secure the area, but there were no Rangers around and it was getting late.

It was starting to get dark. We finally got approval. We didn't want to go ahead on our own and destroy a piece of government equipment that costs that much money, so we waited for approval to burn it. We thought we knew where it was but it was getting dark now. We circled around and expended every bit of ammunition we had trying with our own tracers in hope of burning the Huey. We didn't do that. We decided, "It's so dark. We're out of ammo now. We'd better get out of here." We got ourselves back to Da Nang with the night closing in on us.

Later they told us that more friendly troops were coming in the next day to the area and would take care of that Huey that was on the ground. And you know what? With all of that gunfire that we expended trying to get the Huey burned, when they were able to look at it the next day, the only bullet hole they found in it was the original one that brought it down. We hadn't hit it once. We must have scared the living hell out of everybody around there but we didn't hit it. We didn't lose the Huey because they were able to go out the next day and salvage it and fly it out of there, but they gave us credit for saving the outpost. All in all, it was pretty successful.

I remember how much adrenaline was flowing. At the time, you're pretty calm because of all the training you've had—the aiming and the firing. You're so busy you don't have time to get scared. Once it's over and it gets quiet, and you start to think about what could have happened, when you get on the ground, you just kind of want to explode.

That always happens before and after. You have a tightness in your stomach going in. But once you get into the conflict and get really busy, you're okay. That's why training is so important because you immediately start going through the functions that you've been trained to do. But when it is over, you just want something to release all that adrenaline. After landing, you would sweep all of the grass out of your plane and do all the maintenance, fuel it, check it over, and be ready to fly first thing in the morning, so at least you have something to do to calm you down while that adrenaline is churning.

We were there from the last day of January until the 19th of June, and we lost 12 of our 24 aircraft. It was tough territory to fly in. These aircraft were rotated. We had three Marine UH-34D squadrons in the Orient. One was with the floating battalion, constantly at sea looking for hot spots. One was in Okinawa. One was in Vietnam.

One of the problems with the UH-34D was that, to get the weight down, a lot of it was made out of magnesium. That's lighter by a third than aluminum, so you did gain there. But when you went aboard ship, you get magnesium out of salt water to begin with, and when you get it next to salt water, it wants to go back to its mother. So corrosion is a constant problem around a ship. You're constantly fighting corrosion. It gets under the rivets. It gets everywhere. It gets under everything and starts eating away.

We found that putting a heavy coat of wax on the planes was about the best thing to do to protect them. If you did get corrosion, you would have to scrape it down to bare metal. You would acidize that spot. You would neutralize it. You would then paint it with zinc chromate. And then you would put the olive drab color on top of it.

But when we got on board our ship, the USS *Valley Forge,* somebody had forgotten to bring the olive drab paint. But we had plenty of the zinc chromate, which was kind of a chartreuse color. So here you had Marine olive drab on the helicopter but with all of these cute little spots and speckles of chartreuse all over it. So you would try to be as creative as you could. Some of the guys went a little overboard and actually started designing their planes with chartreuse displayed in strategic places—kind of a response to the boredom of being at sea after fighting in Vietnam.

We were in Subic Bay, Philippines, in August 1964 when the Gulf of Tonkin incident happened. We had been out at sea for carrier quals and pulled back into Subic just as this was happening. We got back to Subic

Who's Who

Cpl. Warren R. Smith, UH-34D Seahorse crew chief

Bay and saw the whole harbor in a frenzy. I got up on deck. I went out to the flight deck. There was just a flurry of activity. There were troops everywhere. There were trucks rolling in. The whole harbor was mad with Seventh Fleet activity, with everybody trying to load up with everything. We took an 1,800-Marine landing force on board the carrier and as much produce and supplies as we could get aboard in a few short hours. By three or four o'clock that afternoon, the whole Seventh Fleet had pulled out of Subic Bay and was headed west going back to Vietnam.

We found out en route that the North Vietnamese had attacked a couple of American destroyers with torpedo boats—we know today that there was just one attack on one destroyer—and that the United States had responded with some air strikes. We were on our way back over there with an expeditionary force, landing teams and all. We were scheduled to make a landing or a show of force, but we didn't go through with it.

We spent two months plus off the coast of Vietnam. I got out of the Marine Corps in November 1964 and the really big buildup in Vietnam took place the following year. It was in April 1965 that the Marines made a huge amphibious landing near Da Nang, and all of a sudden there were thousands of Marines in South Vietnam.

Sikorsky UH-34D Seahorse

The Marine presence in Southeast Asia began on April 9, 1962, with the arrival of Lt. Col. Archie Clapp and a few good men who came into Soc Trang, South Vietnam, in squadron HMM-362 with 24 HUS-1 helicopters.

Crewchief Corporal Warren R. Smith leaned out the door of his Sikorsky UH-34D Seahorse helicopter to snap this portrait of two other helicopters in his squadron, HMM-364, flying over South Vietnamese paddy fields.

[Warren R. Smith]

The squadron was dubbed Archie's Angels after its commander, but the name soon changed to the Ugly Angels. When the system for naming military aircraft was overhauled on October 1, 1962, the HUS-1 became the UH-34D. In civilian parlance, it was an S-58.

The marsh forests of the Mekong Delta were the ideal setting for the Marine Corps's expertise in unconventional warfare. The UH-34D, alias the "Dog," was the right weapon for the Marines at the right time.

In time, the Marines were moved farther north. From 1963 to 1969, they operated UH-34D helicopters at Da Nang, Chu Lai, Marble Mountain, and other locations familiar to Vietnam veterans. The UH-34D was a cantankerous flying machine, but it was also one that Marines loved without reservation. They compared it to the Springfield .03 infantry rifle of World War II. Long after the Army had shifted to the prettier, more efficient M1 Garand, Marines were still in combat with Springfields. When the Army had new Hueys, the Marines were still flying old UH-34Ds.

At many locations, such as the helicopter base at Marble Mountain, UH-34D helicopters operated from MA-2 matting, a flat matting with interlocking sections owing its heritage to the pierced steel planking

(PSP), alias "Marston mat," of World War II. The MA-2 mat had a non-skid surface and no holes. Operations off the matting were excellent. Since there were no holes, the Marines never had a foreign object damage (FOD) problem from dirt or stones coming up through the matting, and braking was excellent.

Ultimately, half a dozen Marine squadrons flew the "Dog" in Vietnam, namely HMM-162, -163, -261, -361, -362, -363, and -365, some for as little as a four-month tour, others for up to two years.

As for the Marine version, even after it was replaced, it wasn't—exactly—replaced. HMM squadrons in Vietnam reequipped with the Boeing CH-46A Sea Knight beginning in 1966. But the CH-46A suffered transmission problems that literally caused the tail of the aircraft

---

Sikorsky UH-34D Seahorse (HUS-1/S-58)

Type: 4-place general-purpose helicopter

Power plant: Wright R-1820-84 or -84B Cyclone 9-cylinder air-cooled radial engine rated at 1,525 hp at 2,800 rpm or 1,275 hp at 2,500 rpm driving 4-blade, 56-ft (17.06-m) rotors on fully articulated rotor heads

Performance: maximum speed, 120 mph (193 km/h) at sea level; cruising speed, 98 mph (125 km/h); maximum rate of climb, 1,100 ft (335 m) per minute at sea level; service ceiling, 9,500 ft (2895 m); hovering ceiling with ground effect, 4,900 ft (1493 m); hovering ceiling without ground effect, 2,400 ft (740 m); range, 225 miles (362 km)

Weights: empty weight, 8,230 lb (3777 kg); gross weight, 13,300 lb (6033 kg); useful load, 5,070 lb (3000 kg)

Dimensions: main rotor diameter, 56 ft (17.06 m); length overall, rotors turning, 56 ft 8½ in (17.27 m); fuselage length, 46 ft 9 in (14.24 m); fuselage width, 5 ft 8 in (17.26 m); tail rotor diameter, 9 ft 6 in (2.90 m); cabin interior length, 13 ft 3 in (4.03 m); cabin interior width, 5 ft 3 in (1.60 m); cabin interior height, 6 ft (1.82 m)

Armament: door-mounted M60 or M2 machine gun

Payload: up to 3,600 lb (1888 kg) of personnel or equipment

Crew: 2 pilots plus 2

First flight: March 8, 1954 (prototype); September 20, 1954 (production)

---

to fall off. During the months that were spent solving this problem, UH-34Ds returned to service. When the Dogs finally had flown their last mission with the Marines, many were turned over to the Vietnamese army.

Chapter Thirteen

Skyhawks Versus the Viet Cong

BILL LUPLOW When the Ninth Marine Expeditionary Brigade landed at Da Nang, South Vietnam, in April 1965—some troops coming ashore from amphibious vessels while the press observed and cameras rolled— it was time to expand the Marine presence in country. Marine aviation was operating from Da Nang, but the base was becoming crowded, its facilities overloaded. The brass found a new spot for a second airfield at Chu Lai, 50 miles (80 kilometers) south of Da Nang. As the war progressed, Chu Lai became the principal Marine air base and the headquarters for land-based A-4 Skyhawk operations.

Seabees went to work at Chu Lai constructing a short airfield for tactical support (SATS) by laying two 12-feet (3.6-meters) sections of aluminum matting over leveled earth. Marines referred to these as Marston mat, or pierced steel planking (PSP). Gerald G. Greulichr of the Carnegie, Illinois, Steel Company designed the product, which drew its name from being first tested during World War II at an airfield near Marston, North Carolina. To cope with shortened takeoff distances, Skyhawks launching from the SATS initially relied on a carrier-like catapult system or on jet-assisted takeoff (JATO) bottles. Recoveries were sometimes made, especially when battle damage was sustained, by a sys-

Capt. Bill Luplow
March 21, 1966
Douglas A-4C Skyhawk
(bureau no. 147808/WL-11)
RED HOG LEAD
Marine Attack Squadron
VMA-311, "Tomcats"
Chu Lai, South Vietnam

This is Bill Luplow as a student naval aviator before going to Vietnam to fly the A-4C Skyhawk for the Marine Corps.

[Bill Luplow]

tem of carrier-like arresting wires. On May 31, 1965, the Seabees finished a 4,000-feet (1215-meter) runway that was 70 feet (21 meters) wide, complete with taxiways and parking ramps. Later, a new construction effort doubled the length of the matted runway. The first Skyhawk to land at Chu Lai made a SATS landing on June 1, 1965, piloted by Col. John D. Noble, commander of Marine Aircraft Group 12, or MAG-12. About 18 months later, a 10,000-feet (3040-meter) concrete runway was belatedly completed at Chu Lai.

Chu Lai became a beehive of activity from which Marine planes took to the air to support Marines on the ground. Because of an early decision not to rotate squadrons, VMA-311, "Tomcats"—the nickname had changed since World War II when the outfit was called Hell's Belles—remained in Vietnam from April 1965 to January 1973, at first with A-4C Skyhawks and later with A-4E models (see chapter 15). The squadron wore the letters *WL* as its tail designator; it was an arbitrary choice, but VMA-311's Marines started calling themselves the Willy Lovers, a nickname that inspired a heart on the squadron patch, although in Korea they had been Whiskey Lovers. During efforts to support the besieged Marine combat base at Khe Sanh, the squadron flew

240 sorties from May 5 to May 8, 1968. By September 1968, VMA-311 had logged 25,000 combat sorties, believed to be the largest number of any Marine combat squadron up to that time.

Flying the Skyhawk

My squadron, VMA-311, had an unusual history with the Skyhawk. The squadron initially had the A-4E model. For reasons having to do with support in the field, VMA-311 traded aircraft with another squadron for their A-4Cs before rotating to Iwakuni, Japan, in December 1965. We took the C model back to Chu Lai in February 1966 and then got new Es over a period of time. In fact, we had a combination of Cs and Es for about 30 to 45 days, I believe, until all the Cs were replaced with E models.

Each flight, whether it was two aircraft (a section) or four (a division) or even a single aircraft, had its own call sign. Mine was RED HOG. Another might have been OSCAR or TRICYCLE or some such. Each squadron had 16 aircraft, but not all in the air at the same time.

They called the A-4 the "Tinkertoy" and the "Scooter" because it was so small. When you closed the cockpit, your shoulders were rubbing right up against the side of the cockpit. The beauty of it was you had your elbows on your thigh and you could reach all the armament switches, the handle for the gear, and just about everything you needed.

The Skyhawk had internal cannons with 200 rounds, but you could put a lot more under the aircraft and under the wing. We usually had bombs hanging underneath, of course. But we had a gun pod that we could put on our centerline station. The A-4C had three ordnance stations (one under the fuselage, one under each wing); the A-4E had five (with two under each wing). You could really make a mark if you carried one of those gun pods. You could hang one of those gun pods under the centerline, and it shot 6,000 rounds per minute.

Before I describe my most memorable 1966 combat mission in the

Skyhawk, I'll say a few words about becoming a Marine aviator and getting into that great airplane.

I was born in 1938 in Michigan, but soon afterward my family moved to Arkansas. I graduated from Parkin High School in Parkin, Arkansas, in 1955 and from the University of Arkansas in 1960 with a degree in chemistry. The Lord blessed me in marriage to Kay Keese (Miss Little Rock of 1957) in 1958, and we have two children and several grandchildren.

As a senior at the university, I was captain of the Razorback football team that won the 1959 Southwest Conference and 1960 Gator Bowl Championship. I played guard on offense and noseguard on defense, as we ran a five-man front. This was in the "olden days" when everyone played both ways. I was the second heaviest man on our team at 202 pounds. Jim Hollander was the heaviest at 212 pounds. Our line averaged 191 pounds and our backs 187. We were small but quick. And in 1960, the Denver Broncos drafted me.

It was the first year of the old American Football League. That was before they started all the big bonuses in the sport; a highly successful linebacker made $11,000 per year. I visited with them about a signing bonus and they "negotiated" me down to a $500 bonus. It turned out they wouldn't even come up with $500. I was recently married and we had our first child, and I couldn't see myself risking an injury and not being able to support my family for what they were paying. So that was the end of my life in professional football.

I attended medical school for a period of time. But I wanted to fly high-performance aircraft, so I visited the recruiters for the Air Force, Army, Marine Corps, and Navy. I decided I also wanted to fly from a carrier. My final decision to be a Marine was because of the esprit de corps. I felt that being a Marine would be something that really mattered.

I entered the Marine Corps, went through platoon leader's course at Quantico, Virginia, from September to December 1962, and received my commission as a second lieutenant there. After that, I reported to Naval Air Station Pensacola, Florida, for primary and basic flight train-

A Marine A-4C Skyhawk practicing short-field operations of the kind that became routine in South Vietnam.

[U.S. Marine Corps]

ing where I flew the T-34B Mentor and T-28B Trojan from January 1963 to June 1964. I then went to Naval Auxiliary Air Station Kingsville, Texas, for advanced jet training and flew the F-9 Cougar and F-11 Tiger from June to November 1964.

Included in our jet aviation training were carrier qualifications aboard the USS *Lexington* (CVT 16). After I qualified aboard the "Lady Lex" and completed the training, Kay pinned on my wings of gold as a naval aviator.

I received orders to Marine Corps Air Station, El Toro, California, to fly the Douglas A-4 Skyhawk. In September 1965, my squadron shipped out to Iwakuni, and from there to Chu Lai, South Vietnam.

So that's how I got there to fly a mission.

Skyhawk into Battle

You taxi down to the end of the runway. You stop short of the active. Prior to takeoff, you check out the instruments. You advance the throttle and make sure you have the thrust you need. You check all the mechanical parts, the stabilizer, the elevators, and all the moving parts. Everybody in the flight does those checks.

You take off one aircraft at a time. The lead aircraft takes off. Once his wheels are in the well, he starts a wide, slow turn. The aircraft following him gets on the inside of that turn, flies up under him, and joins up on him. When you have a third and fourth aircraft, RED HOG 3 does the same, joining up underneath, and 4 follows.

On a typical mission, I'm leading a division of A-4C Skyhawks. We take off. Everybody joins up on my wing. I tell the flight, "RED HOG Flight, check in." Their response is "RED HOG 2 is up," and then, "3, up," and then, "4, up." If anyone fails to check in, we use hand signals from one cockpit to the next to determine if the failure means no radio reception, or if he might be receiving but unable to transmit. If someone in the division can't receive, that means returning to base with RED HOG Leader calling and alerting the tower that an A-4C is returning with no radio. The tower will keep other aircraft out of the pattern until the "no communication" aircraft is safely down on deck. On the other hand, if one of the pilots in a division can receive but not transmit, we can continue with the flight.

You can also continue a mission if you have some minor mechanical problems with the aircraft. Our hardworking maintenance people did an excellent job of keeping those Skyhawks flying, but the airplanes were already more than ten years old and every instrument didn't work perfectly every minute.

On a mission that is scheduled in advance, you have a chart of where you're going. You know the initial direction you're heading and how far it is to the target area. That chart is made of rubberized material. You can keep it in your lap and glance down at it.

From Chu Lai, you go out on a 330-degree heading, 60 or 70 miles. When you're halfway to the target, you check in with the forward air controller, or FAC, in an O-1 Bird Dog spotter plane. You want him to know how many Skyhawks you've got and what kind of bombload you're carrying, so you say something like, "This is RED HOG Flight, of four A-4s, with Snake and 20-mike mike." *Snake* is the term for the Mark 82 Snakeye retarded bomb.

That's when the FAC tells you what you need to know. He says, "I've got a truck in the trees." He uses smoke rockets to mark the target. You can see him pretty easily because the FAC is right there, right over the target, and the top of his aircraft is painted white to make him more visible from above. The FAC tells you what you need in order to bring your Skyhawk flight into position to attack the target, get the target in sight, and begin your bomb run on it.

Hitting the Target

A typical target might be enemy troops on the ground caught up in a firefight with Marines, which calls for close air support. Or it could be North Vietnamese supplies moving south along the Ho Chi Minh Trail. Or intelligence may have word that a certain spot is an ammo dump. On this day, our target is one North Vietnamese truck to begin with, and then we see another truck and another truck and another truck. Our FAC is circling above a big gathering of North Vietnamese vehicles, down there beneath the jungle foliage.

Once the FAC clears us in hot, I roll in. On the A-4C, the gunsight is up on top of the console. The crosshairs in the middle tell you where to release your bomb at a certain speed, dive angle, and altitude. You're strapped to your ejection seat inside that cramped, narrow cockpit, and you have very good control of the aircraft as it goes into the dive.

So I go in and drop a bomb. And then, we see even more North Vietnamese trucks.

I drop a Mark 82 Snakeye. I pull off. I don't actually see the detonation as I come off, but I'm right on target. The FAC in the Bird Dog tells me so in as many words: "You're on target. Put another one in there." He directs RED HOG 2, and then RED HOG 3, as the Skyhawks come in one after another to drop.

A Marine ordnance man of squadron VMA-311 loads 20-mm ammunition aboard an A-4C Skyhawk at Chu Lai, South Vietnam. The Skyhawk was equipped with two 20-mm Mark 12 cannons firing from the wing root. On rare occasion, the Skyhawk also carried a belly gun pod.

[Dept. of Defense]

That's a brief description of bombing North Vietnamese trucks, which is only one of the things we do, flying with VMA-311 out of Chu Lai. As I said, we have several kinds of missions. We go into North Vietnam at night as solo aircraft. On that kind of mission, we check in with our controller, and someone who is using ground-based radar and matching the target to our flight path guides us to the target.

In North Vietnam, the SA-2 Guideline surface-to-air missile, or SAM, added to the other threats we encountered. I never had a SAM shot at me, but I got a lot of small arms. A lot of the time, we couldn't even see it when they were shooting at us. Sometimes, we could see muzzle flashes or tracers.

Now, for my mission of March 21, 1966: It's a close-air-support flight. We're flying close air support to help some Marines in a bind. I have enemy that I can see in the open.

This kind of bombing is completely visual. It's a test of eyes and hands on the controls. We go in to support these Marines and put napalm where it will slow the enemy troops approaching them. The radio traffic tells us that we're being shot at. Our napalm helps, but the situation still isn't decided.

Now we've dropped our napalm, but we still have the 20-millimeter cannon, the 20 mike-mike.

Our Marines down there still have enemy troops within point-blank range. We've thinned out their numbers a little, but it's not yet time to go home. I roll in again and begin my run. I'm looking into the gunsight, coming up on the enemy troops in front of me, when something hits my aircraft.

It's more like a thump than a bang. But that's more than enough. My Skyhawk has really been hit.

I've lost hydraulics. I check again. I have no hydraulics. I start to punch out. I think, "I'm right in the middle of the North Vietnamese." I don't want to eject in the middle of the North Vietnamese if there's any possible choice.

While I'm trying to get control of my A-4C, I fly right through a tree line. I tell the rest of the flight I'm heading back to base. That's when an unexpected radio call comes in. A Marine UH-1E Huey chopper pilot calls and says, "I've got you in sight." He offers to stay as close as he can while I try to coax the A-4C back to Chu Lai.

Letting down toward the base, I drop the tail hook. Without hydraulics, I have to grab the wire to bring the damaged Skyhawk to a stop. The runway at Chu Lai is 8,000 feet of Marston matting, but a lot of the time we only use 4,000 because the monsoon rains get under the runway and eat it away. In an emergency, I don't want to take any chances. I want the hook to halt the airplane, and if there's any danger of a fire or an explosion, I want to get out of the cockpit.

After being nursed home by the UH-1E, who is able to look me over and assure me that I appear to have a chance of surviving a landing, I make the necessary radio calls, line up my airplane, and come down on final approach. I hit the ground. I roll out and the wire pulls back slightly, tugging on the plane. As soon as my aircraft comes to a stop, I have Marines all over me.

I get out of it. I climb down. I think, "I'm safe now." I look back at

This is an A-4C Skyhawk in flight.

[U.S. Marine Corps]

my aircraft and it's pretty badly battered. Even now, I don't fully grasp what happened to me while I was getting ready to strafe with the cannon. I have been assuming that it was North Vietnamese gunfire that struck my Skyhawk. Master Gunnery Sergeant Detly, who is chief of ordnance in our squadron, looks over my aircraft, talks to others about what happened, and concludes that the damage to my aircraft was from shrapnel caused by a mortar round exploding under, and slightly in front of, the aircraft. The mortar round did not strike the aircraft itself.

Much later, I learn that the UH-1E Huey pilot who helped me get back from that mission had been my instructor in the T-34B in primary flight training, a Captain Baldwin. I have never reestablished my acquaintance with him, but I'd like to.

The A-4C Skyhawk I flew on March 21, 1966, was bureau number 147808 and wore the squadron's WL tail code and the side number 11. It survived that near miss from a mortar round, but on May 5, 1966, while being transported to Da Nang by an Army CH-47 Chinook helicopter, it was inadvertently dropped in a swamp north of Chu Lai. Any further attempt to recover the aircraft was now economically impractical, so Marines had to destroy it with satchel charges.

Flying the Skyhawk into the muzzles of enemy guns was only one way to experience danger in Vietnam. Working with jet aircraft is inherently a dangerous business. We were frequently reminded of it.

One night, I was serving as the base duty officer. They later decided not to assign that job to a mere first lieutenant, but I had it that night. I was writing a letter to my wife, Kay, when I heard what I thought was a mortar round. I ran out of the tent. I saw an aircraft burning.

Our aircraft revetments were made of 55-gallon oil drums filled with water, with two aircraft parked in each revetment. It wasn't a mortar round. In one revetment, they were refueling an A-4C when a leak developed in the fuel hose and sent gas cascading into the next revetment. There, one of my squadron mates, Capt. Eugene W. "Gene" Kimmel had just lighted his aircraft to take off on a night mission. They hadn't even pulled the chocks yet. He was loaded with ordnance and was running up his engine, so he had fire inside his aircraft. When the leaking fuel came into contact with his engine and intake, his plane was set ablaze—the cockpit and the top of the aircraft, which had bombs hanging under the wings.

The fire was instantaneous. Gene had no way to taxi his aircraft out of there to get clear. It happened too suddenly, and he was simply engulfed in fire. His aircraft totally burned up.

One of the bravest things I ever saw was a black sergeant—he'd been handling ordnance for a long time and was a bulked-out guy—who went under the aircraft when it was still burning on top and took some of the bombs off the bomb racks. You don't think of a ground crew member being called upon to exhibit that kind of courage, but he did. I put him in for a decoration. The squadron executive officer was also drawn to the scene by the initial, mortarlike sound of the fire igniting. He arrived, took one look, and turned and ran in the opposite direction while the sergeant was performing his heroic deeds. Guess who got the decoration?

Gene was right in the middle of it. Gene got burned real bad. They medevacked him out of there in a hurry. He eventually recovered well enough to return to Marine Air flying.

Who's Who

Capt. Bill Luplow, A-4C Skyhawk pilot, squadron VMA-311

My tour of duty in South Vietnam lasted until September 1966. I flew 186 combat missions in North Vietnam, Laos, and Cambodia, and in close air support for allied troops in South Vietnam. I rotated back to the States in September 1966. They sent me back to Kingsville to naval training squadron VT-22, where, as a flight instructor in the Naval Air Advanced Jet Training Command, I prepared new aviators for combat in Southeast Asia. I instructed in the TF-9J Cougar (originally, F9F-8T), which was a development of the Korean War–era Panther but with swept wings and two seats. One of my fellow instructors during that tour of duty was none other than Gene Kimmel. I instructed from October 1966 to October 1967. I left active duty as a captain on October 15, 1967.

Gene Kimmel volunteered to go back to Vietnam. When he did, they put him in an OV-10A Bronco forward air control aircraft and he got killed. I have a reference source on fixed-wing aircraft losses in Vietnam. The source is the book, *Vietnam Air Losses,* by Chris Hobson (Hinckley, England: Midland Publishing, 2001). Drawing on official records, it tells me that on October 22, 1968, Capt. Eugene William Kimmel and Capt. Rodney Rene Chastant were killed in OV-10A bureau number 155422 belonging to squadron VMO-2, part of Marine Air Group 16. Chastant was a Marine infantry officer. They were hit by ground fire 12 miles from Da Nang. A UH-1E Huey landed and recovered one of the bodies of the crew (unclear which) and subsequently called in an air strike on the area. Gene's widow, Mary Lou, later married another of our squadron members. One of their daughters is an Army helicopter pilot.

This is a Marine A-4C Skyhawk beginning its takeoff roll.

[U.S. Marine Corps]

Douglas A-4C Skyhawk (A4D-2N)

The A-4 Skyhawk (originally the A4D) racked up a unique achievement by meeting requirements established by the U.S. Navy at exactly half the projected gross weight. By paying rigorous attention to detail, Douglas Aircraft Company designer Edward H. Heinemann created a work of art, an aircraft so advanced for its time that some remain in service in other air forces more than 50 years after the Skyhawk's first flight.

Head of the engineering team at Douglas's El Segundo, California, plant in 1951, Heinemann was already the designer of the A-20 Havoc, the A-26 Invader, and the AD Skyraider. At the time he worked on the lightweight Skyhawk, Heinemann was also working on the A3D Skywarrior, the largest and heaviest aircraft ever to operate from an aircraft carrier up to that time. In a letter he wrote later about his design work on the Skyhawk, Heinemann said his goal was to "take the best jet engine I could get, stick a wing underneath, and put a saddle for the jockey on top—and leave out the rest." At the time, many jet engines were still unreliable and Heinemann's goal for a lightweight warplane seemed unattainable. Officers in the Navy's Bureau of Aeronautics said the proposal was downright "irresponsible." Heinemann actually came up with a final design for a nuclear-capable combat airplane that tipped the scales at less than 12,000 pounds (5443 kilograms), or less than half of what most jet fighters weighed. As Heinemann later recalled in the letter, he drew members of his engineering shop together, gave each member a three-view drawing of the planned Skyhawk, and said, "I think this can be done. It will take a tough SOB to do it. I am that man. I would like to have you all join my team. Anyone who does not wish to join, there is the door." No one headed for the exit.

When the Navy challenged Heinemann by increasing the bombload it wanted, the designer warned that gross weight would go up to 14,300 pounds (6486 kilograms), still an extremely light weight for an air-to-ground combat aircraft designed to carry an atomic bomb. It couldn't be done, many said, but on June 21, 1952, with the Korean War raging and the Cold War growing, the Navy gave Douglas an order for a single XA4D-1 Skyhawk prototype, soon followed by an initial order for A4D-1 models, which were to be limited to a maximum weight of 15,000 pounds (6804 kilograms). As the first ship took shape, doubters became believers and the Skyhawk became "Heinemann's Hot Rod," "the Tinkertoy," or "the Scooter."

After rejecting Westinghouse engine designs that were performing poorly for the Navy, Heinemann chose the Wright J65, the American-licensed version of the British Sapphire turbojet engine. As part of his weight-saving campaign, Heinemann dispensed with many of the features found on bombers—for example, an internal weapons bay and an afterburner—and stuck with simplicity as the underpinning of the Skyhawk. The aircraft would eventually perform many missions, including close support with Marine Air, but it was designed from the beginning for just one purpose, to carry a tactical nuclear bomb under the centerline and attack targets in the Soviet Union.

On June 22, 1954, Douglas test pilot Bob Rahn made the first flight of the XA4D-1 prototype. The aircraft performed well from the start, although it needed changes to the vertical tail design. The first production A4D-1 made its maiden flight on August 14, 1954. One of the first Skyhawks set a world speed record over a 310-mile (500-kilometer) closed course later in 1954, reaching a speed of 695 miles per hour (1118 kilometers per hour). A4D-1 and improved A4D-2 models began reaching the Navy in late 1956 and the Marine Corps two years later. From 1959, production focused on a model with more improvements, the A4D-2N. When the Pentagon's system for naming aircraft was overhauled in 1962, the A4D-1, A4D-2, and A4D-2N were redesignated A-4A, A-4B, and A-4C. Douglas never built A4D-3 or A4D-4 models, but did later switch production to the longer-nosed A4D-5, which became the A-4E (see chapter 15).

The A-4C Skyhawk, formerly the A4D-2N, introduced additional equipment to improve all-weather capability, including an advanced autopilot, low-altitude bombing/all-attitude indicating gyro system, AN/APG-53A terrain-clearance radar, and an angle of attack indicator.

The A-4F model, which was used by the Navy but not by the Marine Corps, added nosewheel steering, wing lift spoilers, and an improved Escapac 1-C3 ejection seat. Fleet deliveries began in early 1967. A unique recognition feature was the "bent" aerial fueling probe, configured to preclude electronic interference with the wide-angle target acquisition system. The A-4F acquired an avionics pod "humpback" on its fuselage, also found on the later A-4M, after fleet deliveries began. The A-4F equipped the Navy's Blue Angels flight demonstration team from 1974 to 1990.

There were several two-seat versions of the Skyhawk, including the TA-4F, used as a combat observation post by Marines in Vietnam, and the TA-4J, which was the standard advanced trainer in naval aviation until the late 1990s.

The A-4E model introduced a new engine to the Skyhawk series, an 8,500-pound (3855-kilogram) thrust Pratt & Whitney J52-P-6A twinspool turbojet engine.

The Marine Corps took to the Skyhawk and eventually operated most models of Heinemann's Hot Rod, from the A-4A to the postVietnam A-4M—designed explicitly for, and used only by, the Marine

Corps—which was the final version off the production line in the late 1970s and which introduced a head-up display and computer-aided delivery of its bombload with the angle rate bombing system. To the Marines, the mission of the Skyhawk was to attack and to destroy surface targets in support of the landing force commander, a job that frequently meant close air support over the heads of ground troops.

The A-4M was powered by an 11,200-pound (5080-kilogram) thrust Pratt & Whitney J52-P-408 turbojet about 25 percent more powerful than previous Skyhawk engines, giving the plane much better short-field performance. Smokeless burner cans were introduced to cut down the visible exhaust signature of the aircraft. The A-4M also featured a larger cockpit canopy to improve pilot visibility, especially toward the rear. A new squared-off tip to the vertical tail housed new

---

Douglas A-4C Skyhawk (A4D-2N)

Type: single-seat attack aircraft

Power plant: 1 Wright J65-W-16A or W-20 Sapphire turbojet engine rated at 7,700-lb (3492-kg) thrust (16-A) or 8,400 lb (3810-kg) thrust

Performance: maximum speed, 649 mph (1041 km/h) at sea level; maximum speed carrying a 4,000-lb (1814-kg) bombload, 610 mph (981 km/h) at sea level; initial rate of climb, 8,000 ft (2440 m) per minute; tactical radius carrying a 4,000-lb (1814-kg) bombload, 380 mi (612 km)

Weights: empty, 9,619 lb (4363 kg); maximum takeoff weight, 22,500 lb (10205 kg)

Dimensions: wing span, 27 ft 6 in (8.38 m); length, 40 ft 1 in (12.19 m); height, 15 ft (4.57 m); wheel base, 7 ft 9½ in (2.37 m); wing area, 260 sq ft (24.16 sq m)

Armament: two 20-mm Mark 12 cannons, each with 200 rounds per gun; 3 ordnance stations (1 centerline, 2 wing) for a typically 4,000-lb (1814-kg) bombload

Crew: 1 pilot

First flight: June 22, 1954 (XA4D-1); August 14, 1954 (A4D-1/A-4A); August 21, 1958 (A4D-2/A-4C); 1962 (A4D-2N/A-4E)

Identification Friend or Foe antennas. The A-4M made its initial flight on April 10, 1970, with test pilot Walt Smith at the controls, entered service soon afterward, and was joined by the OA-4M, a two-seat, forward air control derivative of the basic design.

A-4Ms served with active-duty Marine Corps squadrons until February 27, 1990, when VMA-211 transferred its last A-4M to a Reserve unit. The A-4M continued to fly with Marine Corps Reserve units until 1994, when VMA-131 retired its last aircraft. Altogether, Douglas manufactured 2,960 Skyhawks of all models.

Chapter Fourteen

Medal of Honor
in a Huey

What Happened

For the four U.S. soldiers who climbed off an Army CH-47 Chinook troop helicopter on the beach at Quang Ngai, South Vietnam, on August 19, 1967, the trouble began almost immediately. Looking for the cause of a mechanical problem, the crew chief deplaned, accompanied by Army S.Sgt. Lawrence H. Allen and two other soldiers. In keeping with standard practice during an unexpected landing in bad-guy territory, the men set up a defensive perimeter between the Chinook and the inland portion of the beach. The defense was inadequate for the huge number of enemy lurking just beyond the tree line.

The Viet Cong attacked them. A grenade exploded near the glass bubble in front of the CH-47's cockpit. Automatic weapons opened up from behind a tree line. Viet Cong came charging toward the Americans. They scrambled toward the helicopter but the pilot, apparently fearful his aircraft would be destroyed on the spot, took off.

That left the four men stranded and about to be overwhelmed. Knowing it could only be a temporary help, they took cover behind a

**Capt. Stephen W. Pless
August 19, 1967
Bell UH-1E Huey
(bureau no. 154760)
WHISKEY BRAVO 15/CHERRY
6 Marine Observation
Squadron 6 (VMO-6)
Quang Ngai, South Vietnam**

They are the most decorated aviation crew in history. Left to right: Gunnery Sgt. Leroy N. Poulson, gunner; Lance Cpl (later Cpl.) John "Gordo" Phelps, crew chief; Capt. Rupert E. Fairchild, copilot; and Capt. (later Maj.) Stephen W. Pless, pilot. Poulson, Phelps, and Fairchild received the Navy Cross. Pless received the Medal of Honor.

[U.S. Marine Corps.]

sand dune and returned fire with their personal weapons. None had brought reserve ammunition and they were quickly out of ammo.

The CH-47 pilot climbed away. Higher up, he might be able to reach out farther with a plea for help. He put out a radio call on "Guard," the emergency distress channel. There were a number of friendly aircraft in the region, most busy with other missions. One of those who responded to the call was Capt. Stephen W. Pless, piloting a nearby Marine Corps UH-1E Huey. The way one of Pless's crew members recalls it, Viet Cong troops were rushing the Americans with bayonets when the UH-1E Huey arrived in the middle of the fight.

LAWRENCE H. ALLEN A grenade thrown by a Viet Cong exploded near the front of the aircraft. We attempted to withdraw to the helicopter, but the pilot was already lifting off. We then ran back to our position behind a sand dune. We began to receive a barrage of grenades; we returned fire, but soon ran out of ammo.

The Viet Cong moved in close and threw more grenades. Everyone was wounded by this time, when one Viet Cong appeared on our flank with an automatic weapon. His fire struck everyone but me. I crawled next to the sand dune and tried to pass as dead. I could hear the Viet Cong move among us, removing our weapons. At this time, I heard two explosions. I looked up and saw a Huey gunship making rocket and gun runs on the Viet Cong, who were returning the fire as they attempted to flee into the brush along the beach.

At this time, several Hueys were orbiting the area, but Captain Pless's aircraft was the only one to come to our aid. After making several attacks, Captain Pless landed by us on the beach.

STEPHEN W. PLESS On August 19, 1967, I was assigned as escort for the afternoon medical evacuation mission. Initially, at 12:20 p.m., we were launched into the Cochise II operational area. During a pickup from Nui Loc Son, the H-34 we were escorting sustained damage to his tail wheel, so upon completion of our missions, we returned to Ky Ha to exchange aircraft. As the medevac crew was switching aircraft, we received an emergency medevac in an unsecure landing zone in the Republic of Vietnam Marine operational area. Rather than wait for another H-34, I decided to proceed to the zone independently and have it secured for his arrival.

As I approached the medevac zone, I heard a transmission on "Guard" channel: "My aircraft is all shot up and I have a lot of wounded aboard. I'm going to try to make it to Duc Pho." Then after a pause, "I still have four men on the ground. The VC are trying to take them prisoners." Or "God, can somebody help them?" At this time I directed my copilot, Capt. Rupert E. Fairfield, to check on the emergency medevac on FM and see if it could wait. I continued to fly toward the distress area and monitor the UHF. Fairfield said the medevac was a priority, the landing zone was secure, and it could wait. In the meantime, from the radio transmissions, I knew that there were four Americans on the beach one mile north of the mouth of the Song Tra Khuc River, that they were under attack by mortars and automatic weapons, and that a CH-47 had been driven off by severe automatic weapons fire. There

The Marine Corps' UH-1E Huey helicopter performed many functions in Vietnam. This one, belonging to squadron VMO-6, hauled entertainer Anita Bryant to a performance of the Bob Hope show at Da Nang in December 1966.

[James O'Kelley]

were three jets overhead and four Army UH-1s orbiting about a mile out to sea. None of these aircraft could get in close enough to the four besieged Americans due to the mortar fire and severe automatic weapons fire. The Army UH-1s were endeavoring to locate the source of the mortar fire, get a reaction force launched, and get everyone organized.

I made two transmissions offering to help but received no reply. Since the other aircraft seemed reluctant to aid the downed men and unable to get organized, I decided to go in alone and hoped they would follow me and help me.

My crew all knew the situation and were all aware that we had very little chance of survival. Yet when I asked them if anyone objected to a rescue attempt, it was a unanimous and emphatic "Go."

I could see the mortars exploding on the beach and headed for the area. Then the mortars quit and I saw a large group of people swarm the beach from a tree line about 100 meters from the beach.

I made a pass directly over the top of the people at 50 feet of altitude and observed four Americans on the beach. A VC was standing over one man, crushing his head with a rifle stock, and people seemed to be in the process of butchering the other men.

I ordered the door gunner, Gunnery Sgt. Leroy N. Poulson, to open fire on the people. The crew chief, Lance Cpl. John G. "Gordo" Phelps, thinking that I had not seen the Americans, yelled, "Don't fire." I told him to "shut up," and the gunner kept firing.

I pulled the aircraft into a hard climb, switching my armament panel to pods as I did so. A hard wingover put me into a firing position just aft of the mob that had started running for the trees. I could now determine that they were all males and armed, and a few of them had on khaki or green uniforms. I hit in the center of the retreating mob with all 14 rockets. Several of the VC turned to fire at us, but most of them were in full flight. Although the trees were obscured by smoke and debris, I made a number of gun runs into the smoke, praying that I would not hit a tree. Some of the VC ran out of the smoke area, and I shot at point-blank range, firing from so low that my own ordnance was spraying mud on the windshield. As I pulled off of one run, I spotted one of the men on the beach waving his arm. I threw the aircraft into a side flare, continually firing at the VC in the tree line as I lowered the aircraft to a landing.

I landed the aircraft about 15 feet from the nearest man, placing it between the VC and the wounded men so as to offer my crew some protection while picking the men up. Gunnery Sergeant Poulson immediately climbed out of the aircraft and helped the nearest man into the aircraft; returning to pick up the second man, Gunnery Sergeant Poulson was unable to move him due to his large size.

Lance Corporal Phelps was told he could leave his machine gun to

The Marine Corps' UH-1E Huey was a simple, functional aircraft design based on the Army's UH-1B model. The UH-1E was often used for routine transport duty, as shown here. In Vietnam, the UH-1E carried machine guns and rockets, and provided support to troops on the ground.

[U.S. Marine Corps/PHC C. C. Curtis]

aid Poulson. My copilot unstrapped and climbed out to help, also. As Phelps left the aircraft, he handed the wounded man an M60 and told him to cover my left side. As Captain Fairfield exited the right side of the aircraft, he spotted three VC at the rear of the aircraft firing at Poulson and Phelps. Using an M60, he killed the VC, then ran to assist in getting the wounded aboard.

During the rescue, I could see rounds spraying sand around the aircraft and splashing in the water. Although seriously injured, the wounded man had cradled the M60 in his lap, was leaning against the copilot's seat, and was firing at VC who were attempting to close in on the left side of the aircraft. As my crew was dragging the third man into the aircraft, I could see that Fairfield and Phelps were alternately dragging the man and firing their pistols at the VC, who were now within a few feet of the aircraft.

I then noticed that one of the UH-1s had joined us and was making strafing runs around us. Captain Fairfield told me that the fourth man appeared to have his throat cut and was quite dead.

At this point, a Vietnamese air force UH-34 landed next to me. Since I knew he would pick up the dead man, I departed to get to a medical facility. The VC were still firing at us with automatic weapons, and the only route of departure was over the water. I knew that I was well over the maximum payload for the aircraft; I also thought we had been hit, but had no idea as to the extent of damages. The gauges were all normal, so I could only pray that she was okay.

When I first lifted, it appeared that I had overcommitted myself. After about a mile of straightaway and bouncing off the waves four times, I finally started picking up airspeed and building my revolutions per minute, or rpm, back up. I jettisoned my rocket pods and told the crew to throw anything else over the side to lighten the load so we could get more airspeed. During the trip, Lance Corporal Phelps, aided by Gunnery Sergeant Poulson, continued to render first aid to the two most critically wounded men, undoubtedly accounting for the fact that both men were still alive when we reached the First Hospital Company.

JOHN G. "GORDO" PHELPS Let's back up to when we were approaching the area where those men were fighting for survival on the beach. Captain Pless asked our crew, "You all with me?" He knew the answer would be yes. As we approached, we saw four U.S. personnel lying on the beach, and around them not less than 40 or 50 armed Viet Cong. The VC were beating the helpless personnel. As we flew over the group of people, one of the men lying on the beach waved to us, and for his efforts got a rifle butt in the face. The VC were too close to the Americans for us to safely fire at them, but the VC were killing them anyway, so Pless ordered the right door gunner, Gunnery Sergeant Poulson, to fire on the VC. It took only a short burst to send the VC running for cover.

I'll return to that fight on the beach in just a moment, but first a few words about how I got there. I was a crew chief, and the crew chief is often the member of the Marine Air team who doesn't get mentioned in the headlines.

I was born in 1947 in Kentucky. My dad was in the Navy on a minesweeper in World War II. I planned to join the Navy because my father, uncles, and everybody were in the Navy. But when I was a teenager, Marine recruiters came to the high school. When I was 16, an 18-year-old I knew got a draft notice, so we went together to the Navy recruiter. The recruiter told me I was too young. Right across the hall was the Marine recruiter. He took us out to lunch and within weeks had my buddy signed up. I was going to be 17 in two months, so he wanted me to take the entrance exam. Just two weeks after I turned 17, I was in training down at Parris Island. I started boot camp in February 1964.

We had heard of Vietnam, but at that time we were sending only advisors; it was a real small war. I was hoping I would have a chance to get over there, as crazy as that seems today. Boot camp was 12 weeks followed by five weeks of combat training. I was in Platoon 121 in the old buildings that had been there since the 1940s, right by the swamp. There was a row of old white barracks just behind the parade ground and that was where we were. The recruiter told me that if I had a high enough score on my military entrance exam, I would be able to go into aviation. That required a medium-to-high score. Those with higher scores got electronic jobs. I was definitely interested in aviation.

I went to Millington near Memphis for jet school. I wanted to fly and worked real hard in jet school, and then I got into helicopter training. I finished training in late 1964, and in early 1965, I went to New River, North Carolina, working on H-34s. They didn't have very many gas-turbine helicopters in the Marine Corps. I volunteered for a med cruise on the USS *Fort Mandan* (LSD 21) dock landing ship. We could launch eight helicopters at a time from that ship. We had about 60 Marines on the ship, including pilots. We participated in a couple of big NATO operations, one of which was called Operation Steel Spike I, which involved amphibious landings at Sicily and Italy. We spent two weeks at Malta and were in a barracks with Royal Marines. There was extreme partying in that situation, including seeing who could drink the most. Their barracks were like an 18th-century building. One memory that sticks in my mind is flying over Mount Vesuvius. When I was on

This is a Marine UH-1E Huey on a routine flight.

[Thomas N. Bland, Jr.]

liberty, I took a side trip and visited Pompei. For an 18-year-old Kentucky boy that had never been anywhere, that was quite a sight. We were out on that cruise for six or seven months. As soon as I came back, I started looking for some kind of overseas assignment. I hadn't made crew chief yet; I was just a second mechanic in an H-34.

When we got back to New River, the buzz was everybody was going to Vietnam. I was really excited. I wanted to go over. In early 1966, a buddy of mine was in the club, crying in his beer about having orders to Vietnam. He had just bought himself a new double-wide trailer and didn't want to go anywhere. I said, "You lucky bastard!" He said, "Hey, you want to go to Vietnam?" I said, "Hell, yes." So we cooked up this idea that we would go and talk to the Top. The Top said, "I don't care who goes. I need a body. I want somebody to go to Vietnam." I wanted to go. It sounds crazy now. The idea we had was this Vietnam thing was going to be over in a few months, and I thought, "If I don't get there soon, I will never see combat."

I went to Pendleton for jungle refresher training. Then they sent me to Okinawa to get caught up on my shots, records, and such, and then they sent me to Vietnam. I had the idea that the moment we arrived and stepped off the aircraft, we would come under fire. But we flew an old piston aircraft, and I kept looking out of this little bitty window where oil was dripping from the cowling of the engines. We landed at Da Nang. Nobody was firing at us.

I don't think I ever saw a UH-1E until I got to Vietnam. My orders said I would be working on H-34s. They put me in an old Vietnamese piston plane and flew me into Chu Lai, and then I had to walk five miles into Ky Ha. On this walk, I passed a flight line of bright, shiny new Hueys with rocket pods hanging underneath, the first time I had ever seen them. I almost got a woody from looking at them. I thought, "Oh, man, would I like to work on them." I arrived at Ky Ha and said I was a gas-turbine mechanic and shouldn't be working on piston H-34s. So the guy there shrugged and said, "I guess you're right. I'm assigning you to squadron VMO-6." That was the one Marine UH-1E Huey squadron at the time and I was so elated. I just wanted to jump up and down, but I tried not to show them how happy I was because I felt I'd bullshitted my way into that squadron.

I was assigned to VMO-6 in about April 1966. I spent 19 months in Vietnam and came back in December 1967. The Pless Medal of Honor mission was August 19, 1967.

Any time a new, low-enlisted man checks in, he gets all the shit details at first, so I did perimeter guard for a while and got honey bucket detail. That meant emptying the 55-gallon drums used in the outhouses. After this, I became a door gunner and later got my own aircraft and became a crew chief. As a new crew chief, they put me on a "slick" before I was crew chief on a gunship. I became a crew chief in July. I got the Pless aircraft in the spring of 1967. I eventually flew 1,000 combat missions.

Captain Pless—I always call him "captain" because that's what he was when I knew him, though he later became a major—had a rapport with me. He would come down and socialize with us in the enlisted quarters. He was a mustang. He had been in enlisted service before he became an officer, so he kind of identified with us. We would talk about our families. We flew a lot of SOG missions taking Special Forces over into Laos. We were kind of sworn to secrecy. A lot of times the pilots didn't file after-action reports because the Laos operation was kind of secret.

Now, back to those Americans stranded on the beach and being overrun by the Viet Cong until our fire drove the VC back. Before setting down on the beach, Pless pointed the guns of the aircraft into the 'ville and fired off the remaining ammo.

In landing, Captain Pless put the aircraft between the wounded men and the VC. The way he had landed put me facing the VC; I started firing my M60, while the gunner, being on the side next to the wounded, jumped out and ran to the men. Picking up the first man who was the closest, he helped him into the aircraft; this man was still conscious and didn't seem to be in bad shape. Then the gunner, Poulson, ran to the next man, tried to pick him up, but found that the man was far too heavy to carry by himself. The copilot and I, seeing this, jumped from the aircraft and started to run over to Poulson to help him. When several VC, who were out of my line of fire, came running down the beach, Captain Fairfield pulled the other door gun off its mount and fired at the VC, killing all with this first short burst. At this time, Fairfield told me to return to the airplane to provide covering fire.

Then more VC came running at the aircraft from the 'ville, shooting as they came. I fired until they all lay on the sand. Some of the VC were still shooting at the plane; I couldn't see them, but I could see the sand kicking up all around the plane. I kept my gun going, firing in the tree line and under bushes at the end of the beach. About this time, the copilot and gunner came back to the plane with the second man, and then went back for the third. Captain Pless, seeing that the third man was far too much for Fairfield and Poulson to handle, told me to go out and help them.

I gave my gun to the one wounded man who was still conscious and asked him if he thought he could use it; he said, "Yes," so I jumped out and ran to the other men. The three of us could move the last man, and we were about 20 feet from the aircraft when a lone VC with a hand grenade of some kind came running from behind the plane. I let go of the wounded man and drew my pistol, firing all six rounds into the VC. He was only about 10 or 15 feet away, so I knew I was hitting him. We got the last man into the aircraft and started to take off, but the plane

This close-up portrait of a UH-1E Huey, taken stateside, shows the general configuration of the helicopter used with great success by Marines in Vietnam.

[Robert F. Dorr]

was so heavy that we could hardly get it off the ground. We had to take off over the water because we were taking so much fire. One Army gun bird, a UH-1 like ours, tried to suppress the fire and give us cover. After a few frightening moments, we lifted off. On our way to the First Hospital Company, we rendered first aid to the wounded men. We then returned to Ky Ha.

What Happened

Pless separated enemy and U.S. troops by landing his Huey between them, with both only a little more than arm's length from the helicopter.

The moment Pless had the Huey's skids on the ground, copilot Fairfield and gunners Poulson and Phelps found themselves eyeball to eyeball with the enemy.

An official citation describes how Pless's crew pulled off the mission: "During the rescue the enemy directed intense fire at the helicopter and rushed the aircraft again and again, closing to within a few feet before being beaten back. When the wounded men were aboard, Pless maneuvered the helicopter out to sea. Before it became safely airborne, the overloaded aircraft settled four times into the water. Displaying superb airmanship, he finally got the helicopter aloft. Pless's extraordinary heroism coupled with his outstanding flying skill prevented the annihilation of the tiny force."

"As crew chief of the aircraft, and knowing its capabilities, I couldn't believe what Captain Pless was making the UH-1E do," said Phelps. "When the smoke started to clear, I saw enemy bodies everywhere."

For Phelps, now 57 and living in Louisville, Kentucky, that rescue mission on the beach was "typical of the way we fought," but only one of a thousand aerial sorties—inserting special-operations troops, spotting targets, and pulling friendlies out of tight places. Phelps gives much of the credit for success to pilot Pless, and some to the capabilities of the UH-1E Huey helicopter.

President Lyndon B. Johnson awarded the Medal of Honor to Pless in a White House ceremony in 1969. Pless lost his life in a motorcycle mishap later that year.

This UH-1E crew is the most decorated aircrew in U.S. history. As for their helicopter, UH-1E bureau number 154760 is part of the Marine Corps's museum holdings at Quantico, Virginia, and will be displayed at the National Museum of the Marine Corps.

STEPHEN W. PLESS On Sunday, August 20th, I was informed that my gun and rocket runs had left 20 confirmed-killed VC on the beach, with an additional 38 estimated killed. I also learned that a round had severed the tail-rotor driveshaft and an engine oil line, which should have caused the aircraft to crash during the trip home.

JOHN G. "GORDO" PHELPS In one of his last acts as president, on January 16, 1969, Lyndon B. Johnson held a ceremony at the White House

Corporal John Gordon Phelps leans on the nose of UH-1E Huey bureau number 154760 of squadron VMO-6, the aircraft that carried the most decorated crew in Marine Corps history. The location is Ky Ha, South Vietnam, in about September 1967, a month after the Stephen Pless Medal of Honor mission.

[J. G. Phelps]

in which he pinned the Medal of Honor on several recipients, including Steve Pless, and the rest of us were invited. I was nervous in the presence of the president of the United States, especially when he treated us like VIPs. At one point in the ceremony, I was trying not to need to clear my throat, but I couldn't prevent it: I coughed. On the movie film of the award ceremony, you can hear me coughing.

There were four men given the nation's highest award that day: Navy Lt. Clyde E. Lassen, Pless, Air Force Lt. Col. Joe M. Jackson, and Army S.Sgt. Drew Dix.

Fairfield, Poulson, and I were awarded the Navy Cross, which means that altogether ours was the most decorated aircrew from any service branch in U.S. history. I was out of the service by then. They tried to get in touch with me. They wanted to invite me to Camp Lejeune for a big medal ceremony. They couldn't get in touch with me. So when they finally found me, they organized a ceremony in my hometown of Louisville, Kentucky. It was kind of a low-key event.

The whole crew was invited to Washington. We spent a week there. President Johnson's two daughters gave us a guided tour of the White

House. On the second night, we had a big banquet where our old commanding officer, Major Mahoney, appeared.

MARK AUSTIN BYRD Stephen W. Pless was the first and only Marine aviator to receive the Medal of Honor for his service in Vietnam.

There were other "firsts" in Stephen Pless's short life. Something in his character drove him to always strive for excellence in whatever he did. Something led him to enter flight school right out of Marine boot camp, and then to become the youngest aviator in the Marines. When promoted to major, he became the youngest major in the Marines.

Pless was not the first pilot to arrive over the beach where four U.S. Army soldiers were stranded alone and under fierce attack by dozens of VC. Several U.S. Army helicopters had arrived a little earlier, but Pless was the first to take direct action to stop the enemy's assault on the trapped men. If Pless had delayed acting, even for a few seconds, the stranded men would have been killed or dragged away into captivity.

Pless, who survived 780 combat missions in Vietnam, was killed July 20, 1969, when his motorcycle plunged off an open drawbridge into Santa Rosa Sound, which separates Pensacola from Pensacola Beach, Florida.

As a Vietnam helicopter pilot myself, I spent a lot of time and effort researching Pless's story. His official biography tells of a young man who was going places. Pless was born in 1939, in Georgia. He graduated from Georgia Military Academy, College Park, Georgia, in 1957, by which time he had already enlisted in the Marine Corps Reserve. He served with the First Motor Transport Battalion, Atlanta, Georgia, and received recruit training and advanced combat training at Parris Island, South Carolina, graduating in October 1957. He then served as an artillery surveyor until September 1958.

While attending flight training at Pensacola, he was commissioned as a Marine Corps second lieutenant on September 16, 1959. He was promoted to first lieutenant on March 16, 1960, and designated a naval aviator upon graduation from flight training on April 20, 1960. Pless

Who's Who

Capt. (later Maj.) Stephen W. Pless, pilot of the UH-1E Huey, call sign CHERRY 6

Capt. Rupert E. Fairchild, copilot of UH-1E, CHERRY 6

Gunnery Sgt. Leroy N. Poulson, gunner aboard UH-1E, CHERRY 6

Lance Cpl. (later Cpl.) John G. "Gordo" Phelps, crew chief of UH-1E, CHERRY 6

1st Lt. Mark Austin Byrd, a UH-1E pilot in Vietnam

Army S.Sgt. Lawrence H. Allen, one of four soldiers who deplaned from an Army CH-47 Chinook on the at Quang Ngai

then served successively as squadron pilot with squadron HMR (L)-262 at New River, with HMR (L)-264 at sea, and again with HMR (L)-262 at New River. He was squadron adjutant in squadron HMM-162 at New River.

Ordered to the Far East in June 1962, Pless saw duty with squadron HMM-162 in Thailand and Vietnam. He subsequently served as a flight instructor at Pensacola and was promoted to captain on July 1, 1964.

In August 1966, Pless began duties at Chu Lai, Vietnam. In addition to the Medal of Honor, he received the Silver Star and numerous other awards while serving with squadron VMO-6. He had returned to a new assignment at Pensacola at the time of the motorcycle mishap. His wife, Jo Ann Smith, survived Pless, as did three children; a fourth child was born two months after he died.

UH-1E Huey Helicopter

It was probably inevitable that the era's most famous helicopter, introduced to Vietnam by the Army in 1962, would join the Marine Corps in Vietnam as well.

The prototype for the Bell 204 Model UH-1 Iroquois was first flown in 1956 and was designated the XH-40. Later, when it entered service with the U.S. Army in 1959, it was redesignated the HU-1, the source of the Huey nickname. In 1962 the aircraft was again redesignated the UH-1.

The UH-1 was declared the winner of the Marine Corps's Assault Support Helicopter, or ASH, competition on March 3, 1962.

On January 6, 1963, the Marines ordered an initial batch of 76 UH-1E aircraft (of an eventual total of 223), including four test aircraft. In late 1963, the Marine Corps placed a $7 million order for UH-1E helicopters after a demonstration of the Huey's capabilities as a gunship and disappointment with stopgap armed UH-34s. The Marine UH-1E was derived from the U.S. Army's UH-1B. The plan was to replace Cessna O-1B and Kaman OH-43 Huskie aircraft in Marine observation, or VMO, squadrons on a one-to-one basis.

February 1964 marked the delivery of the first UH-1Es to the Marine VMO-1 squadron at New River, North Carolina. The Marines also acquired a few of the Army's UH-1Bs for evaluation.

One of these aircraft was being prepared for flight at Patuxent River, Maryland, when a truck backed into its horizontal stabilizer. There was no time to order a replacement, so the Marines borrowed a horizontal stabilizer from an Army UH-1A at nearby Fort Belvoir, Virginia.

The horizontal stabilizers of the two models were of different size, but the Marines had such confidence in the capabilities of the Huey that after replacement the test pilot, Capt. David A. Spurlock, and aviation boss Col. Marion E. Carl took off and flew the aircraft safely through low clouds and rain to the Pentagon building's helipad.

The helicopter then took a number of Marine officers, including Brig. Gen. Bruno A. Hochmuth, the deputy chief of staff for research and development, for a harrowing demonstration flight, first under the overcast, at treetop level, then on top of the worsening weather and through the cloud bank. Hochmuth, flying in the copilot's seat, was very impressed with the aircraft's performance and maneuverability.

There had been doubts as to the visibility from the Huey's cockpit, but after this and subsequent demonstration flights, no further criticism was uttered.

The UH-1E was externally identical to the UH-1B with that model's shorter fuselage (39 feet, 7½ inches ([12.08 meters] as compared to 41 feet, 10¾ inches ([12.77 meters] for the UH-1H). Its principal difference was the external rescue hoist and a rotor brake system, essential for stopping the blades turning on the crowded deck of an assault ship and for preventing them from moving in the wind when the vessel was underway.

The brake was a simple enough disc brake system fitted to the main transmission shaft and hydraulically hand activated from the cockpit. Radios compatible with air and ground forces' channels also were installed, together with a wiring change from Army direct current (DC) type to Navy–Marine Corps alternating current (AC) type.

The UH-1E also differed from the UH-1B in having an aluminum fuselage and additional saltwater corrosion protection. It was the first turbine-powered helicopter to enter service with the Fleet Marine Force, or FMF.

The Huey was soon to be at the center of a controversy over doctrine within the Corps regarding armed helicopters.

The issue was brought to a head by unique limitations imposed in prosecuting the war in Vietnam. It included the increased success of the Viet Cong, the VC, in shooting up unescorted transport helicopters in "hot" landing zones, and the increasing reliance of Marines on armed Army helicopters as escorts.

As the fighting in Vietnam intensified, VMO-2 was deployed to the Da Nang area from Okinawa as part of the Ninth Marine Expeditionary Brigade. Immediately after arriving there in May 1965, the squadron received six UH-1Es. The arrival of these helicopters inaugurated VMO-2's active participation in the war in Vietnam.

The first major operation in which the squadron participated was Operation Starlight in August 1965. In this engagement, VMO-2 rendered support to Regimental Landing Team RLT-7. Over 600 Viet Cong were killed and 125 captured in the battle.

In order to control costs, Bell had built the initial order of the Huey exactly like the Army UH-1Bs except for changes specified by the Corps. As a result, all the features required to fully arm the Army version were built into the Marine UH-1Es. Thus, once a decision to use the Huey for armed helicopter support was made, this cost control measure greatly expedited the conversion of a portion of the Huey fleet into gunships.

The Marine Corps started looking at the development of "ground-fire suppression armament kits" for the UH-1E. This job went to the squadron HMX-1 at Quantico, Virginia. They had experience developing and fabricating the TK-1 armament kits for use on CH-34s.

Bell UH-1E Iroquois (Huey)

Type: 4-place military utility/transport, general-purpose helicopter

Power plant: one 1,400-shp (1044-kW) Avco Lycoming T53-L-5, L-11, or L-13 turboshaft engine driving a 2-blade 48-ft 0-in (14.63-m) main rotor

Performance: maximum speed, 127 mph (204 km/h); hovering ceiling in ground effect, 13,600 ft (4145 m); service ceiling, 12,600 ft (3840 m); rate of climb at sea level, 2,350 ft (715 m) per minute; range with maximum fuel at sea level, 318 mi (511 km)

Weights: empty, 4,717 lb (2140 kg); normal takeoff weight, 9,039 lb (4100 kg); maximum takeoff weight, 9,500 lb (4309 kg)

Dimensions: main rotor diameter, 48 ft (14.63 m); length overall, rotors turning, 39 ft 7½ in (12.08 m); fuselage length, 44 ft 7 in (13.59 m); height, tail rotor turning, 14 ft 5½ in; tail rotor diameter, 8 ft 6 in (2.59 m); main rotor disc area, 1,809 sq ft (168.06 sq m)

Armament: TK-2 armament kit with two .30-cal (7.62-mm) M60C machine guns and a bomb rack for a 2.75-in rocket pod on each side of the fuselage. Two door-mounted M60 7.62-mm machine guns, one per side. In addition, some aircraft also had the Emerson Electric TAT-101 nose turret with 2 M60C machine guns with 1,000 rounds per gun.

Payload: 8 to 12 armed troops or 4 hospital litters

Crew: 2 pilots plus crew chief and gunner

First flight: April 1960 (HU-1B); February 1963 (UH-1E)

Three kit designs were developed and evaluated. The design that was finally accepted was very much like the TK-1 kits used on the CH-34 and utilized existing UH-1E hard points for mounting.

Many different cockpit gunsight designs were evaluated for use with the new TK-2 armament kits. The one that was used was a simple flip-down ring and post sight that was inexpensive to fabricate, easy to use, and flipped up out of the way when not in use. The pilot would simply align the crosshairs in the ring-sight aperture with etched marks on the windscreen and put that on the intended target.

In late 1965 the "Model 540" rotor system was introduced to the UH-1E, along with some other design improvements. These changes derived from the Army's UH-1C "gunship optimized" variant. Some of the other improvements included in the Model 540 package were a larger fuel cell (noted by the left-side fuel cap), duel hydraulic control systems to handle the larger rotor blade system, asymmetric horizontal stabilizers, and redesigned canted vertical tail pylon. These 204/540 models were the first Hueys specifically designed for Marine gunship use. The same 540 rotor system was later used on the AH-1G Cobras, without the dampers and stabilizer bar.

Even though two additional Marine VMO gunship squadrons were eventually deployed to Vietnam, there were never sufficient Marine gunships in South Vietnam to fulfill all the missions requested of them. Medevac escort, recon, and special-operations-team inserts and extractions, assault operations, direct fire support of engaged Marine ground units, and convoy escort, as well as other missions flying Huey "slicks" had VMO aircrews overcommitted throughout their entire tours.

If ever the Marine Corps got its money's worth out of any aircraft and aircrews, it was with the UH-1E Huey.

Chapter Fifteen

Skyhawks Versus the Viet Cong (II)

MICHAEL SANDLIN We were on the hot pad at Chu Lai. The squadron always kept four Skyhawks on alert, ready to launch. During times of intense activity, we even stayed on alert near the runway's end, with engines running. On this particular day we were called to support an Army of the Republic of Vietnam (ARVN); i.e., South Vietnamese regiment that was in trouble to the south of us. Ninety-nine percent of our missions were to the north of Chu Lai, but this one was south.

I was a section leader of two A-4E Skyhawks. We called the E model the "super" because it had something done to the engine that created more thrust. The other pilot in the section was Capt. Wally Bishop, a descendant of the Bishop cosmetic fortune out of Chicago. There's a myth that Vietnam was a war fought by lower-class minorities who were drafted, but many who fought were volunteers, white, and middle class.

That includes me. I was born in 1942 in California. I lived in Southern California most of my youth. My father served briefly in the Army Signal Corps at the end of World War II. My brother Steve, who is two years my senior, served as an officer in the Air Force between 1962 and

Capt. Michael Sandlin
May 27, 1969
Douglas A-4E Skyhawk
(bureau no. 150091)
HELLBORN 555
Marine Attack Squadron
VMA-311, "Tomcats"
Chu Lai, South Vietnam

Capt. Michael Sandlin, an A-4E Skyhawk, and a load of "Snake and Nape." That's shorthand for four Mark 83 500-pound Snakeye retarded bombs with high-drag tail assembly and two 500-pound napalm canisters. "This combination was used for 'troops in contact' where we had to drop within 100 meters of friendlies," said Sandlin. "Our normal release point was 500 feet altitude at 450 knots." The location is Chu Lai, South Vietnam, which was home base for Marine Skyhawk operations.

[Michael Sandlin]

1966. My younger brother Jeff lost his life in a motorcycle accident in 1969 at age 19.

I married Mary Dawn Scott in 1962; we have four grown children and 13 grandchildren. After attending several schools, one on a football scholarship, I received a bachelor's degree in psychology from San Diego State College in 1964.

I entered Marine Corps officers' candidate school, or OCS, at Quantico, Virginia, in fall 1964. I was encouraged to become a Marine officer by my uncle by marriage, Col. Henry Morgan, a Silver Star recipient at Iwo Jima. I had attempted to enlist in 1959, but was persuaded to attend college first. I did not enter the Marine Corps because of the Vietnam War. In 1964, the war was very low key, and U.S. involvement was not well publicized.

Marine Training

I joined the Marine Corps because I believed, and still do, that becoming a Marine officer is something very special and that not all could achieve that status. I was not ready to sit at a desk and start a career at 21. Being accepted to OCS was the highlight of my life. Becoming a naval aviator as a Marine officer was somewhat of an afterthought. I took the tests, scored high, and was encouraged by my OSO, Captain McManaway, to apply for aviation. I graduated as a second lieutenant in fall 1964 and went directly to flight training at Pensacola, Florida.

I entered ground school at Pensacola NAS in January 1965. Ground school was the first step to becoming a naval aviator. Boy, it was tough. At least 10 percent of those selected for training failed ground school. Eight hours a day for 16 weeks we studied engines, airframes, aerodynamics, meteorology, navigation, aviation safety, Morse code (still used for navigation then), aviation communications, instruments, and so on. It was a graduate course in aviation.

We also had to go to the "pool." Every naval aviator had to go through extensive safety and survival training, which included hours in the swimming pool. We were tested on our ability to swim, tread water, save another downed pilot, get into a life raft, and be picked up by a helo rescue team, and, of course, the "Dilbert dunker."

The Dilbert dunker was a contraption on a set of rails that sat at the edge of the pool. It was an aircraft cockpit mounted at a 45-degree angle on rails that could be slid into the water to simulate a sea landing. The catch was that at the end of the rails was 12 feet of water. The dunker turned upside down, and while upside down the would-be pilot had to release himself and swim to the surface, unaided. Many failed this test and never made it into primary flight training.

Each day, as we sat in class, we could hear the drone of the T-34B Mentor primary trainer airplanes at Saufley Field, where primary flight training was taking place. We could hear the roar of T-2A Buckeye jet trainers taking off and doing field carrier landing practice (FCLP) at Pensacola. As boring and tedious as ground school seemed, most of us

Squadron VMA-311 spent much of the Vietnam war at Chu Lai, but from time to time its aircraft returned to Iwakuni, Japan, where the 1st Marine Aircraft Wing was headquartered. The author snapped this squadron A-4E Skyhawk at Iwakuni just after the squadron returned permanently from Southeast Asia. Date of the photo is August 30, 1973.

[Robert F. Dorr]

were inspired by what we saw and heard around that three-story classroom building.

Primary flight training at Saufley Field had two phases, classroom work and flight training in the T-34B. The classroom work lasted for six weeks and was primarily focused on the aircraft to be flown during this phase. The basic teaching philosophy of naval aviation was to make the students learn everything they could about the aircraft they were going to fly. So, again, we studied engines, airframes, flight characteristics, and safety.

The T-34 Mentor was a single-engine, prop-driven trainer that was fully acrobatic. Some students made it through with flying colors, but many just couldn't get it. When I soloed on my 12th flight, I discovered my love for flying. It wasn't easy learning to fly. Every flight with an instructor carried with it the potential for getting a "down," failing that flight because of a stupid headwork error, or just plain forgetting what you were supposed to do. Believe me, I had my share of downs during flight training. My 24th and final flight went like clockwork, and upon landing I was presented with my solo certificate. Then the waiting began.

The procedure to move to the next level of training was to add the raw scores from ground school at Pensacola, ground school at Saufley, and actual flight training, which created a cutting score. For Marines, the score determined if one would go to Meridian, Mississippi, for basic jet training or to Whiting Field in Pensacola to T-28s and eventually to helicopter training. I waited two long weeks to see where I would go, and as luck would have it, I was the only Marine available when my number came up and I made it to basic jet training.

McCain Field in Meridian was named for Senator John McCain's father, Admiral John Sidney McCain, Jr., who served in three wars and later commanded our Pacific fleet late in the Vietnam era.

In fact, when I was training in the T-2B Buckeye at Meridian, the future Senator McCain was a flight instructor, having been plowed back from the training command after getting his wings and before becoming a Navy A-4 Skyhawk pilot in Vietnam. I never flew with McCain, as I was in a different training squadron. Again, as at Saufley, ground school preceded flight training. By this time, all of us were beginning to feel like we were real pilots and jet flight training changed most for good. No more props! We were "fighter pilots"! At Meridian, we started to learn how to fly on instruments. In naval aviation, being able to fly on instruments is the most important skill one can develop. Where there is water, there is weather!

After completion of basic jet flight training at Meridian, it was back to Pensacola for air-to-air gunnery and carrier qualification. This was the final phase of primary flight training. No ground school this time as the now-familiar T-2B Buckeye was used for this training cycle. There were hours spent in the classroom analyzing the landing safety officer (LSO's) critique of your FCLPs, as when one goes aboard ship, a small error can be fatal. The day you go aboard ship is when you become a true student naval aviator. The day we went out was exciting, and, believe me, when we hit the "charley" pattern above the ship, my heart started to race. The flight deck looked like a small stamp. Compared to the supercarriers of today, this World War II wooden straight deck carrier, the USS *Lexington* (CVT 16), alias the "Lady Lex," was very small. I hit the boat in a T-2B on January 17, 1966—one bolter (a waved-off landing), two touch-and-goes, and four arrestments.

Jet Pilot

On final, my head repeated "meatball, lineup, angle of attack," the phrase that had been pounded into all of us during our field practice. One touch-and-go, four traps, and four cat-shots and bingo, you've operated an aircraft from a carrier deck, and you've made another step toward getting those "wings of gold"!

At last, I went to advanced flight training. By this time, I had not only a wife, but also two children and a couple of dogs. Off we go to Kingsville, Texas, to learn to fly the TF-9J Cougar, a Korean War vintage aircraft converted into an advanced jet trainer by the Navy. Now it was time to learn how to fly a swept-wing airplane, one that was heavy and underpowered, but what did we know of those things? As far as I knew, the F-9 was one heck of a fighter! At the beginning of this assignment, however, it was once again "no flying" for a while because of ground school, again!

The next six months were hard work and a lot of self-evaluation. Until now, one only knew that he was still a student and hadn't washed out. None of us knew our standings or our grades. Everything was pass or fail. We now faced the most difficult task and the pressure was on. Higher expectations were placed on us because when we finished this phase, we would be naval aviators and had to join the fleet.

The highlight of this phase was going aboard the boat in an aircraft that was similar to the one you would fly after graduation. I was chosen to fly the F-9J, the single-seat version of the trainer where we had spent most of our time. I flew this aircraft out to the carrier on August 23, 1966, for one touch-and-go and three arrestments. Going aboard the *Lady Lex* in this airplane signified that the landing signal officer had the

Marines in Vietnam were ecstatic about the performance of the A-4E Skyhawk—like this one, belonging to squadron VMA-311, the "Tomcats"—because it could carry a huge variety of bombs and rockets.

[Robert F. Dorr]

utmost confidence in your ability, and you were being rewarded for your higher achievement.

I received my wings in August 1966. The ceremony was small and very simple. The Navy commander who was CO of my squadron, VT-21, "Redhawks," pinned my wings on and made this simple statement, "God bless you, and remember, to fly with the eagles in the day, you must not fly with the owls at night. Fly safe, and good luck."

Cherry Point Collision

I was assigned to squadron VMA-332, nicknamed the Hat and Cane squadron, in Cherry Point, North Carolina. My pregnant wife, two kids, and dog arrived at Cherry Point in October 1966 in a brand-new Volkswagen Microbus, as our 1956 Ford station wagon had blown an engine in Mobile, Alaska, on the way from California.

The CO of the squadron was Lt. Col. J. J. Walsh, a kindly post-Korea Marine officer of Irish descent. He was a devout Catholic, but liked his booze a little too much. As the story goes, he was medevacked from Vietnam a year later because of this failing. Our XO, or executive officer, was a laid-back Southern gentleman that later turned in his wings so he didn't have to fly missions in Vietnam. Finally, our ops officer was a hard-nosed career Marine who had balls the size of grapefruits, who ended up transitioning into the CH-46 Sea Knight helicopter and flew a million sorties in Vietnam carrying troops and supplies, constantly under fire but never firing a shot in anger. He did make it home, unlike many of his comrades that flew that crazy machine. By the way, his nickname was Rocky, no relation to the fictitious Rocky Balboa.

The squadron was in disarray, with no standard operating procedures and a handful of Vietnam returnee pilots all looking for flight time so they could get out and go to work for the airlines. Nuggets, or new naval aviators like me, found it very hard to get any significant time in the cockpit due to the incessant hole boring that went on to collect those flight-time hours with the least amount of risk to those behind the controls. My experience at VMA-332 was not exactly a happy one. Why would anybody be happy being in the squadron that was referred to by other Marines as "VMA Stupid"?

During my year and a half at Cherry Point, the Second Marine Aircraft Wing was experiencing the highest accident rate in the Marine Corps. At one time we were having two strike accidents per month between Cherry Point and Beaufort, South Carolina. Marine aviation was totally unprepared to train replacement pilots for Vietnam, having just gone through the reduction in force brought on by the end of the Korean conflict. What I joined was not a squadron but a country club.

In August 1967, on my last flight with VMA-332, I was involved in a spectacular midair collision over the Dismal Swamp. During what should have been a routine brief between a senior captain flight leader and a young, inexperienced wingman, there was a discussion of *hassling,* a word and concept forbidden by naval regulations.

This was the common term used for dogfighting, as coined during World War II. After Korea, the practice of going after another airplane as if in air-to-air combat against an enemy was not condoned by any of the top aviation authorities within the U.S. military aviation community. It wasn't until the Navy started the so-called Top Gun school sometime in 1969 that air combat maneuvering, or ACM, was taught so that our naval pilots were prepared to defend themselves against the Sino-Soviet aviation threat. The Marine Corps started its own version of ACM training in 1969 within the Marine Corps combat-readiness training groups (MCCRTGs) at Yuma, Arizona.

At the time I had my midair, it was strictly forbidden to engage in any form of simulated air combat. It is the old story: "You can't do it unless you have done it," which was a phrase that was spoken many times in Vietnam when we were asked to do things we had never done before, such as taking off on the 1,500-foot Marston matting field with jet-assisted takeoff boosters at night in a monsoon.

When my midair occurred, I had lost sight of my flight leader and had decided to take over the fight as I saw my flight leader overshoot the aircraft we had jumped. Instead of rolling wings level, which is standard operating procedure, when I lost sight of him, I pursued the fight. My flight leader did a high yo-yo to reposition himself in the perch position, unaware of my position; the result was two aircraft in the same airspace at the same time going in different directions! His aircraft went through my fuselage behind my cockpit, taking the tail section of my aircraft off, thus making my airplane a great big heavy falling leaf going 400 knots, spinning like a top.

After the initial contact, my aircraft flipped over lengthwise several times, finally stabilizing in the upright position in what could be described as an upright spin (as opposed to inverted). Since I did not know that I had been hit by another airplane, I began applying opposite rudder and neutral stick to stop the spin. Having no tail, my rudder pedals were ineffective. Still thinking I could get out of the spin with my rudder pedals, I applied them in the opposite direction, again with no effect. By this time the plane had started to roll over on its back, spinning like a giant falling leaf! To add to the confusion, I started to go into a zero G condition. All the dirt and trash that had been dropped into the cracks and crevices of the plane started to float up around my head. I had removed my right-hand glove earlier in the flight, and it floated up against the canopy as I strained to get my composure.

After what seemed to be an eternity, I realized I had to eject. Since I was upside down and being pushed against the canopy, I had few options. I couldn't reach the secondary ejection handle that was on the seat between my legs because of the awkward position I was in. I reached for the face curtain behind my head and only retrieved my errant glove. A second try was made with the help of my left hand and arm. I grabbed my right elbow with the left hand and pushed with all my might to extend my right arm and hand far enough back to reach the handle.

Success this time . . . BANG . . . CRACK . . . the canopy was stripped away, and off I went straight down, upside down! Within 8/10 second I separated from my seat, and I was in my chute, upside down. Within seconds I was swinging back and forth from my parachute canopy like a kid on a park swing going as high as he can go. By this time I was checking to see if I had been injured in the ejection as I was going in excess of 400 knots at the time I exited the aircraft. Nothing seemed to be wrong, except I began to lose my sight.

By the time I had stabilized, I had dropped 10,000 feet. My chute had a panel torn due to the force of the ejection, and I was falling at a faster than normal rate. I looked down to see a small farmhouse, some cleared fields, and a million trees. I heard dogs barking and then I went blank. I was alert, but I could not see! Something during the sequence of events caused my sight to go away. I crossed my legs and arms, said a little prayer, and fell! Fell into the trees! I hit an 80-foot pine and was stopped by a large branch at the 50-foot level. I then fell the last 50 feet as my chute had come down around me in the tree. When I landed, I was still unable to see until I rolled over on my back and lifted my feet into the air. Slowly my vision returned, and once again I heard the barking of dogs, and a large voice yelling, "I'll get you. Don't worry. I'll get you!" I tried to stand up but fell as I had broken my ankle in the fall from the tree and couldn't walk.

Soon the voice became a face, and the face became a huge man in bib overalls, tromping through the recently reclaimed swampland. As I recall, he looked down at all 195 pounds of me with 50 pounds of flight equipment on and said, "I'll carry you to the house!" which is exactly what he did. He picked me up in his arms and away we went, the 100 or so yards to the farmhouse where the pilot from the plane that had hit me was hanging in a tree in the backyard, just hanging there in a sitting position, feet flat on the ground, as if he had come by for a visit and took a seat in a tree swing behind the house.

The rest of the story is Navy/Marine Corps investigations, and so on. Needless to say, that was an exciting chapter in my life. Someone was looking out for me that day! As an aside, my wife was at home with our three children when the CO and chaplain came to tell her that I had been in an accident and that the planes had not been found. Her response was, "Don't worry, he's okay! Would you like a cup of coffee?"

She was right!

So how was one to learn how to dogfight if one couldn't dogfight? My response to this wonderful adventure into the forbidden world of air combat maneuvering was to say nothing and just go along for the ride. How was I to know?

I knew absolutely nothing about ACM, and neither did my flight leader, as it turned out. We lost two airplanes and both of us ejected. The *Aviation Safety Magazine,* which wrote the story on our accident after all the dust had settled, showed a picture with a farmer, ax in hand, holding a turkey over a tree stump. You guessed it, I was the "turkey" and my flight leader was the farmer! Well, he was booted out of the Corps and I was forgiven for being just another stupid nugget.

My orders to Vietnam came quickly after I was cleared to fly again. I expected to go to an air intercept control squadron in Da Nang, but the gods were with me, because an old friend was there.

I forgot to say there was a great Marine in VMA-332 by the name of Don Yelek. Maj. Don Yelek was a C-54 Skymaster transport pilot who had transitioned to the A-4 Skyhawk and sat in the S-4 chair, meaning that he was the logistics officer. During the time I was suspended from flying as a first officer, I flew copilot with Don on C-54 flights to Washington, D.C. When I arrived in Vietnam, Don was the XO of VMA-311, and as Paul Harvey says, "And that is the rest of the story." I owe my career and a debt of gratitude to Don for having trust in my ability as a Marine aviator and mostly knowing I was a good Marine officer. It was largely thanks to him that I was assigned to VMA-311 as an A-4E Skyhawk combat pilot.

Vietnam Combat

My tour in Vietnam was from May 1968 to June 1969, at Chu Lai, South Vietnam, where Marine Air Group 12, or MAG-12, was the parent unit of my squadron, VMA-311. Between World War II and Vietnam, the squadron changed from a "fighter" to an "attack" squadron, and its nickname changed from Hell's Belles to Tomcats.

Altogether, MAG-12 had four A-4 Skyhawk squadrons. The air group operated using a pilot-rotation system called LEAN, which meant "late flight, early flight, alert, and night." The frag to the group came from Seventh Air Force in Saigon. At night, you got a frag order that told you what you would be doing the following day, and then the group ops officer assigned missions to each squadron. In addition to missions assigned in advance by the Air Force, we pulled hot-pad alert. We did a four-day cycle on alert.

The day before a mission, the squadron ops officer assigned you a time to be in the ready room. That way, you knew: "Okay, tomorrow I have a 7:00 a.m. takeoff so I have to be in the ready room at 6:00 a.m." The pilots in the flight went into "the Barrel," a Quonset hut for the briefing from the MAG-12 intelligence officer. You went to the ready room. The flight leader would then give a briefing as to the conduct of the flight—safety, emergency issues, what frequencies would be used. In the ready room, you put on a G suit and torso harness and carried your helmet and mask, which you took from your locker.

Thirty or forty minutes before takeoff, you went to the shack and read the yellow sheets. A yellow sheet was a maintenance form on which

This is a bombed-up VMA-311 Skyhawk in Vietnam.

[U.S. Marine Corps]

we wrote down aircraft discrepancies at the end of a mission. There were two sections to the form. The first was the area where we wrote up the "gripes" and the second was where the maintenance department wrote up their corrective action. Prior to a flight, the outgoing crew would review the aircraft log, which contained the yellow sheets for the previous five flights, plus any for which the maintenance actions were not complete. You looked for trends and for inconclusive maintenance "sign-offs:" for example, "Could not duplicate; ground checks OK." These were indicators of things to watch out for on your flight.

There were some discrepancies that were not considered serious enough to render the aircraft unsafe for flight, and they could be "deferred" to a later time. It was important to know these, however, since it meant that something on the airplane you were about to fly wasn't going to work. Good squadrons set a limit on the number of discrepancies that could be deferred.

You signed off on them and went to the airplane and did a preflight on the airplane. You looked at the leading edge flaps to see if they were working. The plane captain followed you around and made note of things that might need to be fixed. This is different from the Air Force, where the pilot takes the crew chief's word for it. Not in the Marine Corps! We used to joke: the Air Force had a starter power unit for each airplane; we had one starter for all of our planes.

You climbed in and did your prestart and pretaxi checklist. The plane captain climbed up behind you and helped you strap in. There were four attachments. You were in a harness already, and you attached the two chest and abdomen points. You plugged in your own oxygen. You pulled in the two pins from the ejection seat.

It was so hot and muggy in Vietnam you didn't want the oxygen mask on your face until you taxied. First you went through a prestart checklist. You used hand signals with the plane captain. He gave you a thumbs-up to start. Once the airplane was started, you used hand signals to indicate readiness to taxi out.

The flight leader always taxied out first. Our call signs were all HELLBORN. All four A-4 squadrons in the MAG used that call sign. The A-4 was the best support aircraft in Vietnam, and when ground troops heard that call sign, they knew help was coming. If it was a 500-series number, it was an alert aircraft. The alert aircraft was expected to be on target within 20 or 30 minutes. In high-intensity activity, like during the Tet of '69 (I missed '68), we would do a CAP or combat air patrol where we would put two A-4s wet over the ocean on airborne alert, with an air-refueling tanker nearby. We were ready to reach the target in a few minutes.

Ninety-nine percent of our missions were to the north, but my memorable sortie of May 27, 1969, took me south of Chu Lai. This particular mission is one that I was very proud of, and I had no indication that I was going to receive any kind of award for it. Normally the Air Force at Cam Ranh operated in that area but today it was given to us. My A-4E Skyhawk that day was bureau number 150091.

Also at Chu Lai was a squadron of Air Force forward air controllers, or FACs. They flew the push-pull O-2. We were on the hot pad. I was called to take a flight out and go south. We were going to be working with a FAC.

Alert Mission

We were on alert, flight suits on, harnesses on, already briefed on potential targets. As things got hot and heavy, with actions taking place at several locations, we sat at the end of the runway with engines running. That's when we heard that some ARVN were being overrun.

We launched. We used color nicknames—red, blue, purple—for the buttons that controlled the frequencies on our radios. So in shorthand, the air control center would say something like, "Two, go button purple," and we would know how to set the radio.

On this day, our target was in a flat valley surrounded by peaks with low clouds and deteriorating weather. By "deteriorating," I mean that the low cloud cover was getting far lower, giving us less space to maneuver in. The FAC, an Air Force O-2, call sign HELIX 23, was barely able to fly in the limited space between the valley floor and the clouds, but it was going to be a lot harder for us in our fast-mover A-4Es.

Bishop and I arrived at the target area at about 10,000 feet. My wingman was in the combat trail position, meaning a diagonal distance of a mile away from me off to the right and to the aft, so that he had a view of both the target area and of my aircraft. I couldn't see him so it was his responsibility to maintain formation and keep his eyes on the situation while we talked with the FAC and tried to find a way to support those besieged ARVN down there.

"We're at angels one zero three minutes from your location," I called to the FAC, who was orbiting above the ARVN on the ground. The FAC had the top of its wings painted white, so I could see him clearly. "We have a regular Viet unit that has been surrounded in an amtrack," the FAC told me. "They've had three people killed."

We got into a racetrack pattern over the target, counterclockwise. I could see the small airplane, the Air Force O-2. Seeing what was happening on the ground was another proposition, which was why we needed the FAC. We began circling over the target, but if we were higher than about 1,500 feet, it was very hard to tell what was what on the ground because people, equipment, and items all blended together. The FAC was saying, "There are three amtracks. They're surrounded and in danger of being overrun." We were in the racetrack setting up to do our run in.

Once the flight leader has established the pattern, you locate the wingman (the "dash two") and stay on the radio with him. You go around the pattern, talking to the controller. We were carrying four 500-pound Snakeye high-drag bombs and two cans of napalm, plus 20-millimeter ammunition for the gun. That's what we call "Snake and nape," plus "twenty mike-mike." The FAC said, "What's your ordnance?" We said, "Snake and nape. Twenty mike-mike." The critical thing about the A-4E is it's so small you can get in close to the ground even with closing weather above you and maneuver, so despite the difficulty of the situation, I felt we could get in and do our job. I called it "wing in the clouds" because you could actually be right under the weather, so close that you would literally have one of your wings poking into the clouds. I have worked under overcast as low as 800 feet. Today it looked like we were heading for exactly that condition.

So this is me, call sign HELLBORN 555, talking to HELIX 23. We're communicating on what separation we would use for our two A-4Es. As flight leader, I decide the level of the downwind pattern. In this case, I find we're able to operate in a downwind pattern at about 1,500 feet. That's still pretty low, with those peaks around. Of course, we go lower when we're making a pass on the besieged amtracks and trying to get the enemy off their backs.

Who's Who

Capt. Michael Sandlin, A-4E Skyhawk pilot, squadron VMA-311

Close Air Support

It's not unusual to get shot at when you're in the pattern to strafe and bomb the bad guys. What is unusual this time is we get shot at not only in the pattern but when we're going around as well. When HELIX 23 keys his mike, you can hear the antiaircraft fire being directed at you.

When you do snake and nape, you do a technique called glide bombing. You approach at 10 degrees instead of 45 degrees when dive-bombing. You roll in at 10 degrees angle to the earth. The distance to the target is dependent on the tightness of your pattern, the angle, and your altitude. The release point is 500 feet above ground level while traveling at a speed of 450 knots in a 10-degree dive angle. The mil deflection is very high because of the dive angle. You need to have a very high mil deflection on your bombsight. We used to always say that "as long as you're there and you have the pipper on the target adjusted for wind direction, you're going to hit that target no matter what process you used to get there." You do a lot of this hard bombing based on your "feel" for the situation based on practice, practice, and practice. Some people never quite get the hang of it because a lot of it is instinct as well as understanding of the capabilities of your airplane.

You don't arm your ordnance until you're on the target and you're told what you're going to do. You're flying downwind at 400 knots at 500 feet, putting four Gs in an airplane being shot at by the enemy, and you know you have to pull out or you'll hit the ground. People get in the middle of all this and forget to turn on the master arm switch. You announce your arrival by saying, "Dash one is in." When the air controller says, "Dash one, you are cleared hot," that's when you put the master arm switch on. The FAC is sitting there in harm's way watching you and telling you if you're going the right way to hit the target.

There are five switches: centerline plus two wing stations. You're going downwind. The FAC says, "On this next run, I want you to drop napalm. Watch my smoke." He fires a Willy Peter. That's a white phosphorus smoke rocket used as a marker. You're going downwind. The FAC gives you instructions: "Hit 30 meters off my smoke at 090 degrees." Let's say you have napalm hanging from your number one py-lon. You turn on the arm switch for pylon one while the master arm is still off. FAC won't give you the authority to drop until you are actually in his sight during your run in. A lot of guys turn on the master arm switch before that, which runs the risk you could release the ordnance while you're still proceeding downwind.

When you're being shot at with small arms, you can't see the rounds coming at you. When it's heavier-caliber stuff, every tenth round is a tracer round. Every tenth .50-caliber round looks like a beer can coming at you. You have to avoid flying through that. It's like flying through a steel net because there are nine other rounds between every one of those beer cans. On this mission there was a hell of a lot of small arms fire while we worked our way into the valley and bombed the enemy swarm-ing over those ARVN amtracks.

It was during this low-level work in the bombing pattern that I got hit. A small arms round went into the wing root on the left side of my aircraft. This is the side on which, normally, you roll in, so you're espe-cially vulnerable there.

I received the Distinguished Flying Cross for that mission in the val-ley, plus the satisfaction of knowing that we saved the lives of friendlies. This was by no means all that remarkable: I flew 43 missions that month alone.

I'm very proud of my squadron. VMA-311 logged 54,625 combat sorties and dropped 105,000 tons of ordnance before its final mission on January 29, 1973.

Douglas A-4E Skyhawk

The long-nosed A-4E Skyhawk, originally called the A4D-5, was the most advanced version of the plane flown by Marines in Vietnam. With a new engine, a different nose shape, and improved navigation and bombing gear, the A-4E, or "Echo," resulted from the Navy's discovery

These are A-4E Skyhawks of squadron VMA-311 in flight in 1964, before the squadron went to Vietnam.

[U.S. Marine Corps]

that it had focused too intently on the nuclear mission. Both the Navy and Marine Corps learned from the Lebanon crisis of 1958 that they needed a light attack aircraft optimized for close air support. The A-4E had about 30 percent newer features not found on the A-4C, including the Pratt & Whitney J52 engine which was lighter, more fuel efficient, and more powerful than the Wright J65. The J52 was also considered to have potential for growth, unlike the J65. Most important, the A-4E had five ordnance stations compared to three for the A-4C.

Marines already loved the Skyhawk. Its cockpit was a cramped fit, something that didn't change with the A-4E, but Marines loved the "Echo" model even more because it was sturdier and better able to bring them home with battle damage. And no one loved the A-4E more than Maj. Robert E. Loftus of VMA-311, who was pressing a low-level attack on January 23, 1968, when his "Echo" was raked with small arms fire. Too far from the coast or from Chu Lai to seek safety there, Loftus nursed his Skyhawk to the Marine combat base at Khe Sanh and ejected over the base. The Skyhawk, which had traveled far enough to save his

Douglas A-4E Skyhawk (A4D-5)

Type: single-seat attack aircraft

Power plant: 1 Pratt & Whitney J52-P-6A or -6B twin-spool turbojet engine rated at 8,500-lb (3855-kg) thrust (8-A) or 9,300-lb (4218-kg) thrust

Performance: maximum speed in clean condition, 674 mph (1084 km/h) at sea level; maximum speed carrying a 4,000-lb (1814-kg) bombload, 631 mph (1015 km/h) at sea level; initial rate of climb, 8,750 ft (2710 m) per minute; tactical radius carrying a 4,000-lb (1814-kg) bombload, 610 mi (988 km); range, 1,400 mi (2270 km)

Weights: empty, 9,853 lb (4469 kg); maximum takeoff weight, 24,500 lb (11112 kg)

Dimensions: wing span, 27 ft 6 in (8.38 m); length, 41 ft 3 in (12.58 m); height, 15 ft (4.57 m); wing area, 260 sq ft (24.16 sq m)

Armament: two 20-mm Mark 12 cannons, each with 200 rounds per gun; 5 ordnance stations (1 centerline, 4 wing) for typically 4,000-lb (1814-kg) bombload

Crew: 1 pilot

First flight: June 22, 1954 (XA4D-1); July 12, 1961 (A4D-5/A-4E)

---

life, vanished beneath jungle foliage, and Loftus landed in Khe Sanh's perimeter wire, where his parachute shroud lines became entangled in the barbed wire. A Marine infantry lieutenant and several platoon members extricated Loftus, who abruptly proclaimed: "Lieutenant, if you weren't so damned ugly, I'd kiss you."

Chapter Sixteen

Flight of the Intruder

JIM HENSHAW We had a plane that some Marines called the Big Ugly, but in Vietnam it was the only plane that could fight at night, and it was decades ahead of its time. The airplane was developed during the middle 1950s using lessons from the Korean War about the need to attack targets in bad weather and at night.

The Grumman Iron Works put the thing together with very prescient technology, including one of the first full computer systems ever installed on a tactical airplane. They had an inertial navigation and weapons system that actually used the computer to release the bombs and hit the target. When it all worked, it did that very well.

The airplane looked like a tadpole, or maybe like a flying fish: it had a side-by-side cockpit with a big dumbo nose with a radome that covered the search radar. The plane's center of gravity was fairly well forward so the wings were, too, which gave it a very long tail and made for a striking-looking airplane. It was also strikingly a great airplane to fly. As for that term Big Ugly, we always took that as a badge of honor.

In the early days, though, it wasn't an easy airplane to learn. The Navy had them and had training squadrons, but in the early days the

**Capt. Jim Henshaw
December 1969
Grumman A-6A Intruder
RINGNECK 6521
Marine All-Weather Attack
   Squadron VMA (AW)-225,
   "Vikings"
Da Nang, South Vietnam**

Capt. Jim Henshaw at Da Nang Air
Base, South Vietnam, Easter 1969.
Henshaw, who later retired as a col-
onel, wears the Marine fatigue uni-
form and poses next to a 500-lb.
Mark 83 general-purpose bomb on
which someone has written SCREW
COMMUNISM. The aircraft is an
A-6A Intruder, which typically car-
ried 28 of these bombs on a
Vietnam mission.

[Jim Henshaw]

Marines trained pilots on a kind of "catch as catch can" basis. The Marine Corps was always tail end Charlie in the A-6 Intruder program. The
two Navy training squadrons had been up and operating for a spell before the Marines had one. And in the early days, we didn't have a decent
simulator to train pilots and bombardier-navigators.

When the Marine Corps set up its very first A-6 squadron, which
was VMA (AW)-242, all instructors went through the Navy training
squadron at Oceana, Virginia. And then, when they set up the second
squadron, the -242 guys trained the VMA (AW)-533 guys—if you could
call it training. That was after the time I came down the road, when operational A-6As were on the flight line at Cherry Point, North Carolina,
but "instructor" was anybody who was ten pages ahead of you in the
handbook. There was no training squadron. There was no real simulator. It was "by guess and by golly" if you wanted to fly the A-6A. I went
in one day and saw my name on the flight schedule. A major came over
from another squadron and put me in the right seat normally occupied
by the bombardier-navigator, and we went for a flight. We landed and

traded seats, and he sat over there and coached me through a few landings, slow flight, and a couple of approaches to stalls and turns.

He said, "You'll do." I flew four more flights with an experienced pilot watching from the right seat until they figured that I had an instrument scan that was good enough to keep me from crashing if I flew into clouds. Then they issued me a bombardier-navigator for the first time and I was on my way. This was not a good way to train people to fly a combat aircraft but it is how we did it.

Flight of the Intruder

I was at Da Nang until we rotated home in early January of 1970. I was in Marine All-Weather Attack Squadron VMA (AW)-225, the "Vikings," that whole time. About 80 percent of the flying was at night. If there were 12 sorties per day on the schedule, generally eight of them would be at night.

All those scheduled to fly at night receive a general "intel and threat" brief at 1600 at group headquarters. We had two A-6 Intruder squadrons, ours and VMA (AW)-242, as well as squadron VMCJ-1 with the EA-6A Intruder electronic warfare aircraft and RF-4B Phantom photo-planes, as well as VMFA-542 with F-4B Phantoms. We were all part of Marine Air Group 11, or MAG-11.

The mission begins when we get briefed. All the night flyers show up at headquarters at a big briefing room where the S-2 and the S-3, or whoever else is pertinent, stands up and gives you the generic portion of what you need to know to get through the night. There are things like coded altitudes and coded frequencies that change every day. Depending on what your mission is, you may have more briefings. If you're doing a PPQ, which is the term for a strike directed by a ground radar site, you need extra briefing and preparation at the group level.

We go from the night flyers' brief over to the squadron ready room. It's located inside a corrugated steel hangar. Three sides of the hangar have office and shop spaces, and one of those spaces is the ready room.

When you walk into the ready room, there's a big grease-pencil board on one side that the operations duty officer keeps up. It has your names and the mission and all, and as soon as the maintenance people know which aircraft will be assigned to you, they put the number up next to your name.

There are only 12 airplanes in a squadron. You fly them all on a pretty regular basis. Some of them have idiosyncrasies, so you say, "Oh, no, not number 9 again!" Each A-6A Intruder is slightly different. For example, there is one airplane that has a problem with its gyro compass. The maintenance guys keep trying to find out what the problem is. They say it wanders off.

Depending on what your takeoff time is, you sit down with your bombardier-navigator and the two of you brief, right there. Or, instead, you say to your bombardier, "I'll see you back here at one o'clock in the morning for a 2:30 takeoff."

We get away until the appropriate time. The MAG-11 living area is separate from the flight line, so there's a shuttle back and forth. That's how you get from one end of Da Nang to the other. So when it's time, you ride back down to the flight line, go to the squadron ready room, sit down, and brief the particulars of your mission. We discuss where we are going and how we are going to get there, and what we'd do if we were going up north—whether it is over land or over water. Almost all of our missions are single ship, so this is just a single, two-man crew doing this. If we fly direct air support, we go with a flight of two aircraft. Otherwise, it's solo.

The bombardier is responsible for all the map planning. If he knows where we're going in advance of takeoff, which he doesn't always, the bombardier will say, "Okay, we're going up here." He'll point out the general area. I flew with the same bombardier-navigator, Dave Brown, for about nine months. We were much better together than either one of us was working with someone else. Eventually, the influx of new guys became so great that flying two experienced guys in the same cockpit just didn't make any sense. So we split up and never flew with each other again.

Now we've finished our briefing. We know where we're going to go

When the A-6A Intruder first appeared on the scene. Grumman and the Navy staged this publicity photo to show the various kinds of ordnance the plane could carry.

[U.S. Navy]

and how we're going to get there, at least in general terms. Still on one side of the squadron ready room, we start putting on our flying gear. The uniform of the day is a Nomex flight suit. Now it's time for everything that goes on top of that.

Suiting Up

You put on your G-suit, the antiblackout coveralls—not really coveralls, they're more like chaps—on your lower legs. Then you put on what they call the integrated torso harness, which is like a harness and parachute straps all at once. Each guy has his own. On top of that, you put a survival kit that has flares, a flotation device, some rudimentary survival items, and extra ammo for your .38. Then, you put your pistol in the pointed pocket in the harness.

You were wearing the pistol on your flight suit during the day, so you take it out of whatever kind of holster you've been using and put it in your survival vest pocket to go flying. I carry a Smith & Wesson .38 revolver. There is some latitude in what you want to carry. The standard issue is the Smith & Wesson with the four-inch barrel. Mine is a snub-nosed version. It has an aluminum frame and is a light weight. You probably can't hit a bear's ass broadside with it, but that's not the important thing. I fill it with signal rounds. Instead of being a regular bullet, this .38-caliber ammo has brass skin over the business end of it and colored pyrotechnics inside. That's really all I carry. I'm not interested in carrying ball ammunition because I figure I'm not going to kill anybody if I have to bail out.

The only thing left of your paraphernalia now is your helmet and your oxygen mask, and you don't put those on until you're in the airplane. You pull your helmet and oxygen mask from their little cubbyhole. The helmet bag is a standard item by now, so we have a little green bag to lug the helmet in. You carry them out to the plane. You'll put them on once you're seated in the cockpit.

You go to the flight line shack, which is a shack located inside the hangar facing the flight line, and look at the paperwork on the airplane. There's a list of discrepancies from about the last ten flights and what has been done to fix them after the aircrew reported that some things weren't working right.

You look for discrepancies that have not been fixed to see whether your plane can be deemed flyable. They have the aircraft logs in a metal binder, so you check to see whether anything is broken and, if it is, whether you can fly with it. If there are any things that have not been fixed but the aircraft is still deemed to be flyable, then you see a list of things that were broken and still are broken. There are a lot of little things that can be broken, and you can still climb into the plane and fly a normal mission. For example, there are a couple of engine gauges, called power trim gauges, on the airplane. On other airplanes they are very important gauges but on the A-6A airplane they're not really relevant. And yet they're forever getting out of calibration. So you see a notation that says, "Trim gauge—inop," meaning inoperable. The gauges are deemed by the maintenance department to be more trouble to maintain than they're worth.

Now we're going out to the airplane. Depending on the time of year, it may be pouring down rain. When we first got to Da Nang, standing at our aircraft in the rain got to be a problem. Parachutes were getting wet. The insides of the cockpits were getting wet. Guys were climbing in and strapping in before they could get the canopy closed. So the flight line guys came up with a bright idea. They used a nose dock, which was kind of an aluminum and canvas parasol arrangement that folded flat for storage and opened up with a thing like the top of a baby carriage. They lay that over the top of the canopy. It was originally designed to do maintenance on the airplane's radar out of doors, to keep dust and stuff out of the sensitive electronic area while they have the radome opened up, but it also worked very well to enable us to get in and out of the airplane when it was raining. That's how we faced that problem.

It's the pilot's responsibility to preflight the aircraft and the bombardier-navigator's job to preflight the ordnance. The standard load is twenty-eight 500-pound bombs. For a lot of the year that we're there, each airplane has its own plane captain. There are actually two, sometimes three, guys assigned to each plane because they work 12-hour shifts. So you get to know those guys very well. Occasionally, when I have one of the good guys, I like to ask him: "Corporal Smaltz, did you preflight this aircraft?" "Yes, sir, I did." "Well, how did it look?" "Looked good to me, sir." "Well, that's good enough for me." I figure it's a pat on the back to this guy if I'm willing to take the plane captain's word for it. But I don't do that very often because the pilot's preflight check is really important.

Doing the preflight check, you look at the whole airplane. In the A-6A, you have a lot of nooks and crannies you're supposed to inspect. You start at the pilot's boarding ladder. There's a pressure gauge in there

The A-6A Intruder was designed to operate from carriers, as seen here aboard the nuclear-powered USS *Enterprise* (CVAN 65). The Navy used it that way in Vietnam, but Marine Corps pilots and bombardier navigators operated from land bases like the giant airfield at Da Nang.

[Grumman]

you need to look at. You climb up into the nosewheel well. There are circuit breakers there, believe it or not. You look to see of there's any hydraulic fluid leaking or dripping. The inertial platform is mounted up there, so you look up at it to make sure somebody has at least checked the plugs on the end of it so it's going to work. You check the latches on the radome. You come out of the nose and check the intakes to make sure there are no foreign objects that will get sucked into the engines when you start cranking. Then you look along the leading edges of the wings and the pylons to make sure there are no big dings. You walk around. You lean against the wing. You check the wingtips and the trailing edge. You stick your head in the tailpipe to make sure there's nothing untoward there. On the aft equipment platform in the rear fuselage, you have to check to make sure that thing is locked and secured. That platform is a monster. It's a hell of a thing if it comes open in flight; you can be in deep kimchi. The official name is the aft extensible equipment platform, but everybody calls it the birdcage because of its framework. It's one part of the airplane you want secured.

You walk along the right side of the fuselage. You check the horizontal stabilizer to make sure it isn't gouged or dinged. You check the rudder and make sure the taillight is in and operating. In the meantime, the bombardier is checking the ordnance to make sure that the fuses are all screwed in tight and that the arming delays are set on the correct number and that there's a correct number of pips on the arming wires. He checks to see that the electrical connectors on the bomb racks are screwed in where they're supposed to be screwed in. Having bombs fall off asymmetrically is a very bad thing, because there are so many and because the wings are so long, you could get yourself in a very unbalanced condition if you got up there and had a whole package of bombs that wouldn't release.

We get into the airplane. There's a ladder that folds into the jet intakes on each side of the airplane. When you unfold it, it makes a neat little ladder that each crew member can use to climb up into the cockpit. You step from the ladder onto the top of the wing. You finish fixing up your gear if you haven't done all that yet. You take a look at the top surface of the fuselage, the top of the wings, and make sure everything is the way it's supposed to be. After you've done a few hundred preflights, you've learned how things are supposed to look. With that experience, you don't eyeball every item, but if something's not where it's supposed to be, it sticks out like a sore thumb. And that's the final part of your preflight inspection.

I climb into the cockpit by stepping right into the middle of the seat and turning to face the nose and sitting down. The plane captain climbs up the ladder behind me and helps me hook up the shoulder harness, which is sometimes a little hard to reach. He helps me plug in the G suit connection because that's always hard to reach.

Once you're all connected to the airplane, you put your helmet on and plug in your oxygen mask. Once you turn on the supply oxygen valve and make sure it's going to work, you turn the oxygen up and attach the oxygen mask to one side of the helmet so that it's dangling in front of your mouth while you finish preparations for flight.

You get ready to start the engines. You start external power. A unit hooks up to a valve underneath the right engine air intake. It blows compressed air across a starter unit that spins the engine up to about 10 or 12 percent rpm. You can see that on your tachometer gauge in the cockpit. When you get up above 10 percent, you bring the throttle around and start counting. You start the engines. You communicate with the bombardier on the intercom and with the plane captain by using hand signals. He has a regular dance that he goes through once you've got both engines turned on.

The revetments at Da Nang are too narrow to park an airplane with the wings spread, and of course the A-6A has wings that fold for stowage on an aircraft carrier. So you wait until your inertial navigation system is aligned, and then you taxi out of the revetment with the wings folded and spread the wings out after you're out in the open area between the two lines of revetments. Once you've got the wings spread, the plane captain checks the flaps and speed brakes and makes sure they open and close. He takes a final look at the airplane and gives you a big salute and sends you on your way.

Taxing is not problem in the A-6A. The landing gear on the A-6A is spread far enough apart that the airplane doesn't have any weird ground-handling characteristics. The airplane is very stable on the ground. Visibility is excellent. Contrary to appearances, I never feel the aircraft is going to tip over if I make a high-speed turnoff or some other sudden movement.

You taxi up to the end of the squadron's parking area. That's when you come under the purview of ground control in the tower. You call ground control and tell him who you are. We use the group callsign, the MAG-11 callsign, which is RINGNECK. So you're RINGNECK, plus whatever your mission number is. So you're RINGNECK 6521. So you say, "RINGNECK 6521, to taxi." Da Nang had only two main runways and they were parallel, so they were both 17/35, running north and south. The airport operator takes us south about 99 percent of the time. So, "You're clear to taxi to runway 17, right." For us, that was only about a hundred yards from our revetment, so it's a short trip. You taxi out and, of course, you're working with the bombardier on the takeoff checklist. You get up to the "hold short" line at the edge of the active runway area, stop the airplane, and switch to the tower controller. When you're done with all your checks and ready to take the runway, you call the tower and say, "Tower, RINGNECK 6521, ready for takeoff."

"You're cleared for takeoff," the tower responds.

You turn right. You taxi out on the runway. You line yourself up with the centerline stripes. You bring the engines up. You watch the instruments come up. You have certain limitations that you had to be within, both maximums and minimums—your engine rpm, exhaust gas temperature, and your fuel flow. Once you're satisfied that the engines are operating normal, you release the brakes and away you go.

We usually have a "line speed check," as we call it: we have a marker and we want to have 120 knots of airspeed by the time we hit the 6,000-foot marker. If we don't, the plane probably is not going to fly. If it looks like you aren't going to get into the air before you run out of runway, you start thinking about lowering the arresting hook and catching the barrier. The Martin Baker GRU-5 ejection seat in the A-6A is not a zero-zero seat. You need 80 knots to use it. So you don't have the option of bailing out if something goes wrong during the takeoff. You can't eject. You have to ride the airplane in, wherever it's going, and hope you can survive.

You don't want to think that you can kill yourself before you've even gotten into the air, tucked in the wheels, and climbed out to cruise to your target, but the thought was ever present that one day, for some reason, that the big and heavy Intruder just wasn't going to get into the sky.

Getting Off the Runway

We had a day when we were sure it wasn't going to fly.

I'm taking off from Da Nang with fifteen 1,000-pounders, which is normally a pretty nice load because it doesn't have as much drag as

A Marine Corps A-6A Intruder takes off from Da Nang in 1968 with a load of twenty-two 500-lb bombs.

[U.S. Marine Corps]

twenty-eight 500-pounders. Rolling down the runway, I want to have 120 knots on the airspeed indicator with 6,000 feet of runway remaining. We don't have any extra today. We have the 120 within a knot or so at the normal place for a go or no-go decision, but then it seems that the airplane just quits accelerating.

So we're coasting down the runway and watching the concrete go by and starting to get nervous as the end of the runway is coming up. All of a sudden, I'm starting to get real nervous.

I tell the bombardier navigator, "If we start to go into the overrun, eject, because once you cross the perimeter road, you're in an old French minefield." I'm thinking, "You can't get through there without something blowing up." The ejection seat may not be completely reliable at this speed and angle, but you don't want to go into those mines.

I don't know what happened. I don't know why we didn't simply lift off with plenty of runway left and climb out routinely, the way we should have. I didn't see any abnormalities with the engine. It was one of those high, cloudy, thunderstormy days when it wasn't raining. We might have gotten a dry microburst, which is a weather phenomenon where a bunch of cold air falls out of the bottom of a cumulus cloud.

Who's Who

Capt. (later, Col.) Jim Henshaw, A-6A Intruder pilot

With that come very strong headwinds or tailwinds for very brief periods of time. It's not as common as a wet microburst, which has a strong rainfall associated with it, but it does happen.

That analysis of our overlong takeoff roll can come later. Right now, it's happening. As we accelerate toward the end of the runway, after I've warned the bombardier, I put the friction lock up on the throttles and put my left hand on the lower firing handle on the ejection seat. I say, "As soon as we go onto the overrun, we're out of here." I can't recall anyone ever surviving a takeoff mishap and ejection like the one I'm contemplating.

And then, much to my amazement, everything changes again. I can actually feel the lift. Our Intruder staggers into the air with about a thousand feet to go. Never in my life have I been happier to feel an airplane get into the air.

I was very glad to get the gear up on that afternoon. As far as being scared, that's probably the most scared I got in Vietnam because I had more time to think about it than the usual "Oh, shit!" situation. Most of the things that happen when you say, "Oh, shit!" are over with before you even get those words out of your mouth, and if you're still alive by then, you know you've made it.

A-6 Intruder

The Grumman A-6A Intruder flown by Capt. Jim Henshaw was the Navy and Marine solution to fighting at night in Southeast Asia. The A-6A, with its fat radar nose, high, thin landing gear, and tapered tail

This is a Marine Corps A-6A Intruder in flight.

[U.S. Marine Corps]

shape, is often accused of looking more like a tadpole than an aircraft. Fast-jet pilots, mocking the slower A-6A, often ask why the pointed end isn't on the front.

Everyone thinks the Intruder looks awkward, with its side-by-side pilot and bombardier-navigator hunkered beneath a clamshell canopy and nudged up against a nonretractable air-refueling probe that makes the plane appear to be attached to a giant fishhook.

The Intruder never won a beauty contest, but a tremendous amount of design work went into finalizing the configuration of the Intruder. Before settling on the two-man-crew, side-by-side arrangement, Grumman had explored a tandem design and a three-seat version. The real thing, with its shoulder wing and twin engines, resulted from thousands of hours at the drawing board and in the wind tunnel. Grumman test pilot Robert Smythe flew the prototype, known then as the A2F-1, on its maiden flight on April 1, 1960. Eisenhower was still president, and it was the world's first warplane with an integrated, onboard computer system.

But from the Vietnam era onward, the Intruder ruled the night. In fact, for long periods during the Southeast Asia war, the Intruder was the *only* warplane that could routinely attack North Vietnamese troops and targets during the nocturnal hours.

The thinking behind the A-6A (as the A2F-1 was renamed in 1962) was both simple and revolutionary. Instead of sleekness and speed, "black boxes" and electronic wizardry would enable the aircraft to take off from a carrier deck—or a sweltering coastal redoubt like Da Nang— journey into darkness and bad weather, and attack targets with a degree of precision unprecedented in warfare.

The A-6A became the standard medium attack aircraft for the U.S. Navy and Marine Corps, a capacity in which it replaced the propeller-driven Douglas A-1 Skyraider, but the Intruder was also intended for more. Its designers believed that if the radar was good enough, if a second crew member with a radar scope was able enough, and if a few technical handicaps could be overcome, the Intruder would be able to bomb an enemy 24 hours a day, 365 days a year. It was no accident that

---

Grumman A-6A Intruder (A2F-1)

Type: 2-seat, carrier-based, all-weather attack aircraft

Power plant: 2 Pratt & Whitney J52-P-8A nonafterburning turbojets of 9,300 lb (4218 kg) static thrust each

Performance: maximum speed, 654 mph (1052 km/h); cruising speed, 551 mph (887 km/h); service ceiling, 44,600 ft (13595 m); combat radius, 1,727 miles (2828 km); maximum endurance, 5 hours

Weights: empty, 26,066 lb (111824 kg); maximum takeoff, 60,626 lb (27450kg)

Dimensions: span, 53 ft (16.15 m); span with wings folded, 25 ft 2 in (7.67 m); length, 54 ft 9 in (16.69 m); height, 15 ft 7 in (4.75 m); wing area, 528.9 sq ft (49.13 sq m)

Armament: up to 18,000 lb (8165 kg) of weapons on 5 external hard points

Crew: 2 (pilot and bombardier-navigator)

First flight: April 19, 1960 (A2F-1)

---

many of the Navy's Intruders were stationed at Whidbey Island, Washington, in the Pacific Northwest, an airfield that has some of the wettest and dreariest weather on the North American continent.

In its early days, the scientific revolution wrought by the Intruder's navigation system and bombing radar was an on-again, off-again proposition. When the Intruder first went to Vietnam, its marvelous electronic gadgetry worked less than half the time. Marines spent more time fixing the aircraft than flying it. In later years, as the rest of the world began switching to tactics that called for fighting at night, the Intruder's electronic prowess was no longer enough to compensate for its subsonic speed or its own glaring radar cross-section. Intruders performed well in Operation Desert Storm in 1991, but took disproportionate casualties. By then, even though improvements had been made to the Intruder over three decades, other aircraft had better radar, infrared, and electro-optical equipment and fought routinely at night.

When the Intruder came along, it had to beat out a lot of competition. Bell, Boeing, Douglas, Lockheed, Martin, North American, and Vought all submitted their own designs for a medium-attack aircraft. Grumman won the contract with a plane that was known initially as the A2F-1 and soon afterward as the A-6A.

Initially, a pair of Pratt & Whitney J52-P-6 engines, each of 8,500 pounds (3856 kilograms) thrust, powered the A2F-1. They were installed inside fairings that might properly be called conformal pods, set low under the fuselage to leave the central structure free for the huge fuel tanks that gave the Intruder its long radius of action. This fuselage configuration was never changed from the first Intruder to the last.

From its first flight at the Grumman factory in 1960 until its final catapult launch from the carrier USS *Enterprise* (CVN 65) in December 1996, the Intruder kept its reputation as a potent night and all-weather bomber. A-6s fought in Vietnam, Lebanon, Grenada, and Libya, and in Operation Desert Storm. Although production ended in January 1992, the Intruder was in service until February 1997.

Chapter Seventeen

Flight of the Intruder (II)

JIM HENSHAW If you can manage to get your heavily laden A-6A Intruder off the ground and into the air at Da Nang, you're into the mission. So it's time to clean up the airplane, tuck everything in, and get some altitude.

Climbing out is one of the things we do very differently at Da Nang than we did back in the States. You do not have to travel very far from our main runway to be over Bad Guy Country. They want us to get aloft, turn, and head for the coast as quickly as possible. The airplane is routinely operating right at its maximum gross weight with all those 28 bombs hanging there, so you have to be conscious of speed and altitude. But with full-span leading edge and trailing edge flaps, the airplane has a really good low-speed wing. It handles really well in the landing pattern when you're at sea, near the aircraft carrier.

You take off. You climb 2,000 feet, still with the flaps in extended position, and you turn to a 270-degree heading, still with the flaps hanging out, and climb 2,000 feet and accelerate to 200 knots and raise the flaps. With all the drag off once the flaps are raised, the aircraft handles pretty much normally after about 300 knots.

You climb out according to whatever altitude the ground control in-

Capt. Jim Henshaw
December 1969
Grumman A-6A Intruder
RINGNECK 6521
Marine All-Weather Attack
  Squadron VMA (AW)-225,
  "Vikings"
Da Nang, South Vietnam

The pilot of the A-6A Intruder sits high above the plane's jet engine air intakes beneath a Plexiglas canopy with the bombardier-navigator (not visible here) to his right. The huge, hook-like device protruding above the nose of the Intruder is an air refueling probe designed to plug into a "basket" dropped by a tanker.

[U.S. Marine Corps]

tercept, or GCI, site tells you. Once you get out over the water, you turn in the appropriate direction for the mission area you've been assigned.

You call a guy named MIKE ONE. He's on top of Monkey Mountain on the southeastern corner of Da Nang harbor. We have a big radar site up there. He has TACAN and other equipment. He can check our transponder for you and make sure all that stuff is working. Sometimes they give you an altitude to transit. If you're going across the fence, you get in touch with an airborne control post over Laos whose call sign is MOONBEAM. That's a C-130 with a big communications box in the back. He doesn't have any radar. He just keeps going with us over there.

Then, depending on what your mission is, after you take off, they might send you to whatever ground control site is currently operating. That site might have targets they've worked up just the day before. They can put you on something on short notice. Or they could hold you for a while. The A-6A has so much fuel and endurance that if it's convenient to their purposes, they can keep you flying around, boring holes in the sky, until they come up with a decision as to what target they want you to hit.

A-6A Intruder Design

I can't emphasize this too much. We had this kind of flexibility because the A-6A Intruder was designed and developed with capabilities that no one had ever seen before. I said some of this before. The airplane was developed in the mid-1950s. It was a requirement that arose during the Korean War for something that could drop bombs on ground targets when the weather was bad. The Grumman Iron Works put it together with what was, at that time, very cutting-edge technology. It had one of the very first digital computer systems ever installed in a tactical airplane. It had very powerful air-to-ground radar. We called it a "search radar," although "ground-map radar" would be a more accurate description. It had an early inertial navigation system that tied all the data together and fed it into the computer. You could use the radar to observe and track the target and you could actually use the computer to release the bombs and hit the target without the flight crew ever seeing it.

It was a striking airplane to fly. The wings had very, very good low-speed performance characteristics. It was easy to land. It was easy to bring aboard the boat. It was like an old shoe after a while: You felt really good when you got back inside the thing after a long absence.

It was very stable—almost too stable for dive-bombing. It was tough to make corrections if you rolled in and you weren't lined up exactly where you wanted to be relative to the target. You'd try to adjust and find yourself rolling back and forth with those big long wings, and you'd kind of get seasick looking through the sight.

It took an incredible amount of punishment. This airplane was built to withstand antiaircraft fire. There were lots of stories and lots of pictures of guys bringing A-6As home with holes in the airplane. It had two good engines and, basically, four hydraulic systems. It got a lot of guys home when a lot of other airplanes wouldn't have.

This view of a Marine Corps A-6A Intruder shows why crews referred to the plane as having a tadpole shape. Supposedly, fighter pilots berated the Intruder's shape by arguing that the "pointy end" was supposed to be on the front. This Marine A-6A is on a stateside flight without bombload.

[U.S. Marine Corps]

That doesn't necessarily mean that the A-6A was the crew-friendliest airplane in the world. With all its black boxes and instruments, it was a busy airplane, even for a two-man crew. You had a lot more work to do in the cockpit, making sure everything was lined up right.

We flew radar-directed missions, which we called PPQ missions, and we also flew visual missions. PPQ comes from the technical designation of the radar set that the ground radar guys were using. It was an AN/PPQ-10. That got shortened to PPQ. It was a fixed ground installation with radar and a computer that took your aircraft to a predetermined bomb-release point. In other words, the ground site had the same kind of system for getting us to the target that we had aboard the A-6, but in this case it was on the ground, so on these missions we were guided by the guy at the PPQ site. You fly out to a certain point and they slew their radar around and lock you up so the radar is tracking you automatically. Now they know where you are. You knew the coordinates for the target so you factored in the winds at your altitude, plus the winds all the way from your airplane down to the ground, and that produced the point that they told you to release the bombs. It was a lot of work and you had to stay involved to assure the accuracy of it. A couple of guys got really good at it. But it wasn't much fun for the flight crews because you were going up there in your A-6 Intruder and doing what they told you. It was almost like ours was a pilotless aircraft with me and the bombardier just going along for the ride and saying, "Roger," on the radio every once in a while.

Our visual missions, meaning daylight missions because we don't do visual at night, are a lot more interesting although there are not as many of them. These sort of defeated the purpose that our airplane was bought and paid for. You take off, go through the check-in procedure and go out to the support center, and check in with them, and they connect you to a forward air controller (FAC) in an aircraft or on the ground.

That FAC is the guy who knows exactly where the target is located. You fly out there and try to establish radio contact with him, and if it's an airborne FAC, you try to establish visual contact with him. That's a nice thing to have if you're going to be buzzing around in the same airspace.

The FAC tries to talk your eyes into the general vicinity of the target so you're looking in the right direction. Then he puts a marker rocket down. The smoke rocket has a white phosphorus head, so it makes a dense white cloud when it impacts. Then the FAC says, "Okay, I hit it. That's the target, I've marked it." Or "The target from that smoke is 20 meters at two o'clock." You try to be in position while that smoke is pretty much where it started from, so you can get your eyeballs in the vicinity of the target, go into a 30-degree dive, drop a couple of bombs, and see how you did.

You're doing all this with the Mark One eyeball and the reticle bombsight in the front of your nose. It's not the most efficient use of the airplane that you could possibly make, but it's one of its many capabilities. Frequently in the A-6A, you had a situation where the airframe was in fine flyable condition but the avionics system that enabled you to do all the night radar stuff was badly broken. So there was always the dilemma of what do you do with the airplane? Do you fly it? Do you do dive-bombing that A-4 Skyhawks and F-4 Phantoms—which lacked our night and all-weather gadgetry—could do just as well? Or do you hold it on the ground and try to fix it? It usually came down to whether or not they had the parts in the avionics shop, which they often didn't.

On a visual bombing mission, you can sometimes see them shooting at you. It's deceptive on night missions because a lot of times you see muzzle flashes but you don't know if they know where you are. If you see tracers in the daytime, you're really getting hosed, because they don't show up very well in daylight. I never took a hit in 65 missions. There were a couple of days when I don't know how they missed.

They shot at us a lot on a mission we flew over in Laos. There was a bulldozer that had been disabled and they wanted us to blow it up. It was a bad-guy bulldozer. We were flying around with a load of 1,000-pound bombs, which is a great weapon for that purpose. We were working underneath the cloud deck doing relatively low-angle stuff. When you're doing low-angle bombing with unretarded bombs, which is what we were doing that particular day, your downrange errors get to be very exaggerated because the angle is so low. You can drop very long or very short. So we were having a hell of a time trying to hit where the guy wanted. Plus, it was almost impossible to see a target that small, so we had to take the info we had and feed in some Kentucky windage and hope we could hit it.

In addition, I was having an electrical problem: the circuit breaker in the cockpit would pop and wouldn't let the bombs release. Something was short-circuited inside the release mechanism that was causing that breaker to pop in the first place. We went around two times without anything coming off. I reset the release button each time, and each time I hit the release it popped and nothing came off. On the third pass, I told the bombardier-navigator to hold it in. I said, "If it doesn't work this time, we're going home." So we set it up to drop ten. So he's holding the circuit breaker in, and I hit the pickle, and he said, "Ouch!" and it popped again, but this time about six bombs came off.

As I was starting to pull off, I looked up and there were tracers going over the canopy over both wings. Those .50-calibers had us really dead to rights. I pulled off and pulled up above the cloud deck. The other aircraft said that the bombs came off this time and detonated, but we still didn't hit the damn target. I said, "Well, we're kind of out of Schlitz up here because of a circuit breaker situation, and, oh, by the way, we're really getting shot at." So we gave it up as a bad job. I don't know if the bulldozer ever got blown up, but we didn't do it. It was not an easy target. It was something that was small enough that you're not really going to see it unless you're really lucky.

Bombing in Laos

In late December 1969 or early January 1970, all the guys who had come over with the squadron were getting ready to go home. The group and the wing had come up with a new tactic using A-6As against trucks on the Ho Chi Minh Trail. This involved listening to the transmitters that the Air Force had dropped along the trail. They were neat little devices—a radio transmitter that had plastic camouflage on top of it. They put them on F-4s. They salted them along the trail. They dropped off the airplane and made their way to the ground like a lawn dart and stuck into the ground. The impact of them hitting the ground set off the batteries and the things would transmit for days. They could actually use these to hear North Vietnamese trucks driving by, which is pretty remarkable for 1969 state of the art.

There was a control center over in Thailand at Nakhon Phanom that monitored these things. They sent an A-6 over to an orbit point just on the Laotian side of the border. You'd be talking to the guy up at Nakhon Phanom, and you just circled around until he heard some trucks coming down the road. There were a series of predetermined choke points where a truck came around the face of a really steep hill or crossed a ford—someplace where the trucks had to go single file and couldn't really get off the road and hide. In the same region, there were terrain features that were more or less easily identifiable on the A-6A radar. The folks who worked this whole thing up had computed the bearing and

In addition to the A-6A Intruder medium-attack aircraft, the Marines operated the EA-6A Intruder electronic warfare platform, which was readily distinguished by the antenna fairing atop its vertical tail. It was the predecessor of the EA-6B Prowler that remains in service today.

[U.S. Marine Corps]

distance from the terrain feature to the choke point. We used the offset bombing capability of the A-6A computer. Once the controller heard the trucks and figured out which choke point was next in line, he did a computation and figured out how long it was going to take them to get there. Then he asked, "Can you drop on Point Alpha Charlie at four-four?" Then, the bombardier got really busy. He typed in the coordinates of the aim point and the coordinates of the choke point and used that to calculate the distance to Point Alpha Charlie. He turned all that over to the computer in the A-6A, and it gave him a readout telling him how long it was going to take to get there. If the number came up four-four or greater, then we did it. We told the guy on the ground at Nakhon Phanom whether we could hit it or not. If we couldn't, we waited for the next one.

I was scheduled to fly one of these deals one night and the latest wrinkle was they had added an F-4 escort. This was the latest in the escalation. When we first started doing this, we were kicking their ass and we were virtually unopposed. But within a couple of weeks, the ridgelines on both sides of the pass coming out of North Vietnam were pretty much wall-to-wall guns. The first guy to hear you go by shoots. When his buddies see his tracers go up, they shoot, too. They aren't shooting at anything; they're just hoping you'll fly into a bullet. That made it a little colorful, and that's why they added the F-4s: once the A-6A was finished with its bombing, we cleared out of the valley and the F-4s ran in and dropped cluster bombs on the guns. That worked pretty good.

So I'm on one of these escorted missions. We get over there. We get into our orbit. Nothing's moving. Remember, you had 20 minutes in a holding pattern with all your bombs. At that point, you had to either go home or drop. You couldn't stay there any longer and have enough gas to get back without cleaning off the airplane. So at the end of 20 minutes, he says, "I've got nothing." So I said, "Well, do you have a secondary?" He said, "Yeah, there's a secondary target at Alpha Delta two-two." My BN did his numbers and said, "Yeah, we can make that." When you start your run, basically, you push over from 20,000 feet with the power full up and try to make it go as fast as it'll go. You could get about 480 or 490 knots out of it, depending on the drag. Once you level off into your bomb run at about 3,000 feet, you are now a lot more vulnerable because you slow down pretty rapidly.

As usual, once we get down inside the valley, the first little guy to hear us shoots. His guns light up. And then others start shooting. Finally the bombs come off the airplane. We pull up at the end of the valley. Now we're 35 degrees nose up and 60 degrees right. I hear the F-4 guy saying, "Son of a bitch!" over the radio. I think, "Oh, man, he's hit." So I roll around back to the left, and I just kind of leave the nose up and work the angle of bank and pull. I look back down into the valley, and here's this humongous orange fireball. I think, "Oh, shit, he went in." And, "Here went the F-4." But then I hear him say, "Boy, you sure hit something!" So now I know it wasn't the F-4. So we kind of just hang in there. I look to see if anything else is going to blow up.

That's when I hear the bombardier say, "So where's 80 knots?" And I think, "Oh, fuck!" And I look back inside the cockpit, and here we are, over on our back, basically, at about 60 degrees nose up, inverted. We're also at about 25 degrees, left wing down. The airspeed indicator is now reading zero. Oops. That goes down as one of the dumber things I did during my tour. Getting us upside down at zero airspeed as a result of being distracted was just as dumb as it could be.

Fortunately, one of the nice things about the A-6A was the airplane really wanted to fly. If you didn't screw around with it overly much, it would fly. The trick, when you got yourself into that situation, particularly if it was inadvertent, was just leave it alone. The throttles were already full up. The bombs were gone off the airplane. The engines were running just fine. So we just sat there. We waited. We watched the airplane go through the horizon and the airspeed indicator start to wiggle its way up. The secret was not to touch anything. The trick, when it happens to you, is don't try to horse the airplane around when you're really too slow to do it. We did nothing but wait until we had about 200 knots and then I rolled it back, right side up, and decided we'd go on home to Da Nang. We never did find out what blew up on the ground. It looked like it was some kind of POL—petroleum oil lubricant—because of the color of the fireball. That was my last out-of-country mission. I was glad of that.

Returning and Landing

Once you've bombed your target, you want to get back over the coast so you're away from Indian country. You follow normal visual flight rules to get back, and the GCI site could warn you if there is other traffic in your area. If you are making a visual arrival, you plan your own descent to arrive five miles from the runway at about a thousand feet and 250 knots, more or less. You call the tower and say, "A-6, five mile initial, for landing." Da Nang operated its runways north to south about 99 percent of the time, so it would be unusual for the tower to ask you to go around and approach from the other direction.

You drop the gear at 230 knots and put the flaps down to 30 degrees. One of the A-6A's fine flying qualities is that it is really stable and forgiving with the flaps down. It is easy to handle. You just slow it down and head for the runway. At about half a mile you see the Fresnel lens that is set up on the runway to guide you down.

If you are bringing back ordnance, you want to be more alert. I came back one night with a 2,000-pounder hung up on the left wing. We had an ordnance jettison area over water about 40 miles south of Da Nang, so if we were in real trouble with hung bombs, we could go out there and drop. The normal way is to arm the ordnance station and push the pickle. If that doesn't work, there's a different selector switch that operates on a different circuit. That's what I used to get rid of my 2,000-pounder. The A-6A had several ways of getting the ordnance off the airplane, including an emergency jettison button that would fire all the explosive lugs on the bomb rack. When you do that, you're going to get rid of a bomb you don't want. If you push the emergency button, you're going to unload all five racks whether they have bombs on them or not. That gets rid of all the ejector sleeves and lugs, so it's an expensive way to clean up your airplane.

Da Nang was blessed with these wonderful, 10,000-foot parallel runways, so you just plopped the airplane down somewhere close to where you're supposed to be, and you had plenty of room. With a cleaned-off airplane, in a typical weight of about 35,000 pounds, you could land within 5,000 feet and make the midfield taxiway to get off the runway. You didn't want to step on the brakes too hard, though: one flaw of the A-6A was that the brakes were very effective in halting the airplane, but if you overreacted you would get hot brakes. You were not allowed to shut down the engine if you had hot brakes because there was a risk of a small leak. I have seen the brakes on other people's airplanes glowing cherry red, with the crew just sitting there, waiting for them to cool down. You could avoid that by not being too eager to make the midfield turnoff.

Once you were off the runway, you taxied to the Marine fuel pits at the north end in Da Nang. The fuel pits were outside the revetted area. You would shut down the plane at the pits and climb out of the airplane. When they finished refueling it, they would tow it into the revetment.

This is a stateside portrait (taken at Cherry Point, N.C., on June 12, 1972), but it does an excellent job of portraying the lines of the Vietnam-era Grumman A-6A Intruder flown by Marine attack squadrons.

[U.S. Marine Corps]

You walked into the hangar and into the line shack, which is a pass-through to the office, where you filled out the yellow sheets on the airplane, reporting what you did on the flight. Part of that document went to operations where they kept your log. On another part of the yellow sheet, you wrote about any discrepancies in the airplane, for the benefit of the maintainers. While the pilot was doing that, the bombardier would sit down with the fire control technicians and debrief the avionics system. The avionics problems with the A-6A were so frequent that you needed a separate reporting vehicle for them.

Having finished all that, you would go into the ready room and look at the schedule for what was happening next. For the year I was in Vietnam, the average mission was 1.2 hours. We would then go to the Marine aircraft group headquarters where they had an intelligence debriefer on duty 24 hours. We would talk through details of the mission with the debriefer, especially anything we had to offer about threats and a bomb damage assessment. After that, we would turn in our gear, get on the shuttle, and head back for the living area.

The A-6A Intruder was awesome. Let me recount an incident to explain how superior the A-6 Intruder was to every other airplane we had "in country" in those days. I remember this mission because of the un-

This is an A-6A Intruder making a carrier-style landing in Vietnam.

[U.S. Marine Corps]

---

usual ordnance load. It was a preplanned landing zone prep, which is usually a pretty dull job since the purpose is to bomb trees and move them out of the way to create a landing spot for helicopters. But on this day, I was the lead aircraft with 12 Mark 82 bombs, four pods of five-inch Zuni rockets, and six Rockeye cluster bombs. My wingman had 28 Mark 82s.

The mission was just south of the airfield at Da Nang, so it only took us about three minutes to get there. When we checked in, we were told by the forward air controller, or FAC, that we could stay on station for an hour. We were still getting the mission brief when a flight of three F-4 Phantoms from Chu Lai checked in on our frequency. They had their usual ten Mark 82s each and told the FAC that they had fuel for ten minutes on station. This was bullshit and we all knew it since they had only come 50 miles themselves, but they (the F-4 guys) were always claiming to be short on time so they could get head-of-the-line privileges.

Well, it didn't work this time. The FAC said, "Why don't you boys go on back and see if somebody can find you a nice target somewhere else. See, these are A-6 Intruders. The wingman in this flight of A-6s has as much ordnance as all of you put together, and they can stick around long enough to do me some good!" I would have given my next pay-check to see the F-4 flight leader's face.

Yet somehow the Intruder never got enough credit for being awe-some. Nowadays, you look through aviation magazines where they're selling paintings and models, and you almost never see anyone offering an Intruder.

In Vietnam, the airframe was still relatively new and it was thor-oughly reliable, so we frequently had a situation where the plane was flying perfectly but the navigation and weapons system wasn't working right. As the Intruder continued with its long and successful career—the more advanced A-6E version came along and was used in Grenada in 1983 and in the Persian Gulf War in 1991—it reached a point where we had the opposite situation. Now the navigation and weapons system was mature and reliable but the airframe was getting old, so sometimes the little black boxes would be working just fine but the plane would be broken.

The Last Flight of the Intruder

Minutes earlier, Capt. Michael D. Malone, skipper of the *Enterprise,* had said that "if anybody were overboard in the sea state we have today, it would be very bad."

The flight deck of an aircraft carrier is cramped, loud, hectic. The flight deck of the USS *Enterprise* (CVN 65) was also caught under low scudding clouds and whipped by an intermittent horizontal rain as the men and women of the Navy gathered on Thursday, December 19, 1996, to say farewell to the Grumman A-6 Intruder, the standard medium attack warplane for the Navy and Marine Corps for the last 30 years.

This was a Navy show, but one of the bombardier-navigators on *En-terprise's* deck was a Marine pulling exchange duty. The Marines had retired their last Intruders a few years earlier, after, as Jim Henshaw pointed out, the planes, rather than the avionics, were breaking.

In the noise, rain, and cold, I watched with the others as the "Sunday Punchers" of Navy squadron VA-75 taxied Intruder after Intruder up to the carrier's powerful steam catapults, worked through their choreographed preflight ritual, and then were slung into the low wet sky with a force so powerful that for a split second it immobilized the crew of the plane. Finally, the last Intruder was on the "cat," piloted by deputy carrier air group commander Capt. Ron Jewett, with VA-75 skipper Comdr. James "Gigs" Gigliotti in the bombardier-navigator's seat. This airplane (A-6E bureau number 162179, side number 501) was hurtled into the wind and rain, the 14th and last of the day and the final Intruder, ever, to be catapulted from a carrier deck.

The gloomy, gray, chilling weather was a challenge for us civilians not accustomed to being pounded by the elements on a carrier deck (the sailors who work there are magnificent), but the rainsquall and the threat of fog were all too appropriate for the A-6 Intruder, the two-seat bomber that took command of the night and bad weather in Vietnam, fought for America in Grenada, Lebanon, Libya, and the Persian Gulf, and thumbed its flat nose at the weather every time. In 1965, when the Intruder was committed to battle in VA-75, it was the only aircraft that could routinely attack targets when darkness and foul conditions closed in—a situation that made a certain Air Force colonel angry, not at the North Vietnamese but at the Navy. "How come," Col. Don Kilgus asked me once, "they have a night and all-weather attack airplane and we don't?"

On October 25, 1967, three Marine Corps A-6A Intruders from squadron VMA (AW)-533 found themselves in a nasty fracas high over North Vietnam during an attack on Phuc Yen Airfield near Hanoi. The action was so furious that all three pilots were awarded the Navy Cross—the only such recognition for fixed-wing Marines during the Vietnam war. The pilots were Maj. Kent C. Bateman of VMA (AW)-533 and Maj. Fred J. Cone and Lt. Col. Lewis H. "Lew" Abrams, both of VMA (AW)-242. The bombardier-navigators who flew with the pilots were not similarly awarded. One pilot explained it this way: "You know what they call a bombardier-navigator without a pilot? An artilleryman, that's what." Abrams, who commanded VMA (AW)-242, was later lost in combat on an A-6A Intruder mission on November 24, 1967.

Americans remember the Intruder for different reasons. The tortured face of bombardier-navigator Lt. Jeffrey Zaun of VA-35, "Black Panthers," made the cover of *Time* magazine during Operation Desert Storm in 1991. After the war, Zaun's pilot, Lt. Robert Wetzel, told me of suffering serious injuries parachuting from his A-6 over Iraq.

In 1982, Lt. (j.g.) Pat Dinkler of VA-42, "Green Pawns," took an A-6E Intruder aboard a carrier off the East Coast on a training flight—the first woman to fly a current jet aircraft "on the boat," in an era when women were generally prohibited from making carrier landings.

The Intruder served the Navy and Marines, but was deemed too sophisticated for foreign sales. Stephen Coonts's novel, *Flight of the Intruder,* was a best-selling flying story but with wooden, one-dimensional characters. It became a poorly executed John Milius movie starring Danny Glover and Willem Dafoe.

There were those who said the Intruder shouldn't have a flat nose: the pointy end should be at the front. The Intruder was not sleek, not supersonic. Until teething troubles were solved, its bombing and navigation system suffered from repeated breakdowns. But the Intruder became the finest combat aircraft in its class. We would all be better off if plans had gone ahead for an advanced, 21st-century version called the A-6F.

Chapter Eighteen

Helicopter in a Hot Zone

JOHN PAUL CRESS The best way to think about the Sea Knight is to remember that it's a big, complex aircraft and one that performs a variety of missions remarkably well.

The letter suffix given to a helicopter in the Sea Knight group can be confusing. During the Vietnam era we had the CH-46A and CH-46D in the war zone and the CH-46F in other locations, yet many years later, and even today, Marines are flying the newer and much-upgraded CH-46E.

I would be hard pressed to find any serious fault in the design of this helicopter. I personally cannot think of any shortcomings in the three models I flew, the CH-46F during stateside operations, the CH-46D in Vietnam, and the CH-46E later.

If you had to find a fault, you'd point to power. The earlier CH-46A model, which we had in abundance in Vietnam, had a significant power deficit. Also if you were looking for faults—and remember, they're hard to find in this aircraft—early Vietnam-era pilots would say that the Sea Knight had a fault in the "hover aft" trim feature of the aircraft. It is my recollection that all the early aircraft (CH-46As and many CH-46Ds, as well) came equipped with a speed trim system that incorporated the

1st Lt. John Paul Cress
October 4, 1969
Vertol CH-46D Sea Knight
  (bureau no. 153987)
CATTLECALL 73
Marine Medium Helicopter
  Squadron HMM-161
South Vietnam

Joan Paul Cress, Marine CH-46 pilot,
in May 1972.

[Jean Paul Cress]

"hover aft" feature. The "hover aft" feature automatically tilted the whole rotor plane aft, depending on airspeed, to keep the Sea Knight's fuselage as close to level as possible. Without it, your helicopter would get very nose high in a quick stop. You weren't supposed to manually engage "hover aft" at a speed faster than 70 knots, but it was easy to do so and it could function as a speed brake, enabling the aircraft to make a steep and rapid approach to a hot landing zone. The trouble was it also overstressed the Sea Knight's airframe. In a combat situation, pilots weren't necessarily going to worry about long-term damage to the airframe—and certainly not about the rules—if they could get the performance they needed in a tight situation. It probably wasn't true that the "hover aft" feature would make the tail come off, as some Marines said, but eventually they installed an airspeed interlock so pilots wouldn't manually engage "hover aft" at speeds that were too high. The interlock precluded actual aft cyclic trimming of the aft rotor head (via "hover aft") until speed decreased below 70 knots indicated airspeed, or KIAS. After the retrofit, the pilot could select "hover aft" above 70 KIAS, but the airspeed interlock would not permit the speed trim actuator to respond to the pilot's selection until speed had decreased to 70 KIAS.

There was a major structural retrofit program for the early Sea Knights that was necessitated in part by the fatiguing effects of "hover aft" use, as well as general combat maneuvering of the CH-46A, which was simply a Marine version of the commercially designed V-107 and wasn't truly ready for the rigors of combat in Southeast Asia. In the CH-46A, and in the early CH-46Ds as well, the aft transmission was mounted to the fuselage via two hardpoints in the tail structure. The "hover aft" experience—five Sea Knights experienced catastrophic structural failure of the aft pylon, as I recall, including two that were airborne at the time—led to a complete redesign of the tail pylon. The primary change was to incorporate a much stronger, four-point aft transmission mount, incorporated in aircraft that were still on the as-sembly line and retrofitted to aircraft in the field at the fastest sustain-able rate. Of course, when it became clear that the entire Sea Knight fleet had a structural problem of this magnitude, and given the Marine Corps's combat responsibilities, other aircraft makers saw a door possi-bly opening for them. Sikorsky, for example, proposed a rear-loading, ramp-equipped CH-3G version of the Sea King as a means for the Ma-rine Corps to extricate itself from what some saw as the service's disas-trous procurement of the CH-46.

Increased Sea Knight Power

It isn't obvious when you look at them from the outside, but the first ver-sion of the Vietnam-era Sea Knight, the CH-46A, bears little resem-blance in terms of performance to the later CH-46D (also used in Vietnam), CH-46F, and CH-46E models. The A model was equipped with dual T58-GE-8 turboshaft engines delivering a maximum of 1,250 shaft horsepower per side, whereas the D and F had the -10 version of the engine, capable of 1,400 shaft horsepower. This made them much more capable, even though they had a higher empty weight. The modern-era CH-46E model uses the -16 version of the engine, capable of a whopping 1,870 shaft horsepower each. Thus, while today's E

The CH-46A Sea Knight helicopter had twin, tandem rotors, one behind the other. It was the workhorse of the Marines in Vietnam. Here, a CH-46A is being refueled at Dong Ha, South Vietnam, in 1966, with an Air Commando A-1E Skyraider in the background.

[U.S. Marine Corps]

model is a significantly heavier bird, in terms of empty weight (probably an average 15,500 pounds, empty), its max gross weight is up to 24,300, with a much more complete "combat suite" (armor, communications and navigation equipment, and electronics) and provides significantly better high/hot performance.

This leads me to one more comment, regarding the "Achilles' heel" of a very fine combat helicopter. The CH-46A, D, and F were equipped with metal blades, as were all helicopters of their era, though the spar on the blades was of corrosion-resistant steel alloy, whereas the H-3 Sea King, CH-53A Sea Stallion, and UH-1E Huey used aluminum spars. While the steel spars provided great strength-to-weight and damage-tolerance benefits, the Sea Knight was victim to no less than 12 rotor blade failures in various stages of flight. Some of these occurred while on the ground, considered "flight" for safety purposes. There were various contributing factors, prime of which were internal corrosion, rework procedures, and battle damage. This vulnerability was very effectively addressed with the composite rotor blades (fiberglass and carbon fiber) introduced in the late 1970s. The entire Sea Knight fleet eventually got them.

Having said a few things about what's wrong with the CH-46 Sea Knight, I want to emphasize that most of what was put into this aircraft design was right from the start. This was one of the first truly successful tandem-rotor helicopters—that's two main rotors, one behind the other, turning in opposite directions, meaning of course that you don't need a tail rotor—and that is a concept that offers a lot.

Let me mention some of the great attributes of tandem rotors versus the more conventional single-rotor/tail-rotor configuration:

1. Tandems are very tolerant of wind from any direction, not so for tail-rotor aircraft! (Thus, the CH-46 Sea Knight is a shipboard operator's dream. Navy pilots who fly vertical replenishment, or vertrep, supply missions love the CH-46 on this score.)

2. Tandems retain control margins through a wide range of center of gravity positions, not so for single rotors!

3. Tandems put a lot of rotor into the wind when it's time to decelerate from a hot approach into a contested landing zone, or LZ. (Ever watch a CH-53 or an H-3 do this? Every enemy in the grid square will get a shot at them!)

4. If you've got to do a two-wheel balancing act on a rock to pick up or drop a medevac or a recon team, you'd better hope you're driving a tandem. (The rear main landing gear is right back there at the ramp hinge, so it's nice and steady for the crew chief and the embarking/debarking passengers, a characteristic further enhanced by the helicopter's rock-solid response to omnidirectional winds.)

5. A tandem, assuming it has speed trim, will provide a much more level cruise attitude than a typical single rotor.

The Sea Knight is a 23,300-pound machine. It will seat 24 troops rather comfortably, plus two pilots in the cockpit and a crew chief. It has a 51-foot rotor diameter, and two main rotors that overlap by about 40 percent. The fuselage is about 44 feet long.

In terms of its tactical capabilities, the aircraft is nothing fancy, but it's extremely flexible and durable. It has many advantages over a single-rotor machine in that, first of all, you have a very broad range of center of gravity choices you can make, depending on how you're loaded.

The tandem-rotor system is ideal for coming into hot landing zones in that you can maintain a relatively high speed until the last moment, and you get very rapid deceleration—in effect, a much quicker approach and landing than you can in a single-rotor helicopter. The comparison would be the CH-53A Sea Stallion helicopter. It's a great machine, but because it's single rotor, and because of its relatively limited center of gravity range, the CH-53A has to come in at a very extreme yaw and a nose-high attitude and it's exposed to enemy fire for quite a while. You don't want to make yourself a target for a moment longer than necessary. The tandem rotor arrangement of the CH-46A has this wonderful advantage in that you can decelerate rapidly and land very precisely.

Marine Helo Pilot

I guess you could consider me typical of Marines who piloted the CH-46A in Vietnam. I was born in 1944 in Ohio. Like all great officers—I have a regular commission in the Marine Corps, having graduated from the NROTC program at Ohio State—I went off to basic school. I got there September 6, 1967. I graduated March 6, 1968. I was a bit of an oddball, in the sense that the demand for helicopter pilots by the Marine Corps was very, very heavy and of course all Marine pilots go through Navy training, but in those days the Navy could not accommodate all the Marines who needed training so, oddly enough, I went to the Army. Our class was one of the first, if not the first, in which we had no one going to Navy training, and all of our would-be candidates for helicopters went off to the U.S. Army and all of our would-be candidates for fast jets went off to the U.S. Air Force. Maybe you could say we were all oddballs in that sense.

I went to Fort Wolters, Texas, west of Fort Worth. It was the primary training spot for all the Army folks in those days. I received four months of primary training in an aircraft known as the Hughes TH-55 Osage. All Marines then went off to Hunter Army Airfield at Fort Stewart, Georgia, where the Army's Third Infantry Division is located. We received additional tactical training and instrument training, and all of that was done in a UH-1 Huey.

At this point in my flying experience, I still hadn't seen a tandem-rotor helicopter, and I must admit that having been an aeronautical engineer by education, I hadn't thought of flying helicopters. Having lived through the era of the space advantage of the Soviet Union, I thought I wanted to be a jet driver and a spaceman. After all, the really important people in aviation are fighter jocks and astronauts, right?

As it turned out, I was meant to be a helicopter pilot. The first time I realized that was when I was exposed to the lifts that we did in basic school. And when I finally had an opportunity to make my first flight in a CH-46A, I thought, "This is pretty cool stuff."

Not all of my fellow helicopter pilots had the best motives. With Vietnam as it was, there were many who had great foresight on how to get ahead in the Marine Corps. They realized early on that the way to get ahead was to become a helicopter pilot. I wasn't that smart. I wasn't thinking of becoming a general in the Marine Corps. I had a very altruistic, patriotic upbringing. My dad was a dogface in the Army. He was in the war long enough to get himself captured by the Germans in France. He was a prisoner of war for five months. I cared more about what I could do as a Marine than where I was actually going to go as a Marine. I don't know how many of my fellow helicopter pilots were motivated by careerism instead of patriotism, but there were some.

When I graduated from the Army flight school on November 19, 1968, I was assigned to the Marine Corps air station at New River, North Carolina. That's adjacent to the city of Jacksonville and to Camp Lejeune, so it's very much a military place. It isn't a place where a lot of people would choose to take their family or to live for the long term, but it was great for my family and we did well there. I was assigned to squadron HMM-264, the "Black Knights," and began flying around the first of December 1968 in the CH-46A.

My experience was initially confusing and stressful for my wife. She wound up having to go through three squadron name changes as we made our way through the learning process in preparing for Vietnam.

I was in -264 through the Christmas and New Year's holidays, until the end of January 1969. I came home and told her that, one, we were quitting the squadron, and, two, I was going to be assigned to a new squadron and it was going to be in the Caribbean. That was the Marine Corps's way of fulfilling its personnel needs and getting us young pilots qualified and able to operate off a ship. So I went and joined squadron HMM-365, or "Yankee Mike," in the Caribbean, deployed aboard the USS *Guam* (LPH 9). In that group, I quickly learned how to bring a helicopter onto a ship. It's a skill that doesn't come intuitively.

I was in that unit until my anniversary, June 11, 1969. I returned to New River, and I was transferred out of HMM-365 to the confusion of my wife, who was getting to remember the name, finally. I got assigned to HMM-162, or "Yankee Sierra," also at New River, until the time I left to go to Vietnam. I arrived in Vietnam on August 24, 1969.

That was the date my sister got married. The Marine Corps was more interested in having me in Vietnam than in having me attend her wedding. I joined squadron HMM-161, or "Yankee Romeo," at Quang Tri, South Vietnam. That was an operations base as far north as any helicopter base in Vietnam. We shared that base with some other Marine Corps outfits and some Army outfits as well, although I don't believe the Army had any helicopters there.

In Marine helicopter flying, the aircraft commander sits in the right seat. I actually didn't make aircraft commander until I'd been in country for a couple of months. You had to learn the ropes a little first. That had to do with flying the aircraft in a tougher environment than I'd been involved with. Certainly, you had to learn the tactics. For example, when you're threatened with small arms, you might want to point your nose at the threat or take some other appropriate action. When you're threatened with a larger-caliber weapon, such as the North Vietnamese .51-caliber machine gun, you want to be up at least 2,500 feet.

CH-46 in Combat

When we went into the areas around Khe Sanh, there were a number of posts up there where the grunts were very high in those mountains. At LZ Sheppard, LZ Pate, Vandegrift base, the Rockpile, all of those places—more often than not, named for previous commandants of the Marine Corps—conditions were very demanding in terms of flying. The grunts were placed up there very precariously. It was difficult to carry out the mission and just hang on the side of the hill. You wanted to position the helicopter in such a way that your downwash was least detrimental to the grunts you were trying to support.

The Vandegrift base was a clearing spot. The Marines had a hospital there. It was an area of pretty significant activity. It was a delivering point for the medevacs.

I can't emphasize too much the fact that the CH-46A was good at many different types of missions. This will sound like a guy who is extremely proud of the aircraft he wound up in, and I am. The CH-46 was by far the most versatile helicopter the Marine Corps flew in Vietnam. On a resupply mission, you brought food in to the grunts. You took in ammunition. You took in water. If you were going to the Rockpile, you had the flexibility of delivering it as an external load, and that was good because there wasn't enough room to get all the landing gear down on the pad, which was on the top of that narrow pinnacle of rocks near Dong Ha. You'd land there and if you were lucky, you could put down the rear wheels and push the supplies out back. If you weren't so lucky, then you'd have to take it in by external, and that was very difficult because visual references were extremely difficult.

Another CH-46A mission was reconnaissance—helping grunts and ground commanders learn more about what the enemy was doing. And then there was recon extract. If a recon team got themselves into some

A Marine CH-46A Sea Knight on a routine flight. In South Vietnam, where karst ridgelines often rose at abrupt angles, the CH-46 sometimes reached a landing zone by parking its rear wheels in the right spot, lowering the ramp, and unloading while the rest of the aircraft remained in a hover.

[U.S. Navy]

sort of trouble, you'd go try to pull them out. Sometimes bad guys might surround them, so you'd pull them aboard and get out of there.

In addition, the CH-46A performed medical evacuation flights. Unlike the Army, which has a dedicated medevac mission known as dust off, the Marines perform medical evacuations with the very same aircraft that fulfill other duties.

Yet another mission was troop lift. We had to take the irregular defense team (CIDG), army of Vietnam (ARVN), or our own Marines into action.

There were also oddball missions. There would be an Arc Light strike by B-52 Stratofortress bombers up along the demilitarized zone, or DMZ, and we'd be given the job of getting a team up there to assess the results. We'd fly up there and we'd literally fly into a bomb crater.

One of my first memorable missions was one of these—the insertion of a battle damage assessment team. I was flying with the commander of the squadron, Maj. (later Col.) Richard Carr, partly because it was time to decide whether I was ready to become an aircraft commander. Carr was a well-known guy, one of the luminaries that came out of that squadron. He ran a squadron in a remote and highly contested area and did a good job.

It was October 4, 1969. October was an extremely wet month. We were deluged in a difficult-to-reach spot, trying to get the job done. There was much flooding and weather bad enough that we had a great deal of trouble getting in to resupply the ground units up in northern I Corps (Quang Tri to the DMZ).

My flight duration that day was 6.5 hours in CH-46D Sea Knight bureau number 153987, and it included two hours of instrument time. Apparently that's because we were flying instrument approaches into Dong Ha and perhaps Landing Zone Vandegrift, a logistical and medical staging area, in an effort to deliver supplies wherever we could before we flew the battle damage assessment, or BDA, mission. The BDA team was typically a team of seven or eight recon Marines. They wanted to see how effective the Arc Light bombing missions had been, which probably meant they were expected to do a body count.

I flew with Carr with a recon team. Our job was to hold outside the DMZ. We were to observe an Arc Light mission in which B-52s flew over and disgorged their bombs. It was one magnificent sight, I can tell you that. We held off to the south and watched. We watched the impact, saw the flashes, and saw the smoke billowing up to two or three thousand feet. When the B-52s had cleared the area, we were given a set of coordinates at which we were supposed to land and put our team out to assess the effectiveness of the Arc Light strike.

B-52 Aftermath

We landed in a crater that was the result of multiple bomb hits. We lowered the ramp. Out went the recon team. They got up to the edges of that pretty large crater and were pretty surprised to find bad guys there shooting at them.

The aftermath of one of those bomb strikes was something to see.

Oddly enough, even though there'd been a three-plane B-52 Arc Light which literally raised the dust some 3,000 feet and shattered eardrums for miles around, when you put the BDA team down into the crater from around the edges, they'd find somewhat delirious but still pretty capable North Vietnamese rising up out of the holes the bombs had made. They would come up with ears and noses bleeding from a concussion but nevertheless ready to fight, almost as if the B-52 hadn't passed overhead at all.

We were taking fire. I remember that particular mission because, as the copilot, one of my responsibilities was to raise the FM antenna, which in those days you could deploy for better reception. In that version of the CH-46, you had a retractable antenna. It was unfortunately not uncommon for the guy in the left-hand seat to forget to pull it up. I don't think the antenna was damaged anyway because we landed in a relatively soft spot and I don't believe we broke it. Still, I was concerned that I might show a lack of professionalism. I did get a little bit of mild butt chewing from the CO but not much because things went well. We had no choice but to take our recon team back on board and pull them out. I remember being so impressed that the bad guys, the North Vietnamese, were still there, still able to carry on with their work.

Here's how our missions were assigned. There was a helicopter direction center, or HDC, that gave us our orders. They would receive the frag, the fragmentary order that was our assignment for our mission. The frag came from the wing and to the group. Our group was called Provisional Marine Aircraft Group 39, or ProvMAG-39, at Quang Tri. We had two squadrons of Hueys and two of CH-46s. We didn't have any H-53s. When we needed H-53s, they had to come up from the south. Anyway, those fragmentary orders from the wing and group would reach the HDC, and they would disseminate them to the squadrons.

Just a few words about the CH-46 Sea Knight and its ability to sustain battle damage in Vietnam: There are famous pix from the Vietnam era (taken by 1st Lt. Paul Pearman of HMM-263, I believe) of a CH-46D having sustained a direct hit by a rocket-propelled grenade, or

RPG. The aircraft, despite a gaping hole three feet in diameter, was flown back to base.

On another occasion, one of my squadron mates took 30-plus hits in the cockpit during an attempted insertion of Civilian Irregular Defense Group (CIDG) troops in Vietnam, but the pilot—sitting next to a copilot, who, as it turned out ultimately, was mortally wounded—was able to fly the aircraft out of the intended zone to a successful landing in a reasonably secure area a mile or so away.

I personally took six hits (mostly in the stub wing area) during a large operation (CH-53Ds dropped napalm and many CH-46Ds followed with successive waves of troop insertion) near Thong Duc, well southwest of Da Nang in bad-guy country. We heard the hits and saw "rosettes" of displaced metal on the upper surface of the stub wings, where the enemy rounds exited. But, of course, the lower third of the stub wings were equipped with self-sealing provisions, which prevented loss of fuel and minimized fire hazard, so we kept going through the multiple waves of troop lifts to be sure "critical mass" (boots on the ground) was achieved.

While assisting with retrieval of one of our birds that had been shot down on Hill 270 at the southern edge of I Corps, we took several hits coming up from the downslope in the cockpit. The hits threw some canopy fragments around. There were light wounds to the copilot and myself. The hits messed up the wiring in the overhead console. I landed to get aid for the copilot, checked the aircraft over, and decided it was fit to fly back. We did so without incident. By the way, the aircraft that was "shot down" at Hill 270, with L. J. Smith as pilot, had been close to the ground when hits were taken to both boost systems. The aircraft became uncontrollable without these. The design was good in that these systems were separated and redundant, but there were critical components (upper and lower dual boost actuators, primarily) where they came close enough together that a well-placed hit could take both out. This was the "Achilles' heel" feared by most of the pilots, I believe. It didn't happen but a few times to my knowledge, but the prospect of uncontrollability was palpable.

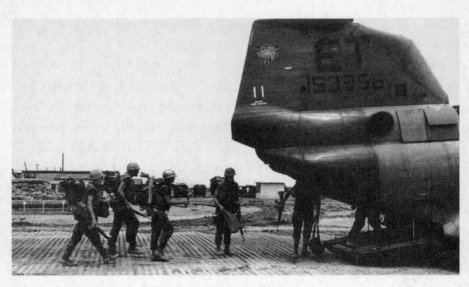

Marines in South Vietnam climbing aboard a Sea Knight helicopter like the one flown by.

[U.S. Marine Corps]

In a busy helicopter cockpit in Vietnam, you encountered a lot of different radio call signs. Our squadron, HMM-161, used CATTLE-CALL. Our sister squadron, HMM-262, was PEACHBUSH on the radio. Squadron HML-167, equipped with the UH-1E Huey, used the call sign COMPRISE. Some of the others were SEAWORTHY for VMO-6, which operated the UH-1E Huey and OV-10 Bronco, and DIMMER for HMH-461, which flew the CH-53D Sea Stallion.

Other Missions

By the way, I didn't fly only missions in the Quang Tri area. After rebasing to the south (MAG-16/Da Nang, with HMM-161), I flew several missions under fire, most "exciting" of which were recon-team extracts. One of these was a night extraction far south and west of Da Nang in "Indian country" in perilous terrain, where all elements of our response team were involved: OV-10 Broncos (overall coordination), a C-130

Who's Who

1st Lt. John Paul Cress, CH-46D Sea Knight pilot, squadron HMM-161

Maj. (later Col.) Richard Carr, squadron commander HMM-161 and CH-46D
Sea Knight pilot

Hercules (dropping flares), and AH-1G Cobras (gunships, with 40-millimeter grenades and a 20-millimeter minigun), along with my CH-46 Sea Knights. There was another daylight extraction I led in a place called Elephant Valley, west of Da Nang, involving artillery assistance and F-4 Phantom–delivered napalm, in which I and my crew pulled a team of seven out of a canyon under fire, via a special patrol insertion-extraction, (SPIE), rig, where we dropped a long nylon strap (with integrated steel rings, strap firmly anchored to the belly of the aircraft) through the "hell hole." As each successive member of the recon team snapped the hook of his torso strap to a ring on the SPIE strap, we'd raise the helicopter another six feet or so. We quickly had all seven recon Marines on the SPIE strap, one above/below the other, with the first attached dangling from the highest ring on the strap, and the last attached on the bottom. We then pulled them up and proceeded (at only about 60 knots, because the drag on their bodies tightened them so much in their torso straps that they couldn't breathe properly over about 60 knots) to the nearest secure landing site, where we lowered them incrementally (each unsnapping himself from the SPIE strap), boarded the team in the belly of the aircraft, and returned uneventfully to the recon landing pad near Da Nang.

There were many other memorable missions. There were big troop lifts involving a dozen CH-46s and half as many gunships, as well as H-53s "prepping" the area via cargo nets full of napalm. There were medevacs into mined areas, where I remember one particular crew chief running with a stretcher through the peril to assist with recovery of troops who suffered multiple amputations as a result of the mines.

There were hovering insertions. Those involved placement of one or two wheels on a promontory, to which the troops jumped from the aircraft. There were recoveries of battle-damaged aircraft. For those, we flew maintenance teams into unsecure (and often under-fire) areas to "prep" damaged aircraft for external lift (via CH-53D) back to secure areas for repair. In one of these, a bad guy got a bead on me and my copilot and peppered our windscreen and overhead panel with AK-47 rounds while we were attempting a second delivery on external lift sling parts. We had to get the copilot and the aircraft patched. Cobras dispatched the bad guy after courageous actions by the ground recovery crew.

You can't say enough to laud the young crew chiefs who fixed these aircraft all night and flew them all day and night into God only knew what. They were smart, hard-driving, courageous young men. They probably didn't even realize what great Marines they were, partially because we forget to tell them at the time, but mostly because they were too busy doing their day and night jobs to spend much time thinking about it. Remember that crew chiefs fix their aircraft AND fly them into harm's way—and come back to fix them again for the next day.

The young man who guided my cabin crew (himself plus two .50-caliber gunners) on one difficult night recon extraction was Cpl. Harry Kersten. Our gunners were Lance Corporals Chris Matisse and Riggs. One of the crew chiefs was Joe Bowling. But there are many others whose service was nothing less than valiant.

In later years, I had the honor of becoming the program manager for the H-46 in the final three years of my career. So I'm familiar with the CH-46E model that is still in use today.

Boeing Vertol CH-46A Sea Knight

In 1961, the Boeing Company's Vertol (formerly Vertol Aircraft and later simply Boeing) won a 1960 competition to build a new assault he-

This is a formation of Marine Corps CH-46A Sea Knight helicopters like the aircraft flown by Cress.

[U.S. Marine Corps]

---

licopter for the Marine Corps. When the Pentagon system for naming aircraft was overhauled on October 1, 1962, the new aircraft known initially as the HRB-1 was renamed the CH-46A. The CH-46A made its first flight 16 days later.

The Sea Knight was the latest in a long line of tandem-rotor helicopters designed in the 1950s by Frank Piasecki and dubbed "flying bananas" by the press. Boeing designed the CH-46A with folding rotors for stowage aboard aircraft carriers.

Boeing began to deliver Sea Knights to Marine squadrons in 1964. The Navy also used the helicopter for delivery of supplies to ships at sea.

The CH-46A arrived in Vietnam in March 1966 and began to replace the Sikorsky UH-34D (see chapter 12). Improved CH-46D models followed soon after. Sea Knights served with squadrons HMM-164, -165, -262, -265, and -364. They were often in the thick of battle. Boeing manufactured 624 of the helicopters, and the North Vietnamese shot down 106 of them. The CH-46E—unlike, for example, the CH-

53E—has been through several modernization programs to introduce new equipment and "zero out" the airframes for longer life. For more than 15 years, the Marine Corps has intended to replace its current Sea Knight fleet with the MV-22B Osprey tilt-rotor aircraft, and plans were still proceeding when this volume went to press.

Boeing-Vertol CH-46A (HRB-1) Sea Knight

Type: 4-place, twin-tandem transport assault helicopter

Power plant: Two 1,250-shp (1010-kW) General Electric T58-GE-8B turboshaft engines driving two separate sets of 3-blade 50-ft (15.24-m) metal main rotors (CH-46A); two 1,400-shp (1200 kW) T58-GE-10 engines with 51-ft (15.54-m) rotors (CH-46D, CH-46F)

Performance: maximum permissible speed, 168 mph (270 km/h); maximum cruising speed, 159 mph (253 km/h); maximum rate of climb at sea level, 1,375 ft (419 m); hovering ceiling in ground effect, 5,250 ft (1600 m); hovering ceiling out of ground effect, 7,400 (2255 m); service ceiling, 17,000 ft (5180 m); range with maximum fuel, 682 miles (1097 km); typical range, 230 mi (370 km)

Weights: empty, equipped, 12,406 lb (5627 kg); maximum takeoff weight, 21,400 lb (9707 kg)

Dimensions: main rotor diameter (both), 50 ft (15.24 m); distance between rotor centers, 33 ft 4 in (25.40 m); length overall, rotors turning, 83 ft 4 in (25.40 m); fuselage length, 44 ft 10 in (13.66 m); height to top of rear rotor hub, 16 ft 8.5 in (5.09 m); rotor disc area, each, 1,963.5 sq ft (182.41 sq m)

Armament: typically, two 7.62-mm or .50-cal (12.7-mm) door-mounted machine guns

Payload: 17 to 24 fully armed combat troops, or 15 litter patients and 2 attendants, or 4,000 lb (1814 kg) of cargo

Crew: 4 (2 pilots, crew chief, gunner)

First flight: October 16, 1962 (CH-46A)

Chapter Nineteen

MiG Kill Near Haiphong

JOHN D. CUMMINGS We went into a trap. I wouldn't call it being suckered. I would compare it to the Charge of the Light Brigade.

The day before our big fight, the MiGs came up to mess with us. One MiG almost got between the strike group and us. I had him locked up, but lost my radar. Our job was to protect the strike group, and if that meant being lured into an area where a lot of MiGs and missiles were waiting for us, that's what we had to do.

My pilot, Bear Lasseter, wanted to get a MiG. I'm not saying I was against it. Of course, I wanted to get a MiG, too. But Bear really, really wanted to get a MiG. He wanted to get a MiG ever since he was a little kid. Nevertheless, there was nothing reckless about what we did on that fateful September 11. We were doing our job.

When we scored our kill that day, it was the only enemy plane shot down during the Vietnam war by Marine aviators flying a Marine aircraft. But the cost was huge.

Capt. John D. "Lil' John"
    Cummings
September 11, 1972
McDonnell F-4J Phantom II (bu-
    reau no. 1555126/AJ-201)
Marine Fighter Attack
    Squadron VMFA-333,
    "Triple Trey"
SHAMROCK
USS *America* (CVA 66), Gulf of
    Tonkin

John D. Cummings is the only Marine radar intercept officer to be
credited with shooting down an enemy aircraft while flying Marine aircraft. Here, Cummings is getting his
first acquaintance with Vietnam at
Da Nang, circa May 1965. He returned in 1972 aboard the aircraft
carrier USS *America* (CVA 66).

[John D. Cummings]

What Happened

The star player in battles over North Vietnam was the Marines' robust,
twin-engine F-4 Phantom fighter. Only the Marine Corps flew the Phantom as an air-to-ground warplane to support its own troops and as an
air-to-air fighter. Two battalions of Marines came ashore at Da Nang
on April 10, 1965, and with them came the first Phantoms, the "Gray
Ghosts" of VMFA-531 under Col. William C. McGraw, Jr., at Da
Nang. Among pilots in McGraw's squadron was Lt. Col. Thomas
Miller, who had set a speed record in the Phantom. Among the backseat
radar intercept officers, or RIOs, in McGraw's squadron was a warrant
officer, John D. Cummings.

Thousands of Marine Air combat missions and seven years later,
Cummings was a captain and was in squadron VMFA-333, the "Triple
Trey," alias "SHAMROCKS," embarked aboard the carrier USS *America*

(CVA 66). Although Marines are trained to fly from ships' decks, this was the only time in the Vietnam War that a Phantom squadron did so.

The Marines used the Phantom to protect an aerial strike force from MiGs. At times, that gave them no real choice about being drawn into the battle.

Pilot Maj. Lee T. "Bear" Lasseter and backseater Cummings launched from the *America* and flew into heavily defended North Vietnam. In a second aircraft were pilot Capt. Scott Dudley and radar intercept officer Capt. James "Diamond Jim" Brady.

The date was September 11, 1972. F-4 crews sought to prevent North Vietnamese from interfering with a nearby air strike.

Things began badly. A planned rendezvous with an air-refueling tanker came too late. Dudley's Phantom was only partly refueled. And then, as a result of what Cummings called "miscommunication" with ships offshore, the two jets were sent to engage North Vietnamese MiG-21 fighters near Haiphong, North Vietnam. The area was rife with enemy surface-to-air missiles (SAMs).

In the book *MiG Killers of Yankee Station,* Michael O'Connor quotes Dudley as preparing to fight. Seven miles from the MiGs, Dudley said, "I got an initial sighting on the MiGs. I don't have atomic eyeballs or anything, but I just happened to look up and see a glint." Lasseter and Dudley each fired a Sparrow radar-guided missile at the lead MiG and missed.

Cummings was carrying a cassette tape recorder strapped to his harness. He recorded a confusing conversation with a radar picket ship during a five-minute dogfight with the MiGs. Lasseter and Cummings fired four missiles without result before a MiG crossed their path and Lasseter saw a clean shot for a Sidewinder. Cummings remembers thinking, "I believe we can get this MiG."

JIM MARTIN I don't think I was involved in that September 11 action. I don't remember, to be honest. In any case, I have vivid memories of that combat cruise with VMFA-333, which was unique in the Vietnam War.

We actually were scheduled for a Mediterranean cruise. The *Amer-*

ica was an East Coast ship. She was Norfolk based. Her squadrons were East Coast Navy squadrons as were our Beaufort, South Carolina—based Marine F-4J squadron. Once through the normal six-month period of workups in the Atlantic, we were ready for what was going to be a Med cruise. Shortly before our departure date, I took my wife, Linda, and son, Jason, down to Panama City, Florida, for a few days on the beach. When we flew back, I was told that our orders had changed and we were going to WestPac, meaning the Western Pacific. Frankly, we didn't believe it. I called squadron commander Lt. Col. John Cochran. He invited me over to his house and explained the situation. We left Norfolk, as I remember, around June 5, 1972, and it was a 30-day trip across the South Atlantic and around the cape of South Africa and through the Indian Ocean.

I remember the first time I flew in combat, in support of Vietnamese troops down south. My recollection is that they were south of Da Nang. We started out flying missions down south. We were a little rusty and down south there was a little less of an enemy threat.

The SA-7 heat-seeking SAM, was in use at that point, so we prepared to deal with it, which meant we were flying at higher-speed and higher-angle bomb deliveries rather than going in at a low angle in a shallow, lower-speed dive. On a typical combat mission, we were making a 45-degree dive with a 5,000-foot bomb release.

Launch from the Carrier

The activity on the flight deck of a carrier is as close to precision as you can imagine. Everybody has to be in the right place at the right time or accidents happen. So sailors and marines in different-colored shirts run around, assisting in the preparation of aircraft for the launch, refueling, respotting, manning emergency equipment, and directing and launching aircraft, but it is all very organized and precise. You and your radar intercept officer proceeded to the assigned aircraft where the pilot met with the plane captain (the enlisted marine/noncommissioned officer re-

Rarely seen in print, this is an in-flight portrait of one of the F-4J Phantoms from Cummings's squadron, VMFA-333, aboard the carrier *America* during the 1972 cruise in Vietnamese waters. This aircraft carries a centerline fuel tank and bombs under-wing, suggesting a long-range mission.

[U.S. Marine Corps]

sponsible for having the plane ready for launch) and together do a walk-around preflight inspection of the aircraft and ordnance. The F-4J had a retractable step that dropped down from the lower left-hand side of the fuselage under the pilot's cockpit. Above that were a couple of small spring-loaded doors in the side of the fuselage that allowed the pilot and RIO hand and foot holds to ascend to their respective cockpits. Once the pilot and RIO climbed in, the plane captain assisted the aircrew in strapping in and arming the ejection seats. The plane captain then descended to the flight deck, where he directed the start-up and poststart flight-control checks through the use of standardized hand signals. Canopies were typically open until taxi unless positioned in a spot where jet blast from other aircraft was an issue. When ready for taxi, the heavy tie-down chains and chocks were removed, and the plane captain handed the aircrew off to a series of yellow-shirted plane directors, who directed the aircraft to the catapult.

The first time you taxi up over that hump to get on the catapult, your heart is definitely beating. The F-4 used a device on the catapult that your front wheel had to go up over, and there was a little bit of a bump when you went over it. If you had to wait for a while on the launch behind planes that were taking off, you were of course getting a lot of heat from the exhausts, plus there was frequently smoke coming down from the stack of the ship. The *America* was an oil burner rather than a nuclear aircraft carrier and it stank.

Typically, F-4s were spotted on the aft part of the deck. This put you in that downdraft if the wind was right. It was not a comfortable environment, especially for the deck crews that weren't sitting inside a closed cockpit. They were out in the elements, getting a lot of jet blast thrown at them, a lot of exhaust gases thrown at them, and a lot of heat thrown at them. Of course, you had to watch out all the time or you could get blown overboard by that. I never saw that happen but it was always a danger.

Preparing for the catapult launch, you have at this point already calculated what your launch weight is going to be. You communicate with one of the plane directors. This is done entirely with hand signals. There's no voice communication. He uses a board to signal your launch weight and you give him thumbs up or thumbs down. The catapult room needs to have your weight right or you won't get launched properly and you may end up in the Gulf of Tonkin. Once you confirm your weight, you signal the catapult officer that you've pulled up tension and you bring it up to military power. You light the afterburner and at that point, if everything looks okay, you give him a left-handed salute. He salutes back and points. That's the signal to launch. You wait for what seems like seconds and then you get the ride of your life, accelerating to 180 knots in just a couple of hundred feet. No matter how much you prepare for that first catapult launch, I don't think anybody's ever quite ready for it.

I guarantee you, that first time off the catapult your knees are going to come back at you. That never ceased to be a thrill. That was a very exciting part of flying off the carrier, the catapult launch. They tried to launch the F-4s last, behind all the other aircraft in the carrier air wing, because we burned more fuel than anybody else did. We launched, climbed to 6,000 feet, and joined on the tanker, which most of the time was a KA-6D Intruder from the carrier. You take on about 4,000 pounds of fuel at that point. One you've made it, your formation takes on fuel and then you're off on the mission.

One target that nobody liked was the notorious Thanh Hoa Bridge in North Vietnam. Typically, the F-4Js provided a MiG combat air patrol, or MiGCAP, between what we understood to be the nearest or the most likely threat—probably one of the MiG airfields—and the strike force. We would also provide a flight of at least four F-4s as flak suppression. The flak suppression aircraft went after antiaircraft guns or antiaircraft trucks.

Rolling in to hit those antiaircraft sites, you point your nose and get into a 45-degree dive and pick up about 500 knots. Then you drop some Rockeye cluster bombs on those gun sites. We got pretty good at dropping bombs. That wasn't our primary mission but we could put bombs on target. Typically, our bombload would always include six Rockeye cluster bomb units, or CBUs, on the outboard stations, and on the inboard stations we'd have four AIM-9 Sidewinder heat-seeking air-to-air missiles and we carried two AIM-7 Sparrow radar-guided air-to-air missiles in the front. With that bombload, you could not carry two additional Sparrows on the rear stations. That was a center of gravity issue.

JOHN D. CUMMINGS The growl of the Sidewinder tone in my earphones—the audio signal that Lasseter and I had locked up this MiG-21—was loud enough to drive you from the cockpit. That's what happens when the missile's seeker head is lined up perfectly. Lasseter fired. The Sidewinder went off its rail in a puff of smoke and went after the MiG.

The missile struck the MiG solidly and blew apart everything aft of its cockpit.

We were now low on fuel. We disengaged. Lasseter and Dudley ran into more communications problems while our earphones boomed with radio warnings of North Vietnamese SAMs being launched at us.

Lasseter and I took a missile hit, ejected, and parachuted into the Gulf of Tonkin, where a helicopter rescued us.

A missile also hit Dudley and his backseater. They ejected and were rescued. Lasseter went on to become commander of VMFA-333, and

The enemy. By 1972, American experts had had a chance to evaluate a Soviet-built MiG-21 fighter obtained by Israel from a defector and seen here at the super-secret U.S. airbase at Groom Lake, Nev., the installation called "Area 51" in the press. The MiG-21 was a formidable adversary for John D. Cummings and his fellow Marines.

[U.S. Air Force]

the squadron racked up a superb record during the remainder of the 1972 combat cruise. The Marines lost two Phantoms that day, but we drew strength from knowing we'd bagged a MiG and protected friendly strike aircraft.

DAVID VAN ESSELSTYN The U.S. combat role in Vietnam officially ended on January 27, 1973, but combat operations in Cambodia continued until August 15. I was in squadron VMFA-115, "Silver Eagles," at Nam Phong, Thailand, flying during that difficult period. Like John Cummings, I was a backseat RIO on an F-4J Phantom.

One of our missions typically starts with a mission briefing. The intel briefing is held at the Group S-2 (Intelligence) in a Southeast Asia hut. Then, for our flight briefing, we go to the only air-conditioned space we have at Nam Phong, which is inside the converted avionics trailers. That's when we look ahead to what we're going to do in the air and talk about crew coordination, navigation to the target area, and tanking, among other things.

And then we go for our equipment. There usually are one or two flight equipment people in there. I get my flight suit on and then don my

David Van Esselstyn (left) and John Pastuf with an F-4 Phantom II of Marine Fighter Attack Squadron 323, the "Death Rattlers," at Marine Corps Air Station Yuma, Ariz., in the fall of 1972.

[David Van Esselstyn]

torso harness plus a separate life vest with my survival gear, and after that I grab my helmet and oxygen mask. We always check these things over very carefully. I always take a good look at my life vest, including checking the pockets to make sure the dye markers have current dates on them. After all that, we go and draw our weapons. Our standard issue is the snub-nosed .38. Some guys carry personal weapons, like nine-millimeters. We have one guy who carries a .45.

Our flight equipment is kept in one of the trailers and our briefing is held in another. So once we've got all the gear together, we talk to maintenance control and look for the outstanding gripes on the airplane. Then, with all our gear in hand, we go out to the airplanes and get started and go.

Nam Phong is called "The Rose Garden," after a popular Marine recruiting slogan of the time. It's the last airfield from which Marine Corps aviation will fight in Southeast Asia. According to lore, it's also the only airfield not adjacent to water from which Marine Air has ever done battle. I arrived after the January 27, 1973, cease-fire ended the American combat role in South Vietnam, but we we're still flying combat in Cambodia. Today is typical.

Today we're going to targets around the Cambodian capital, Phnom Penh. The Khmer Rouge are pushing hard on Phnom Penh, especially from the south side. They're trying to choke off the Mekong River.

On this day, we carry six Mark 82 500-pounders—"slicks," meaning bombs without retarding fins—plus four canisters of Mark 20 Rockeye cluster bomb units, or CBUs. Our fit is a multiple ejector rack, a MER, on the centerline. That's where the six Mark 82s are. We have triple ejector ranks, TERs, on stations two and eight, which are inboard wing stations. Stations one and nine carry external fuel tanks.

My pilot today is Bill "Rat" Cooper, the squadron executive officer. He's a major. We brief. It's a normal brief on en route discipline and lookout doctrine, and on how to fly down to link up with the KC-130F Hercules tankers that have taken off beforehand. The Tonle Sap Lake is the big body of water in the middle of Cambodia (slightly northwest of center) just south of Angkor Wat, and we are going to join on the tankers over the northwestern end of the lake. We fly right over the world-famous temple site at Angkor Wat, which is somewhat frustrating because there's an awful lot of communist activity in and around Angkor Wat. It's a field hospital, resupply facility, and training area, and it's strictly off-limits to us because of its historical significance.

En route, we check in with the airborne command and control, or ABCCC, airplane. We use the call sign BLADE.

The tankers use the call sign RAIDER. They're from squadron VMGR-152, which has a detachment stationed right beside us at Nam Phong. They happen to be the oldest C-130s in the Marine Corps at this time. There are also two F-4 squadrons, an A-6 Intruder squadron, and a CH-46 Sea Knight search and recovery squadron at Nam Phong.

We're at about 12,000 to 15,000 feet when we tank on the KC-130 at about 210 knots, so it's pretty comfortable. The tankers are right where they're supposed to be according to some grand plan. We have two to three tankers on station in echelon. They split us up and we move in to gulp gas. We're about 15 feet above and behind and offset to the tanker, flying behind the tanker in a shallow curve, about three and a half or four feet out from the side of the airplane. The technique in the F-4J is you have to consider the bow wave created by the nose of your own aircraft. As you draw closer to the tanker, there is an aerodynamic bow wave that forces the basket up and to the right: the F-4 pilot has to compensate in order to stick the probe into the basket and receive fuel. This whole thing can be delicate but most of the time there's little danger.

We top off our fuel. As we come off the tanker, we're basically into the mission. We check in again with the ABCCC and get handed off to a forward air controller, or FAC, radio call sign NAIL 25. That's an Air Force OV-10A Bronco of the 23rd Tactical Air Support Squadron flying out of Nakhon Phanom, Thailand. When we talk with him, he's working with a flight of Air Force F-4s out of Ubon, Thailand.

So on this occasion there's a lot of activity, but one thing about missions to Cambodia is their ordinariness. The only threat we have is from small arms fire. The difference is we're dropping bombs on real targets. And real people. Some of whom are shooting at us.

Today, NAIL 25 tells us that we're going to deposit our slick iron bombs on an old fort on the banks of the Mekong River that the Khmer Rouge have overrun. The threat, down there, is small-caliber antiaircraft and small arms, and they could have SA-7 missiles. The OV-10A is circling over the fort and drawing fire while he sets up the target for us. He has a white top on his wings, which makes it easy for us to see him.

When we get into the area, we can see the target. I am doing the communications in the backseat of the airplane. I'm talking to the FAC. Separation of the airplanes is not really an issue for us. There's no danger of us hitting him and no one else is in the immediate neighborhood.

As we exchange quick chatter on the radio, NAIL 25 makes it clear that he wants us to breach one of the fort's walls—the north or northeast wall—and then lay our Rockeye into the center of the fort area. That means we'll be putting the cluster bombs right in the middle of the bad guys. Meanwhile, NAIL 25 has told the Air Force F-4s from Ubon to go up high and orbit around. In effect, he is getting rid of them. He is an Air Force guy himself, but apparently he believes that Marine Corps F-4s are better able to take care of this particular target. We know that's true. We know that Marine F-4s have a reputation for accuracy.

We go ahead and set up. We do our thing with the weapons switches. In the F-4 we have a thing called the "dogbone" on the instrument panel with rotary knobs and toggle switches to select bombs from the ordnance stations, and to set up what station on the airplane we're going to drop from. This is how we determine whether we'll drop from inboard wing or centerline, and the interval at which the bombs will be ejected from the bomb rack.

We do a visual check of everything around us. Once we're set up, we make our first run in a 30-degree dive and release our Mark 82s.

The result is spectacular. With the high humidity and everything, our Mark 82s going off produce a shock wave that we can actually feel inside the cockpit as we're pulling off the target. When we pull off, we look over our shoulder and see the bombs impacting. We see our wingman making his run. We've breached the wall. We wanted to get the Khmer Rouge out into the open so we could use our Rockeye effectively, and we've done it.

We have a standard operating procedure. We'll make no more than two bomb runs over the same target. Yes, it's true that there is a relatively low threat here—although today could become an exception—and absolutely no one wants to lose an airplane over Cambodia. So after our first bomb run, we're thinking we'll do just one more and go home, but the FAC is getting pretty excited. NAIL 25 is telling us that we have hit the wall and blown it into oblivion, which is exactly what he wanted us to do.

The FAC just goes crazy. He thinks this is the greatest thing he's ever seen. Apparently, he hasn't had a lot of opportunities to see Marine Air put bombs squarely on target.

Needless to say, we make another bomb run and plant our Rockeye right in the middle of the chaos that was stirred up by our first run. And then, standard operating procedure or not, we do it again. Hostile fire has been whipping around our airplane but we have taken care of a sig-

Who's Who

Capt. (later, Col.) John D. "Lil' John" Cummings, radar intercept officer, F-4J Phantom, VMFA-333, aboard USS *America* (CVA 66), 1972

Maj. Lee T. Lasseter, pilot, F-4J Phantom, VMFA-333, aboard USS *America* (CVA 66), 1972

Capt. (later Col.) Scott "Scotty" Dudley, pilot, F-4J Phantom, VMFA-333, aboard USS *America* (CVA 66), 1972; pilot, F/A-18A Hornet, commander of squadron VMFA-451, "Warlords," on the first mission of Operation Desert Storm, January 17, 1991 (see chapter 20)

Capt. Jim Martin, pilot, F-4J Phantom, VMFA-333, aboard USS *America* (CVA 66), 1972

Capt. (later Lt. Col.) David "V-Eleven" Van Esselstyn, radar intercept officer, F-4J Phantom, VMFA-115, "Silver Eagles," Nam Phong, Thailand, 1973

nificant number of Khmer Rouge. I'm not sure what the Air Force guys ever did, but maybe they came in and dropped more bombs on our target after we finished it off.

We're now "Winchester," meaning we've expended our ordnance. We turn for home. NAIL 25 comes up on the radio and gives us our battle damage assessment. We have placed 100 percent of our ordnance on the target. Guys joke and say they can put a grease pencil mark on the front of the windscreen and be accurate, but the truth is, we work at it day in and day out. That's why Marine Air F-4s are the most accurate iron bombers over here. Nobody does a better job spreading democracy in 500-pound increments for God and country.

McDonnell F-4J Phantom II

The word *Phantom* is enough to remind Marines—or anyone who knows about fighters—that the McDonnell F-4 was the premier fighter of the Cold War era and the standard against which every other fighter in the world was judged.

Key to the success of the Phantom (originally called the F4H, renamed the F-4 in 1962) was its powerful engines and radar, both the best of their era, the 17,000-pound (7711-kilogram) thrust afterburning General Electric J79-GE-8A/8B and the Westinghouse APG-72. When both appeared on the first production version, the F4H-1 (F-4B) in 1960, they had no match in the world.

The design of the fabulous Phantom began as a study of an improved F3H Demon—a not terribly successful fighter of the 1950s—and went through various name changes as the F3H-(E), F3H-G/H, and AH-1. The prototype F4H-1, later designated F4H-1F (F-4A), took to the air at Saint Louis, Mossuri, on May 27, 1958, piloted by Bob Little. Begun on the drawing board as a multirole fighter, the Phantom was inducted into the Navy as a fleet defense interceptor, but the first production version, the F4H-1 (F-4B), was also capable of air-to-ground work. The Marine Corps embraced it immediately. Lt. Col. (later Lt. Gen.) Thomas Miller was one of several Marine pilots who participated in flight testing and development as the Phantom joined squadrons in the early 1960s. On September 5, 1960, Miller claimed a new 500-kilometer world-class speed record of 1,216.78 miles per hour (1961.43 kilometers per hour) for a flight made in an F4H-1 Phantom at Edwards Air Force Base, California. This bettered the existing record of 816.3 miles per hour (113.7 kilometers per hour) by nearly 50 percent.

F-4B Phantoms were delivered first to the replacement air groups, or RAGs, squadrons charged with training fleet crews. VF-121, "Pacemakers," at Naval Air Station Miramar, California, received its first Phantom (an F4H-1F) on June 30, 1960, and was operating the F4H-1 (F-4B) by early 1961. The first operational Phantom squadron was VF-74, "Bedevilers," in the Atlantic fleet.

The Phantom's combat operational debut came on August 6, 1964, when F-4Bs from VF-142, "Ghostriders," and VF-143, "Pukin' Dogs," aboard the USS *Constellation* (CVA 64) provided cover to warplanes that struck North Vietnamese torpedo boat bases following the Gulf of Tonkin incident. An F-4B scored the Navy's first MiG kill of the Vietnam War in 1965. The Marine Corps's "Gray Ghosts" of VMFA-531

These are F-4 Phantoms of David Van Esselstyn's squadron, VMFA-115 "Silver Eagles," during combat in Southeast Asia.

[U.S. Marine Corps]

began operations at Da Nang in 1965. RF-4B photoreconnaissance Phantoms supplanted, then replaced, EF-10B Skyknights in land-based Marine squadrons in Vietnam. RF-4Bs also served aboard carriers during the immediate post-Vietnam era.

The Navy introduced a new version to Vietnam, the F-4J, with VF-33, "Tarsiers," and VF-102, "Diamondbacks," aboard the USS *America* (CVA 66) in 1968. Marines were soon flying the F-4J, too. Most Marine units rarely had a chance to tangle with MiGs, however: carrier-based Navy jets did the dogfighting.

May 10, 1972, produced the largest air-to-air score of the war—11 MiGs shot down. Lieutenants Randall "Duke" Cunningham and William Driscoll shot down their third, fourth, and fifth MiG-17s to become the only Navy aces of the war. Soon afterward, their F-4J Phantom was tagged by a SAM. The pair ejected and were rescued at sea.

On September 11, 1972, Maj. Lee T. "Bear" Lasseter and Capt. John D. Cummings, flying an F-4 Phantom 155226 of the "Shamrocks" of VMFA-333, shot down a MiG-21 near Hanoi, the only MiG downed by a U.S. Marine aircraft. The Marines lost two Phantoms to ground fire in exchange. Lasseter and Cummings were shot down and rescued.

The 197th and last MiG kill of the war took place on January 12,

1973, when Lt. Victor T. Kovaleski of VF-161, "Chargers," aboard the USS *Midway* (CV 41), used a Sidewinder to shoot down a MiG-17. Lieutenant Kovaleski also suffered the indignity of piloting the last aircraft to be lost over North Vietnam when his Phantom was shot down two days later on January 14. Pilot and backseater were rescued.

The Marine Corps was always a big user and supporter of the F-4B, RF-4B, F-4J, F-4N, and F-4S fighters. Marine Corps Phantom squadrons stayed carrier-capable and occasionally deployed aboard ship. They were VMFAT-101 ("Sharpshooters"), VMFA-112 ("Wolf Pack"), VMFA-115 ("Silver Eagles"), VMFA-122 ("Crusaders"), VMFAT-201, VMFA-212

McDonnell F-4J/S Phantom II

Type: 2-seat all-weather, multirole fighter

Power plant: two 17,000-lb (78.50-kN) thrust afterburning General Electric J79-GE-8A/8B or 17,900-lb (79.62-kN) J79-GE-10B afterburning turbojet engines with 13,500 lb (6124 kg) internal fuel capacity

Performance: maximum speed, 1,277 knots (2365 km/h) at 40,000 ft (12192 m); service ceiling, 61,000 ft (18593 m); operating range, 2,000 nm (3704 km); combat radius, 595 mi (958 km)

Weights: empty, 28,000 lb (12701 kg); maximum takeoff, 62,390 lb (28300 kg)

Dimensions: span, 38 ft 7.5 m (11.77 m); span with wings folded, 27 ft (8.41 m); length, 58 ft 4 in (17.78 m); height, 16 ft 5.5 in (5.02 m); wing area, 530 sq ft (49.24 sq m)

Armament: Typically, 4 AAM-N-3 (AIM-7B) Sparrow radar missiles and 2 AAM-N-7 (AIM-9B) Sidewinder missiles; 1 Mark 28 nuclear weapon; or M117 general-purpose bombs; Mark 81, 82, 83, and 84 conventional and parachute-retarded (Snakeye) bombs; BLU-1, -27, -52, and -76 chemical and incendiary bombs; Mark 77 and Mark 79 napalm bombs; AGM-45 Shrike and AGM-78 Standard Anti-Radiation Missiles; LAU-3 and -10 rocket projectile launchers; AGM-12 Bullpup and AGM-65 Maverick air-to-surface missiles

Crew: 2 (pilot and radar intercept officer)

First flight: May 27, 1959 (F4H-1); May 27, 1966 (F-4J)

("Lancers"), VMFA-232 ("Red Devils"), VMFA-235 ("Death Angels"), VMFA-251 ("Thunderbolts"), VMFA-312 ("Checkerboards"), VMFA-314 ("Black Knights"), VMFA-321 ("Hell's Angels"), VMFA-323 ("Death Rattlers"), VMFA-333 ("Shamrocks"), VMFA-334 ("Falcons"), VMFA-451 ("Warlords"), VMFA-513 ("Flying Nightmares"), VMFA-531 ("Gray Ghosts"), and VMFA-542 ("Bengals"). Marine RF-4B reconnaissance squadrons were VMCJ-1, VMCJ-2 ("Playboys"), VMCJ-3, and VMFP-3 ("Eyes of the Corps").

With about 5,200 Phantoms built, including 1,500 naval variants, the best-known fighter was under constant development for more than two decades.

Chapter Twenty

Hornet Pilots Versus Saddam

JOHN ZUPPAN We didn't know what it was going to be like to fly and fight in combat. We were fortunate to have a commanding officer with Vietnam experience flying the F-4 Phantom II. It was nice to have that corporate knowledge in the squadron. He could tell us what it was going to be like to see a surface-to-air missile coming up at us. We knew we had better technology, airplanes, and systems, but the Iraqis had lots of hardware. It might have been old, but it was very effective when used correctly.

We were in VMFA-451, the "Warlords." We were flying from Shaikh Isa, Bahrain. For night one, we had a 45-minute briefing session. There were a lot of butterflies in everybody's stomach. The mission commander briefed everybody who was a Marine officer; I don't remember who he was. After this mass brief as a Marine Air group, we broke down into smaller groups for smaller briefings.

We were given an interdiction mission to go in and drop bombs on a Scud missile repair facility at Khalil in southern Iraq. Our weapons load was five Mark 83 high-explosive, or HE, 1,000-pound (454-kilogram) bombs, two under each wing and one on the centerline. We also carried two AIM-9 Sidewinder heat-seeking air-to-air missiles, one AIM-7

Capt. John "Z-Man" Zuppan
January 17, 1991
F/A-18A Hornet (bureau no.
   163132)
SWEDE 101
Marine Fighter Attack
   Squadron VMFA-451,
   "Warlords"
Shaikh Isa Airfield, Bahrain

Capt. John "Z-Man" Zuppan strikes a classic fighter-pilot pose with his McDonnell F/A-18A Hornet attack aircraft. The Marines sent single-seat F/A-18As and two-seat F/A-18Ds to Bahrain as part of the Desert Shield build-up only days after Saddam Hussein's Iraqi forces invaded Kuwait on August 2, 1990.

[U.S. Marine Corps]

Sparrow radar-guided air-to-air missile, a forward-looking infrared, or FLIR, pod, and a full load of 567 rounds for our 20-millimeter M61A1 Vulcan cannon.

After our smaller briefing, we went to flight equipment and suited up for the mission with all our gear, including a nine-millimeter pistol.

It was the middle of the night. We walked out to the jets, preflighted them, started them up, and taxied on down to the end of the runway. Our division (four airplanes) was led by Lt. Col. Scott "Scotty" Dudley, our squadron commander. I was number 2, call sign Z-MAN. Our executive officer, Maj. "Dip" Goold, was flying in the number 3 position, and our number 4 was Capt. Gary "Lurch" Thomas.

Because of the weight of our ordnance, we couldn't take off in pairs as we often do in the Hornet. So we took off individually at ten-second intervals. It was probably 250 miles to the border plus 200 more to the target, so that was a good distance for us. We tanked on the way in. We refueled from Marine KC-130F Hercules. We did that in the darkness. We did it "comm out," without voice, so it was done with light signals from the KC-130F when they were ready to have us go plug in and get our gas.

Once we were off from Bahrain, we tanked in Saudi airspace south of the Kuwait border. We tanked in friendly airspace because the KC-130Fs had no protection. At one point we were 90 degrees off the tanker track because Scotty's inertial navigation system, or INS, was messed up, so he passed the lead to me.

Coming off the tanker, now Scott is my wingman and I'm in the lead. Our dash three and four are going to a different target, so Scotty and I proceed toward the "push point." That's a point in space where we hold until the timing is right, working backward from a planned time on target, or TOT.

This is a high-altitude attack on our target. We are listening on common frequencies to things that have been going on prior to us. There is a war beginning all around us and we can listen to it. We hear chatter from F-117s bombing Baghdad and from Wild Weasels using High-Speed Anti-Radiation (HARM) missiles against missile sites.

Now it becomes the designated time for us to go in. We're watching missiles go up and explode on the other side of the border. We push in. We accelerate to 540 knots at 31,000 feet, flying combat spread with lights out except for formation lights, which are a fluorescent green.

We have to get within 40 miles to use air-to-ground radar to find our target. We have a low undercast. We are going to find the target on radar and then hand it off to the FLIR, which will enable us to distinguish roads, buildings, etc. We have seen aerial photos of the target and have those in the airplane with us. I'm flying lead and Scotty's flying wingman on me because his INS is bad. I have to feed him bearings and distance to the target so he can locate it.

As we get closer, we get better resolution. At 22 miles, we realize we can't use the FLIR because there are clouds below everywhere, blocking our vision. So we stay with the radar. This will be a radar attack.

At about eight miles, we roll in, a rolling left-hand turn, and start coming down out of 31,000 feet. This is where Khalil Airfield starts kicking up with air defense. The antiaircraft fire looks like big fuzzy orange tennis balls flying all over the place, and we can also see the smaller white lights of tracers. We're coming down the chute looking for bomb-release parameters in the neighborhood of 15,000 to 17,000 feet.

When the bombs come off, it's a good feeling. You just like to have the lug open up and to have the bombs fall away, because you can pull out.

The bombs are off. They're falling. We go up, nose high. We switch the radar to air-to-air mode to look for other airplanes. The FLIR is still slaved to the target, so pulling off from the target I see my five heat signatures go off on my FLIR display, so that gives me a warm and fuzzy that my bombs are exploding on target.

On the egress, we're climbing to altitude. We're listening to communications about the rest of the missions that are coming out. Our impression is that the missiles the Iraqis are shooting, SA-2s, SA-3s, and SA-6s are not being guided.

South of the border we go. We turn our lights on, safe up the weapons system, and take the long trip back home. Everything worked as advertised. We know we are going to be able to overpower the Iraqis.

I flew close to 40 missions. We flew a lot during Desert Shield. We rehearsed a simulated mission to the real target.

Shaikh Isa was one busy place. It took a long time for a lot of people to take off—50 airplanes taking off from the same base, a lot of assets. Just getting the airplane airborne when you've got a lot of aircraft using the runway, who's going to go to the tanker first, who's going to go first? Who's going to go 21st? Every minute you sit on the taxiway with engines running is 100 pounds of gas you're not going to have later. You never know when a tanker might go down. It's a machine, like anything else. You could have a bad day, or a bad hose. Instead of six tankers up there, you might have four.

I can't claim that I always wanted to be a Marine. I was born in 1962 in San Francisco. They called me in my senior year of high school and asked me what I was going to do when I graduated. I said, "I don't

McDonnell test pilot Jack Krings takes the fourth F/A-18A Hornet aloft for a test flight with a full ordnance load on August 25, 1980. This aircraft is carrying nine Mark 83 1,000-pound bombs (in the form of inert training rounds) and two AIM-9 Sidewinder missiles on the wingtips. Because range and endurance was always an issue, Capt. John Zuppan and other Marines in Operation Desert Storm typically carried five such bombs.

[McDonnell Aircraft Co.]

---

know, but I don't think it's going to be joining the Marine Corps." That was in 1979. There was no draft. I went to the recruiter's office in the suburbs of San Francisco in Walnut Creek, and the recruiter threw all the hard-charging motivational stuff at me. From the beginning, I was talking about becoming an officer and a pilot. They had a picture on the wall of an F4 Phantom and a couple of guys climbing into it. They said, "You want to be an officer, you got to go to college." I signed up for the Reserve at Naval Air Station Alameda, California, in a Marine Reserve A-4 Skyhawk squadron, VMA-133, as a supply clerk. I joined platoon leader class, or PLC, and transferred to San Jose State and finished my degree in communications in 1984. I followed the standard Marine Corps career path to basic school at Quantico, Virginia, and then to flight training. I was commissioned December 1984 and got my wings in August 1987. There were no longer any F-4s, so I went into the F/A-18A as a "Hornet baby."

From the time I signed on the dotted line in high school, I had kept an eight-by-ten photo of the F/A-18A Hornet on my wall above my desk. When I actually got to fly the Hornet, my first impression surprised me. Compared to older, training airplanes, there was an absolute stillness and quiet that came over you as soon as you put down the canopy. I flew the T-2 Buckeye and A-4 Skyhawk in training, but the Hornet was different. My initial impression was the ease of the aircraft. You couldn't tell from sound whether you were going 250 knots or 500 knots. It was a shock.

I went to Naval Air Station Lemoore, California, where a Navy squadron, VFA-125, was training Hornet pilots. Once checked out in the Hornet, I went to VMFA-451, "Warlords," at Beaufort, South Carolina, in April 1988. Being a California boy, I wanted to fly at El Toro, but the Marine Corps thought otherwise.

Beaufort had just received brand-new Lot IX F/A-18As and we were earmarked to join a Navy air wing because the Navy was still transitioning from the A-7E Corsair II to the F-18A Hornet and didn't have enough squadrons of its own. So VMFA-451 "chopped" to Carrier Air Wing CVW-13 on October 1, 1988, operating from the carrier USS *Coral Sea* (CV 43). We did the summer 1989 Med cruise and brought the ship back to put her into mothballs. It was *Coral Sea*'s last trip out. I made about 160 carrier landings and that was the last time I landed on a carrier. We snapped back into standard training. In August 1990, we were chosen to go to Kuwait in part because we had so much experience. That's when I told myself, "Zuppan, you're going to be in a war."

JAY A. STOUT Zuppan was in the bunk below me. He's a good guy, a funny guy, and a real good pilot. We were assigned different targets that first night of Desert Storm, but we spent considerable time together in VMFA-451, the "Warlords."

As for the Hornet, I was very interested to fly it. There was not one thing I missed about the F-4 Phantom when I went to the Hornet. The Hornet was a little slower at the top end, but I never flew the Phantom that fast. The Hornet was much, much more reliable. Best of all, it turned better. It was more maneuverable. Shooting down enemy air-

Capt. Jay A. Stout, seen here as a lieutenant colonel on his last Hornet flight in 2001, was one of the first pilots to cross the fence in Operation Desert Storm in 1991. He later wrote a memoir, "Hornets Over Kuwait."

[Jay A. Stout]

planes was all I wanted to do since I was about four. We didn't get the chance in Desert Storm. The Air Force did such a good job that no enemy plane ever got near us.

I felt being a Marine was important. I was born in 1959 in Indianapolis. I was commissioned through the platoon leader's course between my junior and senior year at Purdue in 1980. After graduation in 1981, I did five months at Quantico until October 1981. I reported for flight school in November 1981 at Pensacola, Florida, aviation indoctrination training at Pensacola, in the T-34C in January 1982. I went to Chase Field, Beeville, Texas, beginning July 1982, flying the T-2C Buckeye and TA-4J Skyhawk. I got my wings May 13, 1983. I went to Yuma, Arizona, to fly the F-4 Phantom. That was with squadron VMFAT-101, "Sharpshooters," the training unit. We sat around for a long time waiting to fly the Phantom. I reported to squadron VMFA-122, "Crusaders," at Beaufort, South Carolina, in March 1984. I flew the F-4S Phantom with VMFA-122 for about a year and then went to VMFA-312 still at Beaufort in 1985. I was at Beeville for three years instructing in the T-2C. I went to VMFAT-101 to transition to the Hornet. I went to VMFA-451. We went for Desert Shield to Shaikh Isa, Bahrain, in August 1990, arriving the 23rd.

The date of my most memorable mission was February 25, 1991. Toward the end of the war, the oil fires had just started to burn. There were a lot of clouds and thunderclouds. It was after the ground war had begun. The weather was horrible. Below all the clouds and oil smoke it was almost pitch black, yet we were able to fly around at 3,000 or 4,000 feet and find Iraqis.

I flew wing on Capt. Carrie "Motto" Venden. I dropped three Mark 83 1,000-pound bombs on three different targets. Venden and I were flying around separately below the clouds. I started to get low on gas and popped up through the clouds. I wanted to get on the KC-130F Hercules to refuel. Now the sun was just going down and the lights from the battlefield and the antiaircraft fire arcing around created an incredibly huge, wonderful light show. We got more gas, went back down, and bombed again. It was remarkable because ten years earlier in Phantoms we wouldn't have been able to fly that mission, in those horrible conditions, with such accuracy. It was the FLIR pod mostly that enabled us to do that.

Going to war in the Hornet, I liked the aircraft every bit as much as I liked it in peacetime. It was a very reliable aircraft. It's real easy to see out of. It has good visibility. It's a great weapons system. If you see something on the ground, you can kill it. We could loiter around at 1,000 feet and kill stuff with the gun. I think I've said, "It's very reliable," about a hundred times. We had five aircraft that were hit, including the two-seat F/A-18D Hornet with Capt. John Scanlan in the backseat (below), and everyone made it back. Not a single Marine Hornet was lost in combat in Desert Storm.

The one shortcoming that it had and still has is it's still a little short legged. It was 250 nautical miles from Shaikh Isa to Kuwait, so we had only 20 to 25 air minutes to root around up there and bomb targets before we had to come back before running out of fuel.

Our squadron, VMFA-451, was only one that painted the false canopies on the bottom of the forward fuselage. I think the Canadians had done it before. We did it to fool enemy pilots but it made it hard to see each other because I never knew whether I was looking at the top or bottom of the other guy's Hornet.

This was nothing like World War II, but when you're getting shot at, it's absolutely frightening. On my first mission, we had a strike of about 50 or 60 aircraft. The war started at midnight and this was 8:00 p.m. It was our first mission. As we were marshaling out over the gulf before pushing on to our target, we got tons of antiaircraft fire. We saw a big curtain of fire ahead of us. As we kept heading towards it, I wondered, "When are we were going to turn around or go around it? We're not going to fly into that, are we?" But we did. A missile's motor will burn out and then you no longer see it, but it's still stalking you. I thought about missiles coming up at us and thought, "I'm not a bad guy. Why are they shooting at me?" It's an absurd feeling to have, but it was, "Why are they trying to hurt me?"

What Happened

In round one against Saddam Hussein, aviators strapped themselves into a variety of aircraft adorned with the word *MARINES*. The helicopters, mostly holdovers from an earlier war and now long in the tooth, were joined in the fight by Bronco forward air control planes that circled over the Iraqi army like gnats, and by Harrier jump jets that needed no runway to take off laden with bombs. All of these aircraft fought in key battles during the First Persian Gulf War, Operation Desert Storm in 1991, but no helicopter, no Harrier, and no Bronco could provide the high-speed capabilities of the sleek, supersonic F/A-18A Hornet.

The Hornet also came in the two-seat variety, and many considered that a groundbreaking innovation. The "Delta," or F/A-18D, was the two-seat version of what was, at the time, the fastest and most versatile jet fighter in inventory. It was an era when the single-seat fighter, flown by a single pilot, was very much the vogue. And in Marine aviation, as in every military air arm, the pilot was the be-all and end-all of the pointy-nose jet set. Still, the F/A-18D had a guy in the rear seat who wasn't a pilot and didn't do anything with stick and rudder. They stripped the flight controls from the back office of the Delta, filled it with electronic wizardry designed to find and kill the bad guys, and installed a backseater called a weapons and sensors officer, or WSO.

One of those WSOs was John M. Scanlan, a South Carolina native and Naval Academy graduate (1983), who stood fully erect to a height of five feet, four inches, went to church more often than he told flying stories at the bar, and knew how to plant a Mark 83 general-purpose bomb into a pickel barrel. When Scanlan graduated from Annapolis, the top 16 percent in his class were offered the chance to become Marines instead of Navy officers, if they wanted. Scanlan wanted. "I felt the Marine Corps was the place to make a contribution," he said. The rear cockpit of an F/A-18D is quite roomy, and Scanlan fit into it with ease.

JOHN M. SCANLAN With the F/A-18D Hornet, the Marine Corps didn't realize what they had. It was a brand-new jet. In 1990, it came off the assembly line and in 1991, boom, boom, there we were, across the pond in Desert Storm. It was a brand-new capability, and we didn't yet know exactly what all it could do or how best to use it. It was a work in progress, or a learn-as-you-go kind of thing.

They intended to use it for the forward air control mission. That was why it was sent over. As far as the night attack mission goes, we wanted to do that, but we didn't have enough guys who were qualified in night-vision goggles. We hadn't sorted out a lot of single-ship night tactics, either.

I was in the first group of WSOs. I was in the very first squadron to operate the F/A-18D. I had previously done three years in the F-4 Phantom II. All backseaters begin their career by going to Pensacola, Florida, for initial training to become naval flight officers, or NFOs. That's about 15 months. After that, they leave Pensacola and go to a fleet replacement squadron, or FRS, for the training that's specific to the aircraft they'll fly in the service. There, they're introduced to the mission. For me, that outfit was Marine Fighter Attack Training Squadron VMFAT-101 at El Toro, California. They always had the training mission for fighter attack jets. I spent about six months there. Once you're qualified in the jet, they boot you out of that squadron and then you go

John M. Scanlan (left) with pilot Capt. Glenn "Lax" Miles, an AIM-120 AMRAAM missile and a 1,000-pound Mark 84 bomb. The aircraft is the F/A-18D Hornet, which the Marines initially used as a fast forward air controller, and then transformed into a night attack aircraft during Operation Desert Storm.

[Lt. Col. John M. Scanlan]

to your real fleet squadron. That's where you learn how to do your real-life mission, based on a program that your training officer has set up.

We were with a new airplane, so everybody in the squadron was new. There were about 35 of us, not just a small number. So it was kind of, "This is how we think you do it."

The F/A-18D Hornet was radically different from the F-4 Phantom II. In the Phantom, I was called a radar intercept officer: I controlled the radar in the backseat. I controlled the intercept of other fighters. But now, in the new F/A-18D, I had all these whizbang toys to play with. The leap in technology was like going from a dinosaur to Star Wars. The F/A-18D has the AN/APG-65 radar and it is very capable. The difference is night and day—phenomenal, the things that radar can do. Plus, there's an infrared display with things I can do. Navigation is easier. Everything is better with the F/A-18D. It's not just radar intercept stuff. The bombing symbology, the infrared symbology, the navigation symbology, and all that stuff was better.

In a normal situation, I would show up as a new guy in the squadron, and there would be 20 experienced guys who'd already been flying this jet. But introducing the F/A-18D to combat was different. I showed up as a new guy and there were 35 other new guys. And, boy, these were some smart, talented guys! Some of them came from test pilot school. There were guys who had been nurturing the F/A-18D program along. But nobody quite knew—nobody was quite sure—what we had and how to employ it.

In August 1990, Saddam Hussein invaded Kuwait. That was about the same time I checked in to my fleet squadron, VMFA (AW)-121, the "Green Knights." We were going to war with those in the squadron. The higher-ups saw us as performing the fast forward air control, or fast FAC, mission. We were supposed to replace the OV-10 Bronco. You had an airplane that flew low and slow controlling the battlefield, and suddenly now you have a two-seat jet that goes ten times faster and five times higher and everything else. Our pilot training officer was a former OV-10 pilot. He tried to train us like they did in the OV-10. In September, October, and November, our unit practiced the fast FAC mission over and over. The Air Force had done a fast FAC mission in Vietnam, but the Marine Corps had never tried it.

Every night we would hold meetings, talking about what worked and what didn't work. We were deployed in the fall of 1990 to Shaikh Isa Airfield, Bahrain. The war kicked off on January 17, 1991.

We were living on the base in a dormitory that may have once belonged to the Bahraini air force. We had eight guys to a room and showers and a latrine down the hall. We had 12 jets and 36 officers flying around the clock. We ate over in a big dining facility when the schedule permitted. Otherwise, we had to grab an MRE. We briefed about two hours ahead of time. If we were going to be controlling single-seat Marine F/A-18 Hornets, we met with them face to face.

After the brief, we go to maintenance control and read the book about the jet to see what maintenance gripes have been written up on the jet. We go to flight equipment. We prepare for a flight by doing things in the following order: the initial briefing, an intel brief, a flight equipment check, a stop at maintenance control, and then to the jet. The jet is within walking distance of maintenance control. We always do a preflight check. The pilot checks one wing and I check the other. It's an unwritten rule that the pilot checks clockwise and the copilot checks counterclockwise. And then you're ready to climb in.

If there's one thing I was impressed with, it was the level of those people who were in the first F/A-18D squadron. It wasn't just an automatic transfer into that squadron. You had to fill out a form. They picked and chose some of the smartest and best people I've ever seen— remarkable people.

Inside the cockpit, I'm attached to my plane by metal devices called Koch fasteners, breathing oxygen, and looking at the rear of the pilot's helmet. We started out the war spotting targets for other warplanes, for naval gunfire, and for Marine land-based artillery, and being an "eye in the sky" for combat commanders. As it turned out, the Delta evolved into a formidable night attack machine.

What Happened

Gen. Norman Schwarzkopf, commander of coalition forces in Desert Storm, called the F/A-18D "a valuable tool." Lt. Gen. Royal N. Moore, Jr., the Marine air commander in Desert Storm, wrote in the November 1991 *Naval Institute Proceedings* that "the intelligence [commanders] were getting was from the F/A-18D that operated deep into the battlefield." The planes flown by Scanlan and his fellow Marines belonged to a squadron with a long and honored history, VMFA-121, the "Green Knights."

"During the ground campaign, late in the afternoon, an F/A-18D or two would come into the fray with no other mission than to look at the battlefield," Moore wrote. "They would go on in, run in the 2nd Division area, run in the 1st Division area, look at the Saudis' area, look at all of Kuwait, come back, tank [refuel], go back, and report to us." Afterward, Moore continued, "We would then catapult them back in—on a couple of occasions with night-vision goggles—to look at the battlefield. After that report—a quick kind of hot look in the air to us—they passed many other hot looks through the system. When they landed, the crews were driven to the Marine Air Group 11 operations center where they picked up the phone and talked directly to one of us with a detailed report."

The "eye in the sky" that became a night attack whiz—the F/A-18D—belonged to a squadron with a shining history. During World War II, the Green Knights flew F4F Wildcats and later F4U Corsairs as part of the Cactus Air Force, fighting alongside Army and Navy squadrons in defense of Guadalcanal. As the war progressed, the squadron fought from Marine airfields at Espiritu Santo Island, Turtle Bay, Bougainville, and Emirau. The squadron produced 14 fighter air aces, more than any other outfit, including Medal of Honor recipient Capt. Joseph J. Foss. Throughout the war, VMF-121 shot down 209 Japanese aircraft, 165 while flying Wildcats and another 44 flying Corsairs.

In later years, the Green Knights of squadron VMFA-121 flew the A-6E Intruder, an improved version of a Vietnam-era attack jet, until they began receiving F/A-18Ds in April 1990. As events in the Middle East moved toward war, the Marines left for Saudi Arabia on January 7, 1991. Within days they were flying their Hornets from Shaikh Isa Air Base in Bahrain. As the war progressed, Hornet crews found themselves facing Iraqis who seemed to be learning how to use their modern weaponry, including surface-to-air missiles, and learning too fast.

JOHN M. SCANLAN We were hit by a surface-to-air missile during a forward air control mission on February 20, 1991. We were in western Kuwait, where a lot of Iraqi forces had gathered. We found lucrative targets to spot for our fellow Marine Air pilots who were flying single-seat F/A-18A Hornets. Our squadron commander at that time was Lt. Col. Steve Mugg, and I was flying in the backseat with Maj. Cheyenne Bode up front.

We were northwest of Kuwait City on a mission as an airborne forward air controller. We discovered this very lucrative group of targets and controlled one section of F/A-18As as they dropped their bombs upon them. However, after their bombs were gone, we had no one else to control. Furthermore, our Marine controllers told us to not expect any more jets for 30 minutes.

For Desert Storm, F/A-18Ds configured in the role of airborne forward air controller carried very little ordnance for their own use—a bomb on the centerline and gun rounds in the nose. Well, our two jets obviously expended the two centerline bombs very quickly, and then Cheyenne and I, as the lead jet, talked intracockpit. We knew that it would be dangerous to descend below 10,000 feet. Cheyenne was a very conscientious pilot when it came to a two-man jet and wasn't going to take risks without consulting. He asked me if I would feel uncomfortable going down to use the gun. I told him, "I'm four feet behind you, Cheyenne!" I always used that phrase whenever he asked my opinion on something over the intercom system, or ICS. Thus, figuring "This is war," we told our wingman of our intention to descend and strafe, and cleared him to do the same.

We got hit in the right rear exhaust by a heat-seeking missile. It worked as advertised. It exploded on impact. In that first instant, we had no way to know how seriously we were hit. Nobody likes the idea of an explosive warhead being in the neighborhood of thousands of pounds of jet fuel.

Cheyenne and I both immediately knew what had happened when we were hit. We had just completed a strafing run and had commenced a climb. I was looking outside, checking our left seven and eight o'clock, and Cheyenne was looking out front trying to get sight of our wingman, who was at our one or two o'clock. As luck—or fate—would have it, the missile was fired at us from where no one was looking, our right four or five o'clock.

We heard an unmistakable explosion that sounded waaaaay too close to have missed. It just sounded like a KA-WHUMP. The jet didn't "shake" or "tremble" or anything like in the movies. Immediately,

Cheyenne came up on the ICS and said in a perfectly calm voice: "Well, Bubba, we've been hit."

My only reply was "Yep," and then we both began the very businesslike procedures of ensuring that we got home. We weren't really scared or worried or panicked or anything like that. We immediately pointed the jet's nose toward the gulf and commenced a climb to an altitude sanctuary. The first thing I did was tell the Marine controllers to hurry up and find us on their radars in case we had to eject.

Cheyenne and I agreed that no matter what, if things suddenly went to shit, we would stick with the jet until we were over the water, and THEN eject. I tightened down my lap restraints just in case one of us had to pull the handle. Cheyenne and I both brought up the engines' parameters on the left screen in each cockpit, and the right engine still seemed to be operating fine. No engine parameters were out of whack. Still, we had our wingman pull up next to us to do a visual inspection, and they confirmed what we felt—the right engine's exhaust pipe (the "turkey feathers") was completely mangled from the explosion. The missile had worked as advertised, guiding on our right engine's infrared exhaust signature. It flew right up our right tailpipe and exploded on contact. Luckily, the missile, we think, was only a two-and-one-half-pound warhead. So just to be safe, we decided to shut down the right engine and fly the 200 or so miles home on just the left engine. On short final into landing at Shaikh Isa, Cheyenne restarted the right engine, and it worked like a champion. The coolest part of the flight was taxiing back into our line. By then, word had reached home base that a crippled jet was coming home, and as we taxied back into our line, it was like a movie, as the entire squadron of maintenance personnel came running out to the flight line to greet us as we parked. It brought tears to my eyes.

As I said after the initial hit, we were able to regain most control functions. There may have been pieces of our plane scattered all over western Kuwait, but we were flying. My pilot, Bode, appeared to have good control. Communications appeared good. Systems were good. We climbed to altitude and had our wingman come up and look us over. There were some terse exchanges over the radio, but the general idea

Who's Who

Capt. John "Z-Man" Zuppan, pilot, F/A-18A Hornet, squadron VMFA-451, "Warlords," on the first mission of Operation Desert Storm, January 17, 1991

Capt. (later, Lt. Col.) Jay A. "Guinness" Stout, pilot, F/A-18A Hornet, squadron VMFA-451, "Warlords," on the first mission of Operation Desert Storm, January 17, 1991

Lt. Col. (later, Col.) Scott "Scotty" Dudley, pilot, F/A-18A Hornet, commander of squadron VMFA-451, "Warlords," on the first mission of Operation Desert Storm, January 17, 1991

Capt. (later Lt. Col.) John M. Scanlan, weapons and sensors officer (WSO), F/A-18D Night Attack Hornet, squadron VMFA-121, "Green Knights," hit by a SAM missile on February 20, 1991

---

was that we were still flying and we could probably coax this jet back to Shaikh Isa.

We remained in good communication and managed to complete the flight back to Bahrain, where we landed with one seriously damaged F/A-18D.

McDonnell F/A-18 Hornet

The Hornet was the result of the U.S. Navy's 1974 requirement, called VFAX, for a low-cost, lightweight, multimission fighter. The design has its origins in the Northrop F-17, the lightweight jet that lost out to the General Dynamics F-16 Fighting Falcon in a competition for an Air Force contract. By the time McDonnell adapted the design, it was no longer quite such a lightweight, and it would forever be criticized for not having enough range, but both the Navy and Marine Corps wanted it.

The first Navy contract was issued on January 22, 1976, covering both single-seat F/A-18As and two-seat aircraft, which were initially

The "Green Knights" of Marine Fighter Attack Squadron 121, otherwise known as VMFA (AW)-121, flew the two-seat night attack version of the F/A-18D Hornet. Marines created new tactics in the field when they discovered that the F/A-18D made an ideal forward air controller as well as a night attack jet.

[Douglas E. Slowiak/Vortex Photo Graphics]

McDonnell F/A-18D Hornet ("Delta")

Type: 2-seat forward air control and night attack aircraft

Power plant: 2 General Electric F404-GE-402 low-bypass turbofan engines, each rated at 11,875 lb static thrust (52.8 kN), increasing to 17,775 lb (71.9 kN) with afterburning

Performance: maximum speed, 1,034 knots (1915 km/h); service ceiling, 50,000 ft (15240 m); range, 1,100 nm (2036 km)

Weights: empty, 25,319 lb (11485 kg); maximum takeoff, 51,900 lb (23541 kg)

Dimensions: wing span, 37 ft 6 in (11.43 m); wing span folded, 17 ft 6 in (8.38 m); fuselage length, 56 ft (17.07 m); height, 15 ft 3½ in (4.66 m); wing area, 400 sq ft (37.16 sq m)

Armament: 1 M61A1 Vulcan 20-mm cannon with 570 rounds; up to 17,000 lb (7711 kg) of external ordnance including AIM-7 Sparrow, AIM-9 Sidewinder, and AIM-120 AMRAAM air-to-air missiles, Mark 82/83/84 conventional bombs, or laser-guided bombs and cluster munitions

Crew: 2 (pilot and weapons and sensors officer)

First flight: November 18, 1978 (F/A-18A); May 6, 1988 (F/A-18D)

called TF-18As but became F/A-18Bs. The first aircraft in the series made its initial flight on November 18, 1978. By the mid-1980s, 12 Marine Corps squadrons were operating the F/A-18A.

Soon the McDonnell production line shifted to the improved, single-seat F/A-18C and the two-seat F/A-18D. The first production F/A-18C made its initial flight on September 2, 1987, but when Marines like John Zuppan and Jay A. Stout went to war four years later, they were still flying the F/A-18A.

The two-seat F/A-18D made its initial flight on May 6, 1988, and deliveries to the Marine Corps began in late 1989. John M. Scanlan's squadron, VMFA-121, was the first to equip itself solely with the Delta model.

Index

Morris, Wayne, 91
Morse code, 178
Mugg, Steve, 341
Muroc Air Base, 166–67, 185
Mussolini, Benito, 50
MV-22B Osprey tilt-rotor aircraft, 310

NA-40/NA-40B bombers, 52
Nam Phong airfield, 318–20
National Museum (Marine Corps), 174, 233
National Museum of Naval Aviation, 187
NATO, 228
Navy, 2, 83. *See also individual carriers*
  Advanced Jet Training Command, 215
  B-25s, 51
  Blue Angels, 218
  Buffalo planes of, 15–16
  Bureau of Aeronautics, 216–17
  Corsairs, 22, 23
  Cross, 162, 222, 234
  Distinguished Flying Cross, 112, 258
  first African-American pilot in, 110–12
  flying aces, 325
  Japan bombed by, 71–72
  National Museum of Aviation, 187
  Philadelphia Aircraft factory, 22, 31–32
  radar development by, 31–32
  Research Laboratory, 31
  Seabees, 13, 43, 77, 204–5
  Top Gun school, 249
  VA-75 squadron, 291
  VFAX requirement of, 344
Neal, George, 107–8
"Nell" (G3M2 Type 96 bomber), 13–15
New Bern, North Carolina, 92–93
New River, North Carolina, 228, 229, 299–30
Nihart, Franklin, 145
Noll, Al, 68, 69
North American Aviation, 51–52, 276
nuclear-capable combat planes, 217, 259
Nukufetau, 76–77, 78

OA-4M, 220
OE-1 Bird Dog liaison plane, 117

Okinawa, 59, 61–69, 66, 72, 97, 99–100, 116, 117, 131, 132, 134
Onishi, Takijiro, 68
Operation Blackbird, 148–49
Operation Desert Storm, 276, 290, 291, 292, 328–46
Operation Windmill, 144–48
O'Rourke, Gerald, 175, 185–86
Oswald, Lee Harvey, 185
OV-10/OV-10A Broncos, 215, 306
OY-1 Sentinel observation planes, 108

P-36 fighters, 4
P-38 Lightnings, 10
P-40 Warhawks, 4, 11
P-47N Thunderbolts, 98
P-61 Black Widows, 27
Page, Bud, 70, *71*, 72–84, 77, *83*, 85, 175–78, 185
Page, R.M., 31
Panthers. *See* F9F/F9F-2 Panthers
Parks, Bill, *38*, 42–45, *47*, 48
Parris Island, South Carolina, 228, 235
Pastuf, John, *319*
PBJs. *See* B-25 Bombers
PBY Catalina, 92, 97
Pearl Harbor, 1–4, *3*, 17, 37, 53, 57, 60, 71, 85, 86, 93–94
Pensacola, Florida, 23, 207–8, 235, 243–45, 334
Persian Gulf War. *See* Operation Desert Storm
Phelps, John "Gordo," 222, 225–33, *234*
Philadelphia, Pennsylvania, Naval Aircraft factory at, 22, 31–32
Philippines, 199
Piasecki, Frank, 309
Pless, Stephen, 222, *222*, 223–27, 230–36
Po-2 night intruder/heckler, 173, 177–78, 182, 183
Pope, Eugene, 109
Poulson, Leroy, 222, 225–27, 231, 232, 234, 236
Power, Tyrone, *93*, 94
Preflight checks, 267–70, 314–15, 318–19

Robert F. Dorr, a veteran and retired American diplomat, has written more than sixty books on air operations, including *Chopper* and *Air Combat*. He lives in Oakton, Virginia, with his family and Labrador retriever.